Fat Lives

Ever caught somebody – or yourself – checking out the content of a 'fat' person's supermarket trolley? Ever wondered what lies behind this behaviour, or what it might be like to be at the receiving end of this judging gaze?

Within the context of the current 'obesity debate', this book investigates the embodied experience of 'being large' from a critical psychological perspective. Using poststructuralist and feminist theories, the author explores the discourses available to and used by self-designated 'fat' individuals, as well as the societal power relationships that these discourses produce.

Using the issues of body size and 'fat' as an illustration, the book describes the benefits of exploring psychological and social matters from a poststructuralist perspective, and the dangers inherent in taking reductionist approaches to public health and other social issues. As such, this book should be of particular interest to anyone working within the disciplines of psychology, sociology and health studies, as well as those involved in the study of health, gender issues and appearance.

Irmgard Tischner is Senior Lecturer in Social Psychology at the University of Worcester and associate member of the Centre for Appearance Research at the University of the West of England, Bristol. Her research focuses on poststructuralist, feminist and critical psychological approaches to the study of embodiment and subjectivity, particularly in relation to (gendered) discourses of body size, health and physical activity in contemporary western societies.

Women and Psychology
Series Editor: Jane Ussher
School of Psychology, University of Western Sydney

This series brings together current theory and research on women and psychology. Drawing on scholarship from a number of different areas of psychology, it bridges the gap between abstract research and the reality of women's lives by integrating theory and practice, research and policy.

Each book addresses a 'cutting edge' issue of research, covering topics such as postnatal depression and eating disorders, and addressing a wide range of theories and methodologies.

The series provides accessible and concise accounts of key issues in the study of women and psychology, and clearly demonstrates the centrality of psychology debates within women's studies or feminism.

Other titles in this series:

The Thin Woman
Helen Malson

The Menstrual Cycle
Anne E. Walker

Post-natal Depression
Paula Nicolson

Re-thinking Abortion
Mary Boyle

Woman and Aging
Linda R. Gannon

Being Married, Doing Gender
Caroline Dryden

Understanding Depression
Janet M. Stoppard

Femininity and the Physically Active Woman
Precilla Y. L. Choi

Gender, Language and Discourse
Anne Weatherall

The Science/Fiction of Sex
Annie Potts

The Psychological Development of Girls and Women
Sheila Greene

Just Sex?
Nicola Gavey

Woman's Relationship with Herself
Helen O'Grady

Gender Talk
Susan A. Speer

Beauty and Misogyny
Sheila Jeffreys

Body Work
Sylvia K. Blood

Managing the Monstrous Feminine
Jane M. Ussher

The Capacity to Care
Wendy Hollway

Sanctioning Pregnancy
Harriet Gross and Helen Pattison

Accounting for Rape
Irina Anderson and Kathy Doherty

The Single Woman
Jill Reynolds

Maternal Encounters
Lisa Baraitser

Women and Depression
Michelle N. Lafrance

Understanding the Effects of Child Sexual Abuse
Sam Warner

The Gendered Unconscious
Louise Gyler

Hard Knocks
Janice Haaken

Domestic Violence and Psychology
Paula Nicolson

'Adolescence', Pregnancy and Abortion
Catriona I. Macleod

The Madness of Women
Jane M. Ussher

Fat Lives

A feminist
psychological exploration

Irmgard Tischner

Routledge
Taylor & Francis Group

LONDON AND NEW YORK

Published 2013
by Routledge
27 Church Road, Hove, East Sussex, BN3 2FA

Simultaneously published in the USA and Canada
by Routledge
711 Third Avenue, New York, NY 10017

Routledge is an imprint of the Taylor & Francis Group, an informa business

© 2013 Psychology Press

British Library Cataloguing in Publication Data
A catalogue record for this book is available from the British Library

Library of Congress Cataloging-in-Publication Data
Tischner, Irmgard.
  Fat lives : a feminist psychological exploration / Irmgard Tischner.
    p. cm.
  Includes bibliographical references.
  1. Body image in women. 2. Weight loss–Social aspects. I. Title.
  RC628.T56 2012
  362.1963′980082–dc23   2012021177

ISBN: 978-0-415-68093-6 (hbk)
ISBN: 978-0-415-68094-3 (pbk)
ISBN: 978-0-203-07989-8 (ebk)

Typeset in Times by
Swales & Willis Ltd, Exeter, Devon

MIX
Paper from
responsible sources
FSC
www.fsc.org   FSC® C004839   Printed and bound by CPI Group (UK) Ltd, Croydon, CR0 4YY

Contents

Acknowledgements   ix

Introduction: a mantra of body weight, health and
lifestyle – setting the scene for fat lives   1

1   Putting the fat body in context   10

2   Exploring fat lives   27

3   Women's in/visible 'large bodies': always visible but
    rarely seen   44

4   'I just wear clothes to keep me warm'   57

5   Health, well-being and the responsible fat woman   74

6   Gendering fat   94

7   Conclusions: the experience of being fat   120

    Appendix 1   Theory in the exploration of fat lives   132
    Appendix 2   Transcription conventions   143

    Notes   144
    References   145
    Index   162

Acknowledgements

My first thanks go to the women and men who participated in my study – without their generous gift of time and trust, this book would not have happened. I am grateful to the University of the West of England (UWE) and the University of Worcester, who provided the funding and time for the research and consequently the book. To everybody at The Centre for Appearance Research (UWE), thanks for your help and support – you will always have a special place in my heart. Very special thanks go to Helen Malson for her guidance, support and friendship. Thanks also to Dominic Upton and Paula Nicholson for your support and encouragement, and to Jane Ussher, whose positive feedback, comments and suggestions at the review stage were invaluable to me. And of course I'm very grateful for all the support and patience provided by my friends and family in Bavaria, Bristol and Worcester; thanks to all of you, and (in no particular order) especially to David, Adrian, Matthew, Gyozo, Laura, Birgit, Geli, Rainer, Joana, Julian, Jonas, Maureen, Derek and Eddy, for your moral support and practical help – you kept me sane. Last but not least, I would like to thank my mother, Irmgard, for her continuous support in many ways. I am dedicating this book to my late father, Hans.

Introduction

A mantra of body weight, health and lifestyle – setting the scene for fat lives

It is January 2012. 'Lose weight without dieting' is promised on the cover of *Cosmopolitan*, 'Lose half a stone' is demanded by *Women's Fitness*, and *Marie Claire* offers help with 'how to stop stress sabotaging your diet – tackle tension to maximize weight-loss'. Women are the prime target of these weight loss directives, and the focus is mainly on the alleged improvement of their appearance through the shedding of body weight. The popular media also encourages men to lose weight, with *Men's Fitness*, for example, wanting them to 'Lose your belly'. However, just the sheer number of women's magazines with weight loss messages, compared to those for men, speaks volumes about where the pressure lies in regard to body size, and appearance generally. You could be forgiven for assuming that this diet frenzy is just the result of publishers capitalising on everybody's new year's resolutions; however, the weight loss mantra is omnipresent all year round. A quick scan of the magazine shelves at WH Smith one October a couple of years ago revealed a similar picture, with ten magazines on offer that specialised in the transformation of one's body: there were those that were clear about their focus on weight loss, with titles such as *Slim at Home*, those that couched it all within discourses of health and fitness (e.g. *Fitness*, *Diet and Health*) and the official magazines of commercial slimming clubs. Headlines such as 'Lose fat fast' and 'Drop a stone' were the rule, as well as 'real-life' accounts of individual women losing large amounts of weight, and promises of 'looking fab' and 'feel fantastic'. All of them featured women, and women were the predominant target reader group. I do not wish to claim that men are not being targeted by the diet industry and the above recent quote on the cover of *Men's Fitness* magazine testifies to the increasing pressure on men to watch their weight, too. However, a distinct gendered focus is undeniable, and the imperative for women to slim and transform their bodies is ubiquitous (Frost, 2005). The spread and content of magazines reflect the gender dualism of men/women, mind/body, active/passive, looking/to be looked at, which is still prevalent in contemporary Western societies, and which I will address at various points throughout this book. Body size is closely and irrefutably linked to the gendered issue of beauty and aesthetics, and while a 'big albeit lean body' can be read as an 'intentionally developed and valued' signifier of masculinity (Monaghan, 2007a, p. 587) the culturally constructed beauty ideal for women is to a greater extent associated with slenderness (Bordo, 1993; Chernin, 1983;

Malson, 1998). My quick look across the magazine shelves highlighted this focus on women's body size, and how the body weight messages aimed at fat men differ (in quantity and quality) from those converging on fat women; and fat women's lives also lie at the centre of this book.

The link between beauty and body weight is not entirely new, of course. Stearns (1997) dates the 'initial crusade against fat' (p. 3) around 1900, with the middle classes in the USA starting their fight against fat between 1890 and 1910. And while this drive for slenderness was mainly seen in the middle and upper classes, geographically it was not restricted to America. One example from European history is Empress Elisabeth (often called Sisi) of Austria-Hungary's documented ambition to be remembered as the most beautiful female monarch. This led her to diet and exercise excessively, in order to maintain a weight of 45 kg (being 172 cm tall) and in addition use corseting to reduce her waist even further. Men were not exempt either, and were reportedly dieting in the nineteenth and into the twentieth century to obtain a large, muscly and fat-free body (Stearns, 1997). Generally, and across genders, body size in the early twentieth century was already being considered a window on the real person (Schwartz, 1986). What is different about today's war on fat is how gendered discourses of beauty, health and responsibility simultaneously converge on fat individuals, with an unequal pressure on women, producing the (predominantly) female abject fat body.

There does not seem to be much good evidence for the generalised and global negative claims against fat and fat individuals (Aphramor, 2005, 2010; Bacon and Aphramor, 2011), which begs the question after their ubiquity and persistence. Other writers from various disciplines (Campos, 2011; Orbach, 2006a; Rich *et al.*, 2011a) are critiquing the current war on obesity and the reductionist approach taken to it in research as well as health promotion and day-to-day discourses. Their writing reflects my personal experience of an increasing embodied body size consciousness over the past 15 years, and particularly during my research. As a woman whose objective it is to stimulate some badly needed critical discussion about weight and stir up some doubt about the taken-for-granted 'truths' around fat, my responses to questions concerning my research interests kept changing in the attempt to pre-empt the often-made assumption that I was either investigating the health risks incurred by 'being fat' or on the lookout for another (weight loss) intervention. Often, even after quite a lot of explaining, the idea that I may not think that fat was bad was obviously so difficult to comprehend that it was simply not accepted. Some people stopped eating in front of me, but the most frequent reaction was the question: why are you interested in that – were you bigger in the past? Or, more bluntly: were you fat yourself once? My body weight history suddenly seemed to become important to friends and participants alike, and also no doubt affected my reaction to people in the interviews (and vice versa), and the way I have analysed and interpreted the data (Burns, 2003). In fact, it probably also affected the choice of research methodology: my own self-consciousness about weight made me more sensitive to how the issue of 'obesity' was being dealt with within the mainstream psychological and medical literature, and to the way body weight, diets, women's body shapes, and so forth are talked about in society.

Over the past 15 years, since having moved to the UK from Germany, where I was brought up, I had also experienced what I may call an increased 'feminisation'. I associate this with the way gender is (or at least was), in my experience, a lot more 'performed' by women through clothes, make-up and demeanour in England than in Germany. The gender rules appear to be stricter here – certain things had to be adhered to if one wanted to call oneself a woman. This applied to behaviours, for example, drinking half pints rather than pints, and particularly to appearance. *Being* a woman and a person was not enough – it was performed femininity that was (not only heterosexually) valued and considered attractive, and the more immersed I got in the English culture and discourses, the more I felt that I literally had to *show* that I was a woman, by wearing the right clothes, preferably having long hair, putting on make-up, and so forth. Interestingly, my research had a similar effect on my weight consciousness; while my thoughts on the topic never strayed from a feminist, fat acceptance and egalitarian take on the issue of body size, I became more and more self-conscious of my own body the more I immersed myself in the literature, i.e. discourses on the topic. For all these reasons, and partly grounded in my own very much embodied experiences of the regulatory power of discourses (which I will reflect on throughout this book), I found that a poststructuralist approach best met the requirement for a badly needed opposition that challenges both the constructions of fat women (and fat individuals generally) as a homogeneous group in need of treatment, and the construction and positioning of (fat) women in contemporary UK and, generally, Western society.

Body size nowadays is not only a matter of beauty, however. According to the World Health Organization (2012), the prevalence of 'overweight' and 'obesity' is increasing globally and in the UK (Rennie and Jebb, 2005), and health professionals and the government are warning of an 'obesity epidemic', with recent headlines claiming that the UK was the fattest nation in Europe (BBC News, 2011). Reasons to slim are frequently embedded in discourses of health (Murray, 2005b) and the alleged 'obesity epidemic' is said to bear not only health risks for the individual, but financial implications for the nation, too. Higher health services costs due to an increase in chronic diseases, for instance, are often blamed on, or at least anticipated by, the growing waistline of western populations (Department of Health, 2004a; McPherson *et al.*, 2007). Thus body weight has become associated with each individual's responsibility for her or his own physical health, as well as a responsibility for the nation's financial health. One report on the BBC news website, based on an article published in the medical journal *The Lancet* (Edwards and Roberts, 2008), took this allocation of responsibility another step further and accused 'obese people' of also 'contributing to the world food crisis and climate change' (www.bbc.co.uk, accessed 16 May 2008). So not only are fat[1] people constituted as responsible for their own health, and the national health services' financial health, but their responsibility/guilt is now being extended globally, affecting the lives of each individual on earth. And in some areas it is both women and men who seem to be (albeit fairly unequal) targets in the current 'war on obesity', driven in part by relentless news bulletins on the impact of an increased body weight on our health, and seemingly more and more drastic measures to counteract this.

In summer 2011, for example, a new report on the threat 'obesity' posed to western populations was published in the medical journal *The Lancet* (The Editor, 2011). A taxation of junk food was – yet again – among the recommended interventions to prevent a further increase, and possibly effect a decrease, in the prevalence of 'obesity'. The report and its recommendations triggered a week's worth of bulletins on news programmes, including interviews with one of the authors of the report, Professor McPhearson, as well as radio panel discussions and call-in radio programmes on what the public perceived as the best measures to slim the UK. A few months on and another campaign, part of the UK National Health Service's (2011) Change4Life programme, sees thousands of leaflets sent out to families advising them on healthy eating and providing recipes. Of course these examples are only snippets of the amount of media coverage on 'obesity' and its risks, not even counting the number of mentions of it in many media items on other health-related issues, often, it seems, just to increase the report's news worthiness. A recent Sky News headline, for instance, read 'Cancer "caused by obesity and bad diet"' (Brady, 2011). On closer inspection, the main cause of cancer was reported as smoking, there were links made to nutrition, and weight was just one smaller contributor among several. Body weight now seems to be made a factor in almost all health matters and the word 'obesity' is worth adding to any report or headline for impact's sake – there is no getting away from it.

Within all these reports, news bulletins and popular magazine articles, there is rarely a critical voice against the weight loss mantra to be heard. Fat discourses are so prevalent, and knowledges produced therein so taken for granted, that not even peer-reviewed journal articles, for example in the fields of dietetics and medicine, need to be explicit about the risks or health benefits of weight loss, and the lack of references for these is often not challenged (for one example, see Wang *et al.*, 2011); the 'facts about fat' seem clear and obvious to everybody and as such no evidence is necessary. As Bacon and Aphramor (2011) contend, weight loss seems to enjoy a special immunity from scrutiny of facts (p. 1).

Most of these reports point towards the individual as the target of remedial action, which reflects the message delivered by health promotion agencies and the Department of Health. Initiatives like Healthy Town, for example, at first sight are aiming to change people's living environment (Department of Health, 2008b). The focus here is on improving people's health through an increase in activity levels, by providing more opportunities for cycling and walking, and making healthy food more accessible. These initiatives are presented as good ways of improving people's quality of life and nine towns and cities were chosen as Healthy Towns to share the £30 million Healthy Community Challenge Fund. However, while the stated aims are improved health and quality of life, the outcome measure, the target of this initiative, is individuals' weight loss. This is just one part of the Department of Health's Healthy Weight, Healthy Lives programme (Department of Health, 2008b, p. 23) which in turn comes under the umbrella of the Change4Life campaign. In the Department of Health's (2008a) press release promoting this initiative, ill health and 'obesity' are consistently equated and the main objective of the Change4Life programme seems to be to 'combat the obesity epidemic'

(Department of Health, 2008a) by encouraging 'healthy' living. The blanket generalisation and equation of 'health' with body weight disregard people's individual life circumstances and lifestyles, the gender issues associated with social contexts, people's well-being and health status, as well as their subjective experiences of being 'large' or fat in contemporary society. Being the focus of health promotion campaigns also seems to make fat individuals 'legitimate' targets for discrimination and stigmatisation, the extent and effect of which are well documented in the literature (Annis *et al.*, 2004; Puhl and Brownell, 2003a; Rogge *et al.*, 2004; Vartanian and Shaprow, 2008). Fat individuals, admittedly, are not the only ones affected by this 'healthism', as smokers (especially in terms of second-hand smoking) and other social groups with less than medically sanctioned 'ideal lifestyles' have been targeted in similar ways (Department of Health, 2004b). However, smokers, for example, can put their cigarettes out of sight, while 'large' individuals always carry their bodies around with them (Monaghan, 2007b, personal communication; Stearns, 1997). As such, they are always visible and always-already constituted as 'health offenders' in a culture where mutual policing (and hence stigma and discrimination) seem 'justified' in the name of the 'war on obesity'. For more on the issue of visibility and fat, see Chapter 3.

The focus on the individual (and more often than not, on the individual woman) in this 'war on obesity' is also evident in the medical and psychological literature which, within medicine, concentrates on the health risks, causes and treatment of 'obesity' (Lawrence and Kopelman, 2004; Miles *et al.*, 2001; World Health Organization, 2012) and, within psychology, the links between eating behaviour and mental health, psychological causes of fat, psychological weight loss interventions and attitudes towards 'large' individuals (Blaine, 2008; Cramer and Steinwert, 1998; Henderson and Huon, 2002; Heo *et al.*, 2006; Puhl and Brownell, 2003a; Shaw *et al.*, 2005). A more detailed literature review follows in Chapter 2; however, it is fair to say that within the mainstream medical and psychological literatures, being 'fat', 'large' or 'obese' is discussed as a problem in need of treatment or 'cure'. Its causes are seen as located primarily within, and interventions are aimed at, individuals and their lifestyle choices, with an emphasis on a simplistic energy balance equation, or the injunctions 'eat less!' and 'move more!'.

This individualism is not only a characteristic of mainstream (health) psychology but a general feature of all aspects of life in neoliberal societies like the UK. Here, freedom and autonomy of the individual are highly valued, and defended against any potential risk of restriction. However, this freedom is not simply a right but also an obligation (Rose, 1996) – an obligation to consider oneself free and autonomous in one's choices, and consequently also responsible for the outcomes of the latter. As I will argue later, the state's responsibility in this has been reduced to providing adequate information for the neoliberal citizen to make the right, informed choices. This is also evident in the popular media, for example, in a new BBC Radio 4 programme for the year 2012, entitled Inside Health. In one of the promotional clips for the programme, its presenter, Dr Mark Porter, promised to provide clarity about health issues and thus to empower people to make informed decisions about their own health. Implied here is that health is indeed something concrete and achievable, rather than mysterious, and above all, a matter of choice rather than fate. Thus, the liberty promised by neoliberalism is also a regulated and regulative freedom: while people are, as Nikolas Rose (1996) maintains, free to choose their own way in life, including lifestyle, the choices open to individuals are restricted by what is considered normative as well as beneficial to the individual and society within a certain culture. The 'ideal' person regulates her/himself according to societal rules, based on expert advice, to achieve the highest level possible of 'self-realization, self-esteem and self-fulfilment' (Rose, 1996, p. 2); being 'healthy' is part of each individual's duty (Cheek, 2008) within this project of self-perfection. From a neoliberal perspective, health is constituted as an achievable and obligatory outcome of lifestyle choice, as something that can be performed rather than something that one enjoys. The body, or rather the appearance of one's body, serves as a symbol of how well a woman performs in her ongoing 'health project', with the slim body symbolising (among other things) self-control and her ability to stick to a healthy diet (Lupton, 1996). Julianne Cheek (2008) calls this the 'what if approach to health' rather than 'what is' (p. 974), where the absence of any physical disease is no longer enough to be considered healthy, and health is something we have the freedom and choice, as well as the responsibility, to perform:

> Health has become . . . a new form of badge of honor by which we can claim to be responsible and worthy both as citizens and individuals.
>
> (Cheek, 2008, p. 974)

Making the right (healthy) lifestyle choices produces individuals as 'successful, moral [and] disciplined citizens' (Murray, 2005b, p. 111), who take responsibility for their 'health' and lifestyle, in the knowledge that they owe it not only to themselves to be the best 'self' possible, but also to society generally and their close family and friends in particular. A stark illustration of this latter point was offered by a recent instalment of the British weight loss reality show *The Biggest Loser* (ITV, 2012). Here participants were competing against each other for the biggest weight loss as well as a £25,000 cash price. During the first screening of this programme, each contestant was weighed publicly, i.e. literally in a very public place like a town square, surrounded by family, friends and presumably unrelated onlookers. After having had their weight displayed on a big screen, for everybody to see, contestants stated their weight loss motivation and many, often in tears, promised their family and friends 'the wife/daughter/mum that [they] so desperately, desperately deserve' (Gemma). Many spoke of disgust and hate for themselves and their unsexy and unattractive bodies, and of shame and guilt, whilst the coaches they would be working with (all looking toned, slim and no-nonsense) 'don't apologise for what [they] are going to do to them' as the programme was going to be 'tough but worth it'.

Within these individual health projects, what counts as healthy lifestyle is based on the notion that physical health is only possible in a slim body that stays within certain medically defined body weight limits (Campos, 2004; Kim and Popkin,

2006; Lawrence and Kopelman, 2004). This notion, as mentioned earlier, does not go unchallenged by academics (Campos *et al.*, 2006a; Cogan and Ernsberger, 1999; Lyons and Miller, 1999; Miller, 1999), health professionals (Aphramor, 2005; Ernsberger and Koletsky, 1999) or pro-fat activists (Cooper, 1998), however. One of the critics' arguments is that weight is not a reliable indicator of health (Campos *et al.*, 2006a) and an emphasis on weight loss is deemed not only ineffective but also potentially harmful (Austin, 1999; Campos, 2004; Orbach, 2006a). There is no consistent and reliable evidence for the extreme risks health promotion agencies continuously associate with 'obesity' which would justify the use of the term 'epidemic', and rarely are confounding factors such as weight cycling taken into account in the interpretation of the evidence (Campos, 2004; Campos *et al.*, 2006a; Ernsberger, 2004). At the same time, the benefits of weight loss are deemed at best contentious (Aphramor, 2005), with some critics associating dieting, weight loss and the general pursuit of slimness with a number of risks to the individual's well-being, such as the development of eating disorders, generally negative impacts on psychological health (Cogan and Ernsberger, 1999) and physical effects such as loss of bone mass (Aphramor, 2008b).

Another strand of critical literature engages with the cultural and sociopolitical background to, and the implications of, the current focus in health policy on body weight and size (Burns and Gavey, 2008; Gard and Wright, 2005; Malson, 2008; Murray, 2005a; Orbach, 2006a). They are asserting that in the current neoliberal atmosphere of healthism, health and healthcare have been made the individual's responsibility and body weight has become the prime indicator of a person's health status (Malson, 2008) and, by extension, moral standing. According to Samantha Murray (2005b), Western societies have developed what she calls a 'collective "knowingness" about fatness' (Malson, 2008, p. 154) in as much as there is the assumption that we are able to discern a fat person's history and lifestyle from her or his body size. This collective 'knowingness', mobilised by the health promotion and media messages disseminated on a day-to-day basis, can function to legitimise an increased stigmatisation and discrimination of 'large' individuals (Gard and Wright, 2005; Puhl and Brownell, 2003a). The vilification of fat together with the individualisation of the responsibility for health can thus lead to the exclusion, marginalisation and oppression of individuals who do not fit within the narrow socially accepted body weight bracket.

A lot of the critical literature in relation to body size is of a feminist nature, which is not surprising if one considers that appearance, the body and health are all highly gendered issues (Bordo, 1993, 1998; Craik, 1994; Lupton, 1996; Malson, 2008; Wolf, 1991). Since writings as early as Aristotle, women have been associated with the body, while men were associated with the mind, and throughout history women's bodies were 'political' in as much as they were implicated in the politics of gendered power relations (Weitz, 2003). Women and women's bodies have been construed as incomplete, lacking, 'other' to men and their bodies (Weitz, 2003), and even today physical experiences that are specific to women (for example, pregnancy and postnatal depression) are frequently pathologised, with the cause being sought in the alleged inferior biological make-up of a woman's body

(Nicolson, 2004; Ussher, 2006, 2008; Weitz, 2003). Efforts to define premenstrual and postmenopausal experiences as illness may also be seen as backlash reactions to the feminist movement and as attempts to keep women in 'their place', the family home (Weitz, 2003; Wilkinson, 2004). Similar connections between feminist achievements and the increasing focus on a slim female body that is shaped to 'perfection' by means of exercise, diet and/or plastic surgery, have been made by Naomi Wolf (1991) and others. And while some may contend that we are now living in a postfeminist era, with women having access to the same opportunities and choices as men, not that much has changed in the underlying unequal power relations. The difference lies in the perception of female agency: women are now seen as freely choosing to carry out the exactly same beautification practices as always (or more, considering aesthetic surgery) purely for their own benefits, rather than for men or due to patriarchal oppression (Braun, 2009; Gill, 2007). Despite an increasing focus on men's appearance, it is thus undeniable that the issues of appearance and health are highly gendered and political, and that women are under greater and qualitatively different pressures to conform to a socially constructed 'beauty' and body size norm.

With this book I would like to extend the critical literature on fat and gender further, aiming to inspire a reform in the way we think about and treat fat (female) bodies. Most of the critical literature in regard to body size either remains within the theoretical domain, or critiques the current dominant take on 'obesity' from a medical or individualistic psychological perspective. My aim is to build on and extend this research by taking a critical social psychological and feminist standpoint, exploring how the dominant discourses within the current fat-phobic and healthist cultural atmosphere play out on fat individuals and women in particular. Multiple gendered discourses converge on fat women (and men) and I was curious to look at how 'large' women are positioned within them and how they discursively manage their subjectivities and subject positions within the politics of 'obesity'. As such I am exploring how 'fat women' and (to a lesser degree) 'fat men' are discursively constituted (in both women's and men's talk), as well as the gendered constructions of embodied fat, health and well-being, and the power relations and conditions of possibilities produced in discourses of body size and gender in contemporary Western cultures.

While being concerned with more global discourses on fat, I also wanted to involve fat individuals and their stories and have interviewed 'large' women and men, individually and in focus groups, on topics such as the language of fat, the media, appearance, lifestyle and health. The audio-recordings of these discussions were transcribed and analysed using Foucauldian discourse analysis. Fat individuals, and fat women in particular, seem to be caught in an interwoven nexus of discourses of beauty/aesthetics, health, self-perfection and individual responsibility, which seems to marginalise and disempower them within a number of fields. Reform, according to Foucault, cannot be achieved through the direct call for reform, but only through critique by uncovering the origins of the prevailing 'regimes of truth' and the power relations inherent in them (Foucault, 2002a). Taking a critical psychological perspective, based on poststructuralist and feminist theories, exploring the discourses at play within the articulations of fat individuals will enable me to add to this important process of disclosure, and thus contribute to a reform in our societal take on fat. As such, the analysis of my participants' narratives will form the biggest part of this book.

Following on from these introductory pages, I will continue with a review and critique of the literature in Chapter 1. Given the abundance of literature on 'obesity', this review will inevitably be very focused on the narrow range of publications relevant to my research. I will give a brief overview of the mainstream medical and psychological literature on 'obesity', after which I will concentrate on the critical and feminist literature dealing with body weight and body size. In Chapter 2, I will then outline the epistemological framework and related theories my research was based on, namely, as mentioned above, a critical psychological perspective grounded in poststructuralist and feminist theory. There are many overlaps between the critical literature discussed in Chapter 1 and the theoretical literature covered in Chapter 2, and the decision to present them in two different chapters was a purely pragmatic and structural one. Although I am using a similar perspective to many of the critical publications covered in Chapter 1, I feel that it is useful to concentrate on 'obesity' and 'body weight' in the literature review while laying out the general theories and perspectives my research is based on in Chapter 2.

Chapters 3–6 form the main content and heart of this book. In these four chapters I am concentrating on the data of my research, focusing in its analysis on the following main themes: the in/visibility of fat women, issues of clothing choice and availability, the constructions of health, responsibility (for both health and weight) and the responsible neoliberal citizen, and, finally, gender and fat. It may seem curious to have a separate chapter on 'gender' within a book that deals with the clearly gendered topic of fat, and issues of 'gender' and 'gender politics' indeed run through all chapters. However, there was not much direct or outspoken engagement with 'gender' in the interviews with the women, while all the men made mention, for example, of the increased pressures women are under in regard to body weight. The general lack of mention of 'gender' in the women's interviews and the noted difference in engagement with this topic (which I in part would attribute to an interview-specific artefact) guided my decision to dedicate some focus groups and a separate chapter to the issue of 'gendering fat'.

I round up this book in Chapter 7 by providing a summary and brief discussion of the main concerns identified in this publication, their (political and health promotion) implications, and the importance for critical and poststructuralist feminist psychology to be involved in the exploration and improvement of fat lives.

1   Putting the fat body in context

Outlining a context for the fat body in contemporary Western society could be seen as both unnecessary and impossible. It could be viewed as unnecessary with media reports on the alleged 'obesity epidemic' and related topics surrounding us all on a daily basis – surely there cannot be anybody who does not know the common view on fat. At the same time it is near impossible to provide a review of the literature that does justice to the amount and complexity of knowledge production on the subject matter, particularly if one wants to avoid the trap of reproducing the taken-for-granted 'truths' which I endeavour to challenge. As anybody can imagine, the amount of literature on the topic of 'fat' is immense and ranges from reports on medical research findings to books and articles written and edited by fat acceptance activists. A comprehensive review of this literature would constitute a book in itself. The objective here thus is to provide a context for the ongoing debate around body weight, by drawing out the different voices involved in this discussion, with a particular focus on adult fat individuals and their fat embodiment. With this in mind I will briefly summarise the mainstream medical and psychological literature on the subject matter, as well as its critics in the form of the Health at Every Size (HAES), the fat studies and fat acceptance movements, before moving on to explore the critical psychological, sociological and feminist literature on body size and 'being large' in more detail.

Fat is bad and weight loss the global objective: the biomedical view

This is no doubt the most prominent voice on the issue: In addition to general medical journals, like the *British Medical Journal,* for example, which all publish reports of research into body weight and its alleged correlations with ill health, there are a variety of publications that take 'obesity' as the (or one of their) focal point. Among these are titles with a relatively narrow focus, such as *Current Opinion in Endocrinology, Diabetes and Obesity*, and others that are covering a broad range of disciplines engaged with the topic of body weight, such as the *International Journal of Obesity* and *Obesity Review*. Within the medical literature, both 'obesity' and 'overweight' are defined as measures based on a weight-to-height ratio, the body mass index (BMI), which is calculated with the formula: weight (kilograms) / (height (metres))^2. Based on this calculation, a BMI of less than 18.5 is considered 'underweight', 18.5–24.9 as 'healthy', 25–29.9 as 'overweight' and anything above 30 as 'obese' (with varying degrees). Whilst a grading of 'overweight' and 'obese' exists in theory, the (academic and popular) literature generally collapses the categories of 'overweight' and 'obesity' into one when talking about the risks and consequences of 'high' body weights.

The variety of subtopics covered on the issue of fat is immense, ranging from research into biochemical factors in the determination of body weight to reviews on the efficacy of weight loss surgery (Colquitt *et al.*, 2009). They include research into the biomedical and biochemical processes associated with 'large' bodies, for example the biochemical processes involved in energy homeostasis, that is, the regulation of energy intake and energy expenditure (Hivert *et al.*, 2007; Morris *et al.*, 2008; Yang and Harmon, 2003); investigations into possible appetite or food choice regulation through medication, food supplementation and other biochemical substances (Hallschmid *et al.*, 2008; Zhao *et al.*, 2005); and genetic factors believed to be implicated in 'obesity' (Beckers *et al.*, 2006; Farooqi and O'Rahilly, 2007; Stutzmann *et al.*, 2009).

Not surprisingly, a great number of studies are carried out into surgical and non-surgical weight loss interventions and their evaluation. Apart from bariatric surgery, these may focus on the efficacy of weight loss medication (Porter *et al.*, 2004; Poston *et al.*, 2003; Wangsness, 2000), dieting and exercise (separately and in combination) (Riebe *et al.*, 2005; Shaw *et al.*, 2006) and the use of certain nutritional combinations (Thomas *et al.*, 2007). Despite the abundance of literature, Glenny and O'Meara (1997) concluded from their research that, while there may be effective weight loss interventions available, no conclusive evidence for their efficacy (or otherwise) could be found owing to methodological problems in the studies reviewed. A scanning of the Cochrane Reviews available on the topic of 'obesity' (in non-clinical populations) confirms this not to be an isolated issue, and a frequent statement in the authors' conclusions is one of caution. They warn that no clear recommendations could be made based on the evaluation of the majority of medical interventions, often due to poor methodological or reporting quality of the studies reviewed (Colquitt *et al.*, 2009; Flodgren *et al.*, 2010).

A similar picture is drawn by Paul Campos in his book *The Obesity Myth* (2004), where he argues that the vast body of research on weight loss interventions was inconclusive and frequently methodologically flawed, and asserts that the same is true for other anti-obesity research (Campos, 2004). More on Paul Campos and other critics of the biomedical view later.

Another strand of biomedical anti-obesity research concerns itself with the links between body weight and health. 'Obesity' is allegedly associated with a number of health conditions (Yanovski, 2000), such as type 2 diabetes and other endocrinological conditions (Rana *et al.*, 2007), cancer (Bianchini *et al.*, 2002; Harvie *et al.*, 2003) and cardiovascular disease (Wilson *et al.*, 2002), to name the most commonly mentioned (Field *et al.*, 2002; Wang *et al.*, 2011).

One of the conclusions commonly drawn from this abundance of research is that the human physiological system in itself is very complex, including vast individual genetic and other physical differences. Add to this any economic, societal or systemic factors and it becomes ever more apparent that generalisations are very difficult to make, if at all possible, and a lot more research is suggested by many, before any conclusive recommendations can be made (Elliott and Johnson, 2007; Moreno-Aliaga *et al.*, 2005). Interestingly, this notion of complexity is shared by most researchers and activists involved in the field of fat studies. However, the interpretations of this complexity, and resulting conclusions, vary to a great extent across the disciplines and perspectives on fat. The critics of anti-obesity activists and researchers (Saguy and Riley, 2005) would assert that the 'war on obesity', with its focus on body weight, is a harmful overreaction (see below); they are asking for a focus on health rather than weight, at least until there is some clear evidence (if this is at all possible to achieve) that body weights designated as 'overweight' or 'obese' are harmful *per se*.

On the other side, a recent series on 'obesity' published in the *Lancet* (vol. 387, 2011), can probably be seen as a good representation of the general biomedical view on this matter and 'obesity' in general. The series comprises four scholarly articles on different aspects of the alleged 'obesity epidemic', drawing out what they see as the drivers, burdens and possible solution to the problem (Gortmaker *et al.*, 2011; Hall *et al.*, 2011; Swinburn *et al.*, 2011; The Editor, 2011; Wang *et al.*, 2011). In response to the multifaceted nature of the 'obesity' issue, which in their view cannot be solved with one intervention, they are asking for a systems approach to 'obesity' prevention. This approach would involve every single part of contemporary global society, from individuals to the United Nations (Gortmaker *et al.*, 2011). A prevention of obesity, rather than weight loss interventions, is seen as more cost-effective, with the overall goal to reduce the population's weight. Whilst the authors of the series still include weight loss interventions in their list of recommendations, a weight loss simulation model, presented in one of the series' papers (Hall *et al.*, 2011) confirms what many critics have voiced before: weight loss is difficult to achieve and takes a long time; as such, the majority of the funding should be put into 'getting them young'. Preventing children becoming 'obese' adults is seen as the most promising avenue, as 'policy makers begin each year with a new birth cohort, a low rate of obesity, and the opportunity to maintain this situation in the future' (Gortmaker *et al.*, 2011, p. 839).

Generally, the *Lancet* obesity series (2011) reiterates what has been the predominant view of the medical establishment on 'obesity': we are in the middle of a four-decade-old 'obesity epidemic', which, if not stopped, will cost individuals and economies dearly. The alleged burdens range from an increase in type 2 diabetes, various forms of cancer and cardiovascular diseases, to an increased cost not only for the healthcare services but also for the economy, due to an overall loss in productivity (Wang *et al.*, 2011). Based on these predictions, and that is all they are, the last paper in the series calls for global action involving every aspect of societal life, including individual behaviour change, new governmental and global policies, and an integrated and cross-national systems approach, including improved monitoring systems to ensure accurate data of every population's weight and their 'obese' state. The suggested and highly rated interventions range from a taxation of what are deemed unhealthy food stuffs to gastric banding for adolescents. The objective here seems to be exclusively a reduction in population weight in the long term – not population health.

Interestingly, this is in contrast to the most recent Department of Health (for England) paper on public health, Healthy Lives, Healthy People (Department of Health, 2010) which seems to have turned to an increased focus on health rather than weight – at least in choice of language. This begs the question whether the series in the *Lancet* had another objective: to reanimate the focus on, if not to reignite the panic about, the alleged 'obesity epidemic', which after all keeps many anti-obesity researchers and a substantial diet industry in business. The urgent need for anti-obesity action was underlined with 'facts' about health and fat, some of which seem to have obtained such a truth status in the health and popular literature that they do not require further evidence in the form of citations any more – not even in highly regarded scientific journals. One such example is the assertion that a high prevalence of 'obesity' leads to an increase in mortality (Wang *et al.*, 2011, p. 815); a statement that is highly contested and can be challenged with research evidence (Flegal *et al.*, 2005). 'Facts' about fat seem to enjoy immunity from scrutiny, which has been noted by researchers in a variety of publications (Aphramor, 2010) and certainly emphasises the need for a critical exploration of the alleged truths about fat.

The assertions of the medical mainstream, or indeed their use of epidemiological and other research findings, do not go unchallenged, however. I have already mentioned Paul Campos (Campos, 2004; Campos *et al.*, 2006a), who in his book *The Obesity Myth* (2004) investigates and contests the claims made by medical scientists in relation to both the health risks incurred by being fat and their claims that weight loss is beneficial and possible. And the medical establishment also finds critics of their take on body weight within the ranks of health professionals. There is no hard-and-fast, and methodologically sound, evidence for the health benefits of major weight loss (Aphramor, 2005, 2010; Lawrence and Kopelman, 2004), for example, and whilst mortality rates are drawn on for anti-obesity purposes, there is some evidence that the mortality rate for people within the 'overweight' BMI bracket is in fact lower than that for the 'healthy' BMI bracket (Flegal *et al.*, 2005).

Health At Every Size

This lack of evidence for the benefits of weight loss as well as the notion that diets and weight loss can in fact be harmful to people's health, are the focus of the HAES paradigm, which is advocated by a group of academics and health professionals, including Linda Bacon, Lucy Aphramor, Paul Campos, Paul Ernsberger and Wayne Miller. They assert that the current 'war on obesity' is based on a number of assumptions, which Paul Campos (2011) summarises as follows.

1. A strong correlation exists between weight and health risk.
2. This correlation reflects a direct causal relationship. People within the narrow range of 'ideal' weight are healthier than people who are not, because they avoid the detrimental causal effects of overweight and obesity.

3. Significant long-term weight loss is a practical goal, and will improve health.
4. The cost–benefit ratio involved in trying to make people thinner justifies using scarce public health funding to pursue this outcome.

Challenging the above assumptions, critics of the weight-centred approach to health claim that the focus on weight loss can have negative consequences in relation to a person's mental as well as physical health (Bacon and Aphramor, 2011). These 'side-effects' of the weight loss approach are mostly ignored by health professionals and policy makers, to the extent that Lucy Aphramor considers the current practice of recommending weight loss interventions to patients referred for cardiac health advice not only as inefficient but also as unethical (Aphramor, 2005, 2008b; Bacon and Aphramor, 2011). According to Aphramor, the weight loss approach to health can be said to violate the principles of professional good practice by not adhering to the requirements of treatment beneficence and of not inflicting any harm. Above all, the current weight loss focus falls down on issues of patient information, which demands that patients are made fully aware of any potential side-effects of medical treatments as well as their potential for success. Patients are rarely fully informed of the health risks associated with weight loss diets, for example, loss of bone mass (Aphramor, 2008b; Shapses and Cifuentes, 2003), or negative effects on psychological well-being (Bacon and Aphramor, 2011; McFarlane *et al.*, 1999). This lack of information prevents individuals from giving truly informed consent, which is another requirement of ethical professional practice.

Similarly, though coming from an approach that is less focused on clinical practice in dietetics, Cogan and Ernsberger (1999), among many others, maintain that the pursuit of thinness can lead to disordered eating practices (Austin, 1999; Bordo, 1993; Burns and Gavey, 2004; Rich and Evans, 2005; Wooley and Garner, 1994) and a deterioration in mental health in the form of depression and body dissatisfaction (Kiefer *et al.*, 2000). All these side-effects of dieting and weight loss seem to get eclipsed, however, with weight loss taking centre stage in the current predominant approach to health. It seems like the persistently replayed message that any degree of 'adiposity' is bad and that we have to lose weight 'at any cost' (Kiefer *et al.*, 2000, p. 90) has created a society where people would rather live with a number of disabilities or diseases (including leg amputation and blindness) than be 'fat' (Rand and MacGregor, 1991, cited by Miller, 2005).

An alternative approach advocated by Miller and other critics (Aphramor, 2008b; Bacon and Aphramor, 2011; Burgard, 2006; Miller and Jacob, 2001) is the HAES approach, which maintains that health is possible for people of any size and calls for a focus on increasing the health of the population through the promotion of healthy diets (not to be confused with weight loss diets) and exercise, regardless of body weight. According to the advocates of this approach, there is plenty of evidence that:

(1) there is no direct association between adiposity and disease,
(2) mortality risk is more strongly associated with fitness than with fatness,
(3) weight loss is not necessary for an improved metabolic profile,

(4)   the fat person responds to exercise training just as the lean person does, and
(5)   you can be fit and fat.

(Miller, 2005, p. S90)

The HAES paradigm asserts that weight loss is not required for health improvement, and that a salutogenic lifestyle benefits individuals of any size. Lifestyle changes can improve a person's health where this is necessary, while weight loss may or may not be a side-effect of these changes, but should not be seen as an objective. There is, in fact, a good amount of evidence that challenges the benefits of weight loss in relation to mortality and morbidity (see Aphramor, 2010; Bacon and Aphramor, 2011 for a comprehensive review). This evidence not only questions the value in weight loss but generally contests the alleged causal links between body fat and morbidity. Bacon and Aphramor summarise the leitmotifs of the HAES paradigm as follows.

1.   HAES encourages body acceptance as opposed to weight loss or weight maintenance.
2.   HAES supports reliance on internal regulatory processes, such as hunger and satiety, as opposed to encouraging cognitively imposed dietary restriction.
3.   HAES supports active embodiment as opposed to encouraging structured exercise

(Bacon and Aphramor, 2011, p. 6).

The HAES approach still advocates, however, that 'health is a result of behaviours' (Miller, 2005, p. S89) and, while it opposes the vilification of 'large' individuals as unhealthy, it still places the responsibility for a person's health, albeit under consideration of potential constraints through the cultural and physical environment, with the individual.

Fat acceptance and activism

The first point of the above HAES leitmotivs will certainly resonate with most fat acceptance researchers and activists, although there are disagreements as to where this acceptance should emanate from – society or the individual fat person. The fat acceptance movement is often said to have started with the foundation of NAAFA (the National Association to Aid Fat Americans, subsequently renamed the National Association for the Advancement of Fat Acceptance) in 1969 – starting out in the USA, from where it expanded globally. NAAFA's mission is to 'eliminate discrimination based on body size and provide fat people with the tools for self-empowerment through public education, advocacy, and support' (NAAFA, 2011). This mission is followed both on a national and policy level, e.g. by campaigning for a change in equality laws or against offensive media representation; and on a personal level by providing support and advocacy to individuals, running support groups and workshops (Saguy and Riley, 2005).

For some, however, NAAFA and its activities are not radical enough. This was first evident in a splinter group, the Fat Underground (FU), which formed in the 1970s and followed a more radical feminist line. This connection between fat acceptance, fat activism and feminism has remained constant ever since, despite the fact that the FU in its original format ceased to exist in the late 1980s.

And it should be noted that not all fat activism is exclusively bound to official organisations. There are a great number of individual fat activists, from Charlotte Cooper in the UK to Marilyn Wann in the USA, who draw attention to and fight against fat phobia, fat discrimination and the stereotypes often held against fat individuals by writing books and through direct action.

For a comprehensive account on the history of the fat movement I would like to direct the reader to Charlotte Cooper's book *Fat and Proud* (1998), as well as publications by Saguy and Riley (2005) and Samantha Murray. In her book *The Fat Female Body* (2008), Murray in fact criticises certain aspects of the fat acceptance movement for trying to change the world for fat people on a purely cognitive basis, ignoring the facts that we are embodied beings, and that none of us exists in a societal or interactional vacuum. Drawing on Linda Alcoff, Murray asserts that we are reading and creating meaning off each other's bodies, i.e. on an intercorporeal level. It is impossible to change the world for fat people by individually accepting our (fat) bodies. Whilst I would agree with this statement, it is exactly the intercorporeality and complex societal world we live in which calls for an equally complex and multifaceted approach to activism – within which individual fat and body acceptance has a big role to play.

And Samantha Murray would not want these activities to be abandoned either. She also calls for an acknowledgement of and dealing with the complicated and intercorporeal nature of social life, which currently produces processes of disempowerment and discrimination for fat individuals. As such, to effect change, activism equally has to happen at this complicated, societal and intercorporeal level, as well as the individual level.

This seems an apt place to add a little qualifier to the structure of this chapter. I have presented my overview of the contributions of the fat acceptance movement as a separate section because I wanted to draw attention to their work, and it could be seen as one of the more distinct 'voices' engaged in the 'obesity' debate. This division into distinct sections is an artificial and pragmatic one, however; we will find critics of the weight-focused approach to health in the mainstream medical camp, just as we will find feminists among fat acceptance activists, and those engaged in work based in sociology as well as critical and mainstream psychology. And it is the latter I will turn my attention to now.

What does psychology have to say about 'being large'?

Mainstream psychological work has a strong focus on the individual and deviance, and in relation to 'obesity' broadly speaking is trying to answer the following questions: 'Why are people fat?' (Blaine, 2008; Henderson and Huon, 2002), 'How does "being large" affect people's lives?' (Engel *et al.*, 2003; Friedman *et al.*, 2005;

Heo *et al.*, 2006) and, often drawing on answers to the first two questions: 'How can we help people to lose weight?' (Shaw *et al.*, 2005). In the UK, the professional body of psychologists (the British Psychological Society) feels that psychology currently is underinvolved in the 'war on obesity', and stated in a recent report on the issue that:

> whilst Cognitive Behavioural Therapy is briefly mentioned in the NICE [National Institute for Clinical Excellence] (2006) obesity guidelines as the recommended way to address behavioural change through psychological issues associated with obesity, psychological issues are generally not receiving as much attention as sociological and diet issues as ways of tackling this growing epidemic. . . . [T]he British Psychological Society attempts to redress this with a cohesive approach between academic and applied work by producing a report on psychological approaches to obesity.
>
> (BPS Obesity Working Group, 2011, p. 3)

'Approaches to obesity' in this context can be taken as interventions for weight loss and behaviour change. As psychology is considered the science of human behaviour, questions after the 'why' are mostly based on the assumption that, biomedically, weight gain is caused by overeating and a lack of exercise. As such, the task for psychology is often seen as that of discovering the reasons why individuals behave in 'obesogenic' ways and subsequently apply this knowledge to facilitate behaviour change in fat individuals, with the aim of weight loss. Fat individuals' health beliefs, and perceptions of weight gain and weight loss, are also psychological factors under investigation (Befort *et al.*, 2008; Cachelin *et al.*, 1998; Holt *et al.*, 2001). These studies have the aim to establish common beliefs and cognitive and behavioural attributes among 'large' individuals, which are not shared with individuals of 'normative' weight. Finding such shared attributes is believed to help in the development of new, successful psychological weight loss treatments. Most psychological weight loss interventions are based on cognitive and behavioural theories (Melchionda *et al.*, 2003; Shaw *et al.*, 2005), and it is hoped that finding behavioural or cognitive attributes common in, but specific to, 'large' individuals will explain their eating behaviours, and provide targets for psychological behaviour change treatments.

Similar to medical studies mentioned earlier, a recent review of psychological interventions for childhood 'obesity' (Bogle and Sykes, 2011) concluded that, whilst some promising strategies were identified (e.g. interventions aimed at increasing physical activity, or population-based school-wide campaigns), the limitations and heterogeneity of the studies reviewed meant that no firm recommendations could be gleaned from the review. In another review, the quality of the research included was equally criticised (Shaw *et al.*, 2005); however, cognitive behavioural therapy was in fact identified as more successful in psychological weight loss interventions than other forms of treatment. Of course, underlying all these interventions are the assumptions that 'being large' is detrimental for our health and weight loss is beneficial for everybody (Cogan and Ernsberger, 1999); from this putatively follows that the fat individual's shared behavioural and cognitive attributes must be flawed and consequently corrected.

Apart from influences on eating behaviour, 'obesity'-related psychological research looks into affective responses such as depression, self-esteem and anger, which are frequently associated with 'obesity' or its treatments. 'Obese' individuals are more prone to depression than non-obese individuals (Heo *et al.*, 2006), but there are divided opinions on whether depression causes 'obesity' or 'obesity' causes depression (Blaine, 2008; Stunkard *et al.*, 2003). Receiving weight loss treatment seems to reduce the severity of depression; however, this is independent of the amount of weight loss achieved, which indicates that depression may pre-exist 'obesity' and that the psychotherapeutic attention in itself results in psychological benefits (Blaine *et al.*, 2007). On the other hand, dieting, that is reducing one's energy intake to a very low level, has also been shown to have detrimental effects on people's psychological well-being (McFarlane *et al.*, 1999). So here, too, no consensus has been found yet, and there are many confounding factors involved in the link between depression and 'being large' (Heo *et al.*, 2006; Siegel *et al.*, 2000).

Weight stigma and its effects

The psychological interest in 'obesity' does not end with weight loss treatments. Body image has been a growing field within psychology for decades, and as we are living in a society where fat is considered ugly and disgusting (Foster *et al.*, 2003; LeBesco and Braziel, 2001; Malson, 1998; Russell-Mayhew, 2006), it comes as no surprise that 'being large' has been found to have negative effects on body image (Annis *et al.*, 2004; Matz *et al.*, 2002; Schwartz and Brownell, 2004). Negative body image, or body dissatisfaction, is often linked with anti-fat attitudes or the stigmatisation of 'large' individuals (Friedman *et al.*, 2005; Ogden, 2006; Pepper and Ruiz, 2007), and there is a vast amount of social psychological literature on the topic of weight-based stereotypes and stigma. 'Large' people are the subject of numerous negative and damaging stereotypes, including being considered stupid, less likable, ugly, lazy and less self-disciplined, sexless and less feminine, less friendly or popular, less happy or self-confident, unhealthy – the list goes on (Cordell and Ronai, 1999; Latner and Stunkard, 2003; Puhl and Brownell, 2003b). These stereotypes feed into the stigmatisation and discrimination of 'large' individuals in a variety of settings and across a diversity of people (Puhl and Brownell, 2001, 2003b). Health professionals like nurses and doctors are not exempt from holding anti-fat biases, and while they are slightly less pronounced than those of the general public (Teachman and Brownell, 2001), these biases are still very strong and pervasive and include health professionals who specialise in working with 'obese' patients (Brown, 2006; Schwartz *et al.*, 2003; Teachman and Brownell, 2001).

Anti-fat attitudes, stigmatisation and experiences of discrimination have also been found to have negative effects on 'large' individuals' psychological well-being in regard to depression, body image and self-esteem (Annis *et al.*, 2004;

Friedman *et al.*, 2005) as well as on their exercise behaviour (Vartanian and Shaprow, 2008). Contrary to findings that stigma experiences may increase motivation for and practices of weight loss (Latner *et al.*, 2009; Ogden, 2006), other studies suggest that weight stigma could deter 'large' individuals from exercise and thus be counterproductive in relation to a healthy lifestyle (Seacat and Mickelson, 2009; Vartanian and Shaprow, 2008). An interesting area within the research on weight stigma and discrimination is the investigation into the links between anti-fat biases and an attribution of controllability of body weight. As I have already mentioned in the previous chapter, and will further discuss below, current health promotion strategies are based on the notion of choice in relation to health and lifestyle (Department of Health, 2004a, 2006) and as such the individual is made responsible for her or his body weight and by extension for her or his health. In addition to being assigned this responsibility for their own health, 'large' individuals are currently also, at least implicitly, given responsibility for the financial health of the National Health Service. With repeated reports on how much the treatment of conditions associated with 'obesity' cost (Wang *et al.*, 2011), the link is easily made to the individual 'large' person representing a drain on the National Health Service's budget, and thus on the nation's wealth.

One of the more recent warnings came from epidemiologists who claim that the global increase in the prevalence of 'obesity' has implications for the environment (Edwards and Roberts, 2009), which was made into an even more alarming headline in some newspapers, for example *Metro*: 'Being fat is bad for you – and the environment' (Taylor, 2009). Considering this, it is not surprising that studies found that anti-fat prejudice was predicted by attributions of controllability of body weight – the more people thought fat people were in control of their weight, and by extension responsible for their weight and health, the more anti-fat bias there was (Crandall and Martinez, 1996; Crandall *et al.*, 2001).

It could thus be argued that the current focus on individual responsibility for health and body weight within health promotion discourses increases the stigma and discrimination faced by 'large' individuals (Orbach, 2006a). The perpetuated negative stereotypes about 'large' individuals can in turn affect their behaviours and they may not engage in activities or take up 'healthy' active lifestyles because they believe that they and their 'large' bodies are not suited to them, or that they are perceived as unacceptable in certain settings (Carryer, 2001; Cordell and Ronai, 1999).

And there is another side to this: Due to the responsibility and blame attached to 'large' individuals in relation to health, many also will not seek medical treatment for any medical conditions; they fear being blamed for their suffering and dismissed as simply too fat, with their body weight being made the sole cause for their health status (Joanisse and Synnott, 1999; Saguy and Riley, 2005). Underpinned by psychological theories of behaviour change and agency generally, the weight-focused health promotion discourses at play within society today thus construct being fat as unhealthy and individuals as responsible and to blame for their own physical as well as the nation's financial health; this in turn can have detrimental effects on the 'large' individual's well-being.

Neoliberal constructions of fat

This emphasis on an individual's free choice and subsequently responsibility in all matters of life, including health, is a characteristic of contemporary neoliberal societies, and contributes to the discrimination and oppression of fat individuals. 'Large' (as well as 'thin') bodies are socially inscribed with a myriad of meanings, which in terms of the fat body are mostly negative (Malson, 1998; Probyn, 2009). Samantha Murray (2005a, p. 154) refers to these cultural meanings as 'collective knowingness' (p. 1562). She argues that we collectively, as a society, believe that we know a fat person, her or his lifestyle and habits, just from looking at that person. Others refer to the same phenomenon as 'fat as master status' (Cordell and Ronai, 1999, p. 29) or consider 'body size as metonymic of everything' (Malson, 2008, p. 37). 'Large' individuals, in short, are assumed to eat too much and move too little, they are allegedly weak and lacking self-control, they are indifferent to and/or irresponsible about their health (Cordell and Ronai, 1999; Levene and Gleeson, 2003; Malson, 2008; Murray, 2005a, 2005b), and thus morally abject.

However, the issues of who is considered fat and what meanings are attached to being 'large' are culturally, historically and socioeconomically located (LeBesco and Braziel, 2001). In contemporary Western industrialised nations the negative values associated with the fat body are compounded by a healthist neoliberal atmosphere. Here, continuous striving for the best possible healthy body and lifestyle are a 'free' choice we are all obliged to make (Rose, 1996). According to Rose (1996), while we are compelled to see our choices as freely made within this neoliberal culture, social constraints and values dictate the 'right' healthy choice to be made if one does not want to be marginalised by or excluded from society. This applies to a variety of lifestyle choices, of course, and to a certain extent to the entire population. However, as mentioned in the previous chapter, due to the visibility of the 'large' body, in contrast (for example) to the cigarette as the 'health signifier' for smokers, fat individuals are always-already constituted as 'health offenders'. The self and the postmodern body have become inseparable from each other and, according to Gwen Chapman, 'shaping one's body has become a way to shape one's self' (1999, p. 82), and this 'self', including all its 'inner' characteristics, is then assumed to be represented in one's physical appearance (Jutel, 2005).

In Western industrialised nations, being 'large' is thus considered to represent a loss or lack of self-control (Germov and Williams, 1999) and the fat body has been made a 'site of moral decay and failure' (Murray, 2005b, p. 112). Looking after one's body and managing one's weight to medicalised standards has more and more become an 'act of good citizenship' (Throsby, 2009, p. 322), which will ensure that one can efficiently contribute to the economy rather than costing the health system any money. In this scheme of things, it is up to all individuals to make the 'free' choice to look after their bodies in a responsible and 'healthy' way. In her research on the experience of weight loss surgery, Karen Throsby (2007, 2008, 2009) found that her participants oriented towards these discourses of responsibility and health, and while reinforcing the notion that fat is bad and weight loss desirable, they also rejected the subject positions of the irresponsible overeater.

Weight loss surgery patients, however, not only have to negotiate discourses in which they are positioned as a diseased and morally defective fat person (Herndon, 2005) but equally, weight loss surgery is often seen as 'cheating' (Throsby, 2009) in one's body project towards a healthy and healthily shaped body. Surgery means avoiding the hard work usually involved in keeping one's body in 'good shape'. In relation to body weight, 'shaping of the body' is assumed to be achievable through the means of dieting and exercise (Campos, 2004; Cogan and Ernsberger, 1999), and this notion of a controllable body weight is perpetuated by the prevailing and ubiquitous discourse of dieting (Chapman, 1999). Although the term 'diet' is increasingly replaced by such terms as 'healthy eating' (Chapman, 1999), health promotion messages are still telling us to slim down to or stay at a 'healthy weight' by eating less and 'healthier' food (Burns and Gavey, 2004; Department of Health, 2008b).

These discourses of weight loss and dieting still persist despite a substantial body of literature that suggests that dieting does not work (Campos, 2004; Cogan and Ernsberger, 1999; Garner and Wooley, 1991) in terms of weight loss or health benefits. They are circulated in day-to-day talk, the media and by health professionals alike, and further reinforced by the diet industry. Gwen Chapman asserts (1999) that dieting and talking about dieting have now become so common that they belong to the normal repertoire of behaviours of every woman, and according to Lee Monaghan (2007b, 2008a), they are becoming more and more acceptable and common practice for men, too. This latter expansion of dieting practices to men is probably also reflecting the shift in the construction of weight loss purpose from an enhancement of one's appearance to a maintenance of health. The vice of vanity has become a pursuit of 'health', and has led to very few people actually being happy with their bodies (Campos, 2004, p. xviii).

However, this does not mean that appearance concerns as such are abolished, and some authors believe that 'health' discourses simply hide the underlying ambition for aesthetic appeal (Murray, 2005b). As such, fat individuals are caught up in what Deborah Lupton (1996, p. 137) calls a food/health/beauty triplex, within which they are positioned as 'failures' on all three axes. They are positioned as inferior and lacking in terms of the nutritional quality and quantity of the food they eat, and they are constituted as both unhealthy and unattractive. This moral and aesthetic condemnation of 'large' individuals, according to Susie Orbach (2006a), causes widespread psychological harm, to people of all sizes, who either are medically demed, or believe themselves to be fat. We are collectively becoming food- and fat-phobic and very few people, and even fewer women, have a positive and undisturbed relationship with food and eating nowadays (Malson and Swann, 1999; Orbach, 2008). Dieting and topics like eating disorders, women's bodies and embodiment have long been a big part of the feminist literature, which I will turn to now.

Feminist contributions

First published in 1978, *Fat is a Feminist Issue* is Susie Orbach's (2006b) now classic book on women's troubled relationships with food and their bodies, our obsession with dieting and the negative meanings that are now so ingrained in 'fat' in Western societies that we see the constant need to criticise our bodies and ourselves. While critiqued by some writers within the fat acceptance movement for treating being 'large' as a personal problem for women, and most fat women as overeaters (Cooper, 1998), *Fat is a Feminist Issue* was one of the first feminist publications that linked women's body size with patriarchal power systems, with the aim of helping women free themselves of size oppression. Feminist literature on fat is part of the broader feminist work on the gendered politics of food, eating, women's bodies and embodiment, and the power relationships symbolised and produced within them (LeBesco, 2009). While feminism is sometimes perceived by younger generations as not really relevant to their lives any more, as inequalities are perceived as not posing a problem any longer (Rich, 2005), this reluctance to identify as a feminist also seems to be grounded in the embodiment of feminism and the social construction of a feminist as unattractive and not feminine (Rudolfsdottir and Jolliffe, 2008). The links between women's rights on the one hand and what is socially held up as beautiful and feminine in terms of appearance lies at the heart of Naomi Wolf's *Beauty Myth* (1991). The 'beauty myth' is about the way women's self-esteem and identity in patriarchal societies are grounded in their appearance, their beauty. And while women have perhaps become more and more successful and powerful within society generally, increasingly gaining access to education and employment, the criteria for feminine beauty have become tighter and tighter (Nicolson, 2002; Wolf, 1991). Women are being controlled and regulated in their new 'freedoms' through the imposition of subject positions of femininity that require self-scrutiny and self-regulation in relation to appearance, and in a similar vein a regulation of their appetites and eating. This is often termed the backlash against feminism (Bordo, 1993; Weitz, 2003; Wolf, 1991), as the more feminism achieved in terms of gender equality, the more women's oppression through prescribed efforts and standards of femininity and beauty increased, including the requirement to be slim (Chapman, 1999; Lupton, 1996; Malson, 1998; Tyner and Ogle, 2007; Weedon, 1997). Wolf writes:

> The closer women come to power, the more physical self-consciousness and sacrifice are asked of them. 'Beauty' becomes the condition for a woman to take the next step. You are now too rich. Therefore, you cannot be too thin.
>
> (Wolf, 1991, p. 28)

Women and their advance within society had to be controlled through their bodies – an obsession with slimness, that is, the constant striving to become or stay slim, according to Wolf (1991), was, or rather is, doing just that. As such, while the pressure to conform to a certain body shape on men is undeniably also increasing (Bell and McNaughton, 2007; Gill, 2008a; Monaghan, 2008a), women are under notably more pressure to be slim (Bordo, 1993; Campos, 2004; Cordell and Ronai, 1999) and subject to the dictum 'thin is feminine and beautiful and fat is ugly and repulsive' (Germov and Williams, 1999; LeBesco and Braziel, 2001; Malson, 1998).

As mentioned in my introductory chapter, women's bodies have always been political and implicated in the politics of gender equality. Whether in discourses of appearance or physical health, women, through their/our bodies, have been constituted as the weaker, inferior, less capable 'other' sex of the human species. Within the discourse of Cartesian dualism, mind and body are produced as two distinct entities, with the rational mind being superior to the irrational body, and the latter thus needing to be controlled by the mind. Women, since Aristotle, in Western cultures have been associated with the body (Weitz, 2003) and by extension are thus made inferior to and to be controlled by men, who are associated with the rational mind (Bordo, 1993). By being associated with the irrational body, women are rendered unrestrained and volatile and in need of control (Grosz, 1994), with the slim body signifying a disciplined body/woman (Bordo, 1993; Germov and Williams, 1999; Lupton, 1996).

Susan Bordo (1993) asserts that this gendered construction is produced and maintained by representations of eating women in the media, and particularly in advertisements. Men are allowed to eat heartily and with passion while the ideal woman is preparing food for men and children, but herself has 'achieved a state beyond craving' (Bordo, 1993, p. 102). Susie Orbach (2006b) makes a similar point in maintaining that fat women through their embodiment reject the social constructions of women as frail, meek, demure and weak and that being fat represents strength and capability for them, and as such a rejection of the subject position of the smaller and weaker 'other' to men.

These feminist critiques of the pressures on women to conform to a normative or rather idealistic body size and shape have been seemingly weakened by the recent shifts in weight loss 'justifications' away from appearance and on to 'health' (Malson, 2008). However, while a shift of focus on to health may now increasingly include men as targets in the 'war on obesity', the conflation of health and beauty (Lupton, 1996; Malson, 2008) simply means that two discourses – that of health *and* beauty – now converge on women with the same message: that only a slim and healthy-looking woman is a (heteronormatively) attractive and feminine woman. Women are caught up in these discourses, however, not as mere victims or dupes (Frost, 2005); rather they play a part in the perpetuation of the thin ideal (Germov and Williams, 1999; Levene and Gleeson, 2003; Smith, 1998) by engaging in 'doing femininity' (Smith, 1990) and by scrutinising their own and other women's bodies. This is not to say that women intentionally maintain and reinforce the regulation of women through the 'thin ideal'. Rather, women, their bodies and embodied experiences, are an active and at the same time regulated part of the discursively constituted cultural power systems at play. Within the prevailing, gendered discourses of health and beauty, women and men, femininity and masculinity, as well as the meanings of 'fat' and 'slim', are dynamically produced in forever-shifting, complex and varied ways. The dominant discourses of food, health and beauty that converge on women in contemporary Western industrialised nations, however, still produce femininities and embodied subject positions for women that are restrictive, oppressive and damaging.

Often the media are seen as the main culprits in the dissemination of these discourses, particularly by promulgating idealised images of thin women. However, like other theorists (Coleman, 2008; Paquette and Raine, 2004), Elspeth Probyn (2009) sees the issues of fat and feminism as much more complex than a pure matter of representation and would like feminist research and theory to move away from this focus on body image. Women's relationship with their bodies as well as food and eating practices is influenced by lived embodied and interrelational experiences, some of them in relation to and with images (Coleman, 2008) but not as static images that are passively awaiting discursive inscription. Women's embodied experiences, including the constitution of certain bodies as feeling disgusting or out of place, are culturally, economically and geopolitically located (Probyn, 2009) and, while the media are part of a culture, so are individuals and the political and economic circumstances they interact within. Just as women cannot be considered a homogeneous group who are subject to the same conditions and have the same experiences across the board just because they are biologically women (Butler, 1999), fat women equally cannot all be considered as all the same. How a woman experiences herself is not simply produced in media discourses or pictures, but also in social practices and everyday relationships (Paquette and Raine, 2004), which in turn are economically and culturally located. The focus and concentration on a static image of *the* 'large' woman does not do the individual fat person justice in her embodied experience of being 'large', and does not sufficiently acknowledge the problems associated with this that she may or may not have. The unilateral engagement with 'fat' also reinforces the metonymy of the 'large' body, which re/produces the negative stereotypical meanings of 'fat' which cause so much harm. The damage a focus on body shape can have is also recognised by Paul Campos (2004).

> We live in a culture that tells the average American woman, dozens of times a day, that the shape of her body is the most important thing about her, and that she should be disgusted by it. How can one begin to calculate the full emotional, financial and physiological toll exacted by such messages?
>
> (Campos, 2004, p. xviii)

A little later he adds: 'increasingly, men are beginning to show signs of the damage that is done to people when they are told constantly that there is something fundamentally wrong with them' (Campos, 2004, p. xviii); and it is on men, masculinities and fat that I want to focus in the last section of this chapter.

Masculinities and fat

As outlined above, being 'large' nowadays is commonly associated with a variety of health risks, which allegedly not only affect the individual but also the whole nation, and it is considered each and every individual's responsibility to counteract these ill effects with disciplined eating and exercise practices. Thus, in a culture where the body is seen as 'an indicator of self-control and self-discipline' (Gill, 2008a, p. 114), the fat body is often seen as a sign of excess and a lack of self-control. As such, in relation to moral judgements aimed at the fat body, both women and men are targets in this 'war on obesity' (Monaghan, 2008a). In fact, the societal scrutiny of men's bodies is not a new phenomenon (Stearns, 1997). As far back as the nineteenth century, Bell and McNaughton (2007) found that men had been 'archetypal dieters' (p. 113) and, despite being near invisible in the literature in that respect, men have always been under pressure to shape their bodies according to societal norms. So, although they agree with many writers (Bordo, 1993; Campos, 2004; Schwartz, 1986; Sobal and Maurer, 1999) that women's bodies are more scrutinised in relation to body weight, Bell and McNaughton (2007) challenge the notions that men are under minimal pressure to conform to a socially prescribed body shape or that there has only recently been a shift towards a focus on men's bodies.

'Large' men may not experience the same degree of hostility and pressures as women in relation to their appearance, but men's bodies nowadays are more and more on public display, with a young, toned, eroticised ideal being constructed as the norm to strive for (Gill, 2008a). As such, men's identity is increasingly also built around their bodies, and more and more men are becoming dissatisfied with their bodies (Gill, 2008a; Grogan, 1999). However, things are more complicated than that and men struggle with several discourses of masculinity converging on them. Gill (2008a) found that men had to manage various dilemmas around masculinity and body image. For example, while men are not supposed to be vain or to look after their appearance, they should still be seen to look after themselves in terms of health and fitness. This is also reflected in other research (Frith and Gleeson, 2004; Robertson, 2006) and, considering the current 'moral panic' (Campos *et al.*, 2006a) about health and body weight, may also explain the shift to an increased focus on men in society's concern with body weight (Monaghan, 2007a, 2008a). Similarly, while hegemonic masculinity is still signified in physical strength, excluding a weak and thin physique (Monaghan, 2007a; Robertson, 2006), being fat also has negative connotations in relation to a masculine identity. Bell and McNaughton (2007), quoting Durgadas (1998), assert that 'In males, [fleshy bulk or stoutness] represents womanlike weakness or physical impressionability' (Bell and McNaughton, 2007, p. 123). Drawing on this, and considering the social construction of female bodies as inferior in patriarchal societies, Bell and McNaughton (2007) argue that the feminisation of the male fat body is doubly bad for men as not only are they demasculinised but they are also inscribed with inferior 'feminine' characteristics (Monaghan, 2008a). 'Large' men's struggles with their embodied identity thus seem connected to and similar to women's, in that their bodies carry significations of ill health and other negative associations made with 'obesity'. It is a gendered struggle, in as much as embodied gender identities are at stake in the discursive constitution of fat bodies, but also because there is a qualitative gendered difference between the struggles of men and women with body size. While being 'large' for women has solely negative connotations (Bordo, 1993; LeBesco and Braziel, 2001) for men both fat and 'thin' can carry negative meanings but 'bodily bigness' does not have to 'spoil masculine identities' (Monaghan, 2007b, p. 587).

Generally, while there is an increased focus now on men's bodies generally, men in their construction of masculine identities seem to have more resources to draw on than their physique, and are able to create what Toni Coles (2008, p. 238) calls 'mosaic masculinities'. That is, by drawing on those fragments of available constructions of hegemonic masculinity that they can perform, they can assemble a satisfactory masculinity of their own making, which may or may not include body size. Women, on the other side are very much defined by their bodies (Bordo, 1993, 1998; Levene and Gleeson, 2003; Weitz, 2003) and consequently body shape takes on a very different significance for them than for men.

To summarise, then, there seems to be a general agreement that the issue of body weight and its associations with health and well-being is a complex matter with many interrelating factors to be considered. The consent ends there, however, with the medical and psychological mainstream in the meantime treating 'large' individuals (mostly unsuccessfully) with the aim of losing weight. The assumptions these approaches are based on, such as 'fat is unhealthy; slim is healthy' and 'weight loss is achievable and beneficial for everybody', are challenged by researchers and healthcare professionals advocating for an HAES approach, who believe that the focus should be on a healthy lifestyle regardless of an individual's weight. Criticisms of the mainstream also come from other areas, however, in particular feminist and poststructuralist researchers who draw attention to the damaging negative stereotypes and meanings associated with fat, and the oppressive unequal power relations produced through the dominant body size and health discourses. Women seem to be still more negatively affected by these discourses but the pressure is increasing for men, too.

While the amount of research on 'obesity' is vast, there does not seem to be much work that considers fat individuals' narratives and their lived embodied experience of being 'large'. I wanted to expand the research base in this area by exploring how 'large' individuals are positioned within the multiple gendered discourses that converge on them, and how they discursively manage their subjectivities and sub-ject positions within the politics of 'obesity'. To this end I am exploring how 'fat women' and 'fat men' are discursively constituted, in both women's and men's talk, derived from interviews and focus groups. It is important to note that this book represents and interprets the facets of fat lives that I found most striking in my data, but can never provide a true reflection of the experience of fat embodiment. I will, however, endeavour to challenge the reductionist, individualist and gendered 'knowledges' about fat lives, constituted and reconstituted in contemporary Western neoliberal discourses of the body, health and well-being, and draw attention to the resulting sociopolitical consequences.

2 Exploring fat lives

Not surprisingly, it seems the issue of being fat is a complex one, with popular discourse, media content and various health disciplines contributing to the current societal panic (in my view) about 'obesity'. The multiple campaigns related to the 'war on obesity' rest on evidence gained via mostly biomedical or scientific methods. The 'scientific' foundations on which this 'war' is built are highly contested, however. Despite their reputation for rigour and objectivity, they do not seem to provide us with a 'true' picture of the situation in regard to fat and health, and cannot shed any light on the embodied experience of being 'large'. As such, researchers and writers from a number of disciplines, including health professionals, lawyers, sociologists and psychologists (Campos, 2011; Orbach, 2006a; Rich *et al.*, 2011b; Throsby, 2009), challenge the medical 'facts' that are disseminated, as well as the general scientific, reductionist and individualistic approaches taken in research, health promotion and practice.

As to psychology, the mainstream in the discipline cannot, and will not, challenge the generalised and reductionist 'scientific' findings most health promotion and media projects on 'obesity' are based on. With its focus on the 'effects of being fat' on the individual's mental health, psychological and behaviourist causes of 'obesity', as well as weight loss interventions, the mainstream psychological approach used for the bulk of psychological research in this field has added to the potentially harmful focus on body weight as a problem to be solved by/through the individual. It does not provide us with any insight into the subjective experience of 'being large', or the complex interactions between society/culture (including language) and individuals. Mainstream psychology thereby not only may play a part in the over-simplification of the issues of fat and health, but also promotes a neoliberalist and healthist culture in Western societies, which contributes to the marginalisation, oppression and vilification of fat individuals.

Grounded in this critique of the currently predominant approaches to issues around body weight, my aim was to explore women's experience of being fat in contemporary UK (and, in extension, Western) society, to raise awareness of the complexity of this issue and the potential harm the current 'war on obesity' is causing us all in general, and fat women (and men) in particular. Taking a feminist poststructuralist perspective informed by Michel Foucault's as well as feminist theories, I am neither claiming nor aiming to find generalisable truths. Like other (feminist) critical psychologists, I would argue that individuals, knowledge, health and illness are socially and politically located and produced, and thus subject to multiple and shifting power dynamics in society. I would like to support Ros Gill's assertion (1995, drawing on works by Jane Flax and Judith Butler) that 'what we as feminists want is not truth but *justice'*, which may not be attainable by establishing another 'truth'. It is crucial, however, to question, challenge and deconstruct the truth claims and values which are often at the basis of oppression and discrimination, and thereby to enable transformation. By making it harder for people to believe taken-for-granted truths or thoughts, we can make change possible. Or, in Michel Foucault's words, 'as soon as people begin to have trouble thinking things the way they have been thought, transformation becomes at the same time very urgent, very difficult, and entirely possible' (Foucault, 2002a, p. 457). This point is particularly important for the subject matter explored in this book: the embodied experience of being fat. We cannot offer an opposing 'truth' to the discursively produced, but taken-for-granted, 'fact' that being fat is always bad for us. Just as there is no proof for this statement, we cannot offer a counter-argument, like, for example, that fat is good for us, against this ill-evidenced (see Chapter 1) but nevertheless strong and dominant piece of health 'knowledge'. However, we can try and deconstruct it, dismantle and contest the basis of its truth claim. For the sake of justice and equality, we need to throw as much doubt at it as possible, to make it difficult for people to think and utter automatically the taken-for-granted statements that equate (ill) health with body size, and a great number of negative characteristics and behaviours with the fat individual. As such, I believe that Foucauldian and feminist theories, with their focus on a complex analysis of governmentality, disciplinarity, control and power relationships, lend themselves particularly well to an exploration of fat embodiment, in the context of the current 'war on obesity'. As most readers will be familiar with the theories and perspectives referred to in this chapter, I will not elaborate on them here. However, for those who would like more detail, and as there are multiple variances of poststructuralism as well as feminism, I have included an extended version of this section, with a more detailed discussion of the approaches taken in this book, in Appendix 1.

For Foucault, power is universal and dynamic, and cannot be constituted as purely a negative force of oppression, but is also productive. In contemporary Western societies, this complex web of power relationships is evident in the domination of women, which is the result of discipline and governance, effected through processes of self-discipline and self-regulation, rather than unilateral power relations and direct oppression (Saukko and Reed, 2010). This (self) governance is to a great extent played out on women's bodies, and it is body politics which I am turning to in the following section.

The significance of the (female) body

The body, its meaning and significance in the social sciences clearly is a 'bewildering field of study' (Welton, 1998, p. 1). As such, my aim here is to interpret the meaning of, and situate, the body in the context of this book, and the exploration of fat lives.

Body and psychology

Over the last century, the consideration of the body in psychology has moved from a behaviourist model, focusing on stimulus–reflex mechanisms where biology and psychophysical processes still played a major role, to a cognitivist model, with a focus on signals and information processing, where the body merely housed the mind (Brown *et al.*, 2009; Stam, 1998). When the body re-entered the psychological stage, it was within mostly individualistic notions of identity production. However, the body as both subject and object, both the self and the other, to a large extent evades traditional psychological theories and methodology, which in their often reductionist approaches simply cannot do justice to the complexity of embodied experiences.

While critical psychology's turn to qualitative methods and 'to language' avoids the reduction of participants to mere stimulus–response or information-processing units, and thus brings us closer to the complexities of people's lived experience within their social environments, the material body and related embodied experiences in interrelation with the (social) world around it often failed to be represented satisfactorily here, too. The focus on language and text within discursive methodologies means that we have to rely on the expression and representation of embodied experiences through the spoken word. Whatever transcription methods we use for this, and however detailed our notes are on embodied experiences, for example, the physical expressions of emotions, we cannot adequately remove the gap between this experience and its representation in language. Or, as Brown and colleagues (Brown *et al.,* 2009) put it, we are left with the 'gulf between language and embodied experience intact whilst nevertheless giving the superficial appearance of bridging it' (p. 202). In their paper on 'some methodological experiments' around the notion of embodiment, they describe their difficulties in finding a methodology that would allow us to analyse embodied experiences in a way that does them justice. Using memory work (Haug, 1987, cited in Brown *et al.*, 2009) they are trying to analyse how certain situations were experienced rather than thought about, but come to the conclusion that they still ended up analysing these memories in a discursive way, i.e. treating the experiences as text. I found it difficult to follow their initial anticipation of being able to get away from such an approach in the analysis of experience which was written down from memory and thus thought about; if disappointed, I was thus not surprised by their conclusions. It seems to be nearly impossible to avoid an objectification of the body in the exploration of embodied experiences.

Any engagement with the subject of 'the body', or indeed embodiment, seems to come back to the problem of objectification, couched in a discussion of Cartesian dualism and traditional Western philosophy's notion that body and mind were separate entities, with the mind controlling the body. But perhaps it is more a question of our limited capacities for experiencing the world and ourselves, and an even greater limitation in our representational abilities and in how we then express these representations externally? We do not seem to have the language, the words required to write and theorise embodiment without creating dichotomies of biology and society, body and mind (Braun, 2000). And even outside the limits of language, it seems that in order to make sense of our experiences, we need a certain framework, some foundation to work with, and Cartesian dualism provides such a structure. Or, as Brown and colleagues (2009) express it: 'Cartesianism, like "control", is part of the psychological grammar of Western sense-making practices around the body. It is scarcely surprising to see it emerging in our own analyses as a means of organizing a disparate set of materials' (p. 206). So exploring, thinking and talking about 'the body' always seems to objectify it and separate it from the mind, and this in part because we take a binary structure of our lived world for granted.

For Merleau-Ponty this separation and the subsequent objectification of 'the body' were not as clear-cut, however, particularly in reference to psychological investigations. In fact he believed that psychology could have gone a different, non-Cartesian way, had the classical psychologists explored the question of 'the body as object' with more scrutiny rather than succumbing to the urge to 'imitate the scientist' (Merleau-Ponty, 1962, p. 109). Using the examples of phantom limbs and anosognosia, Merleau-Ponty (1962) draws out how, in his mind, such a separation is inconceivable, as we experience the world through our bodies in relation with the world. Using terms such as 'organic thought' (Merleau-Ponty, 1962, p. 89), he argues that phenomena such as the phantom limb are neither 'the mere outcome of objective causality; no more . . . a cogitatio' (p. 89). In other words, they are neither purely physical processes nor pure thoughts or mental representations. This mode of simultaneous existing in and experiencing the world he terms 'being-in-the-world', a flow of energy and activity towards and in relation with the world, which also anchors us in our 'environment' (p. 90). Consequently, the body as the experiencing as well as experienced entity is 'subject-object' (p. 109). Others, not Merleau-Ponty, but no doubt influenced by his work, later called this intertwined psychophysiological 'being-in-the-world' embodiment.

With his insistence on the relational nature of our embodied being, I do not see Merleau-Ponty's theories as directly contradicting or opposing poststructuralist perspectives. Others, however, turn to his phenomenological theories in their critique that poststructuralism and postmodernism, including poststructuralist feminist perspectives, neglect the material body. Bodies should not be seen as just texts, or as inscribed with text, but as lived, experienced, active, dynamic and relational agents and crucial signifiers in political struggles around gender, race and religion (Bordo, 1998, 1999; Csordas, 1994). And of course phenomenology does offer us a more integrated theorisation of the body. However, what is lacking in phenomenology, despite its consideration of embodied relationships, is a temporal aspect, i.e. the relevance of history, as well as the importance of culture and community (Sampson, 1998). Culture, to my mind, is of particular importance here, as it provides the connections, the links between the already enmeshed body and representations. It provides the 'horizon' (to stay with Merleau-Ponty) or backdrop to our 'being-in-the-world', and gives meaning to representations. These meanings, on the other hand, are constituted in culturally and historically contingent discourses. Thus, an analytical integration of poststructuralism with a phenomenological take on embodiment seems to offer itself (Brown *et al.*, 2009; Gillies *et al.*, 2004; Sampson, 1998).

Of course an interest in the experience and the meaning of the body as well as poststructuralism has been a feature of feminism and feminist theory for a long time. Traditionally, in philosophy, psychology and medicine, 'being a women' and what this means has been associated with women's biology, with their bodies, and how these distinguish them from men (Bordo, 1999; Butler, 1999; Weedon, 1999). Men, and male bodies, were the norm, the standard, against which women and their bodies were considered and measured. 'Woman' was not only constructed as 'the other' and different from men, but also as generally physically weaker, and mentally less able and less rational than 'man', who was/is associated with the rational mind. As such, woman, or the feminine, has always also been easily associated with pathology – with both physical and mental illness (Malson, 1998; Ussher, 1991, 2011). A lot of the differences, and pathologies, were seen as stemming from women's reproductive role and associated biological make-up, with Plato and Hippocrates, for example, warning of the deleterious effects of a 'wandering womb' on a woman's physical and mental health (Ussher, 2006). These days, the associations made between women, their bodies and pathology are more subtle but nevertheless still present and active in gender politics (Reed, 2010).

Women's bodies are constituted as 'problem bodies' (Bayer and Malone, 1998) which harbour many (psychological) conditions such as premenstrual and menopausal syndromes and postnatal depression (Ussher, 2006, 2008). Not surprisingly, therefore, the body features as a focal point in a lot of feminist theory and in feminist discourse. The meaning of the body and of the biological differences between women and men, constructed in these feminist discourses, however, varies within and across historical times and feminist standpoints (Weedon, 1999). What most feminist perspectives, certainly from the early 1970s, have in common in relation to the body, however, is the recognition of the body's role in the production and maintenance of power relations, and the reverse shaping and regulation of the body through the latter. This holds true not only where gender is concerned but also concerning racial, class and ethnic relations. Within the efforts to eradicate these power inequalities, based on biological differences, the body, however, became more and more dematerialised – a mere social and discursive construction, rather than lived and experienced flesh and blood. So when Susan Bordo was among the first to reintroduce 'the material' in feminist discussions on the body, she was not greeted with open arms – who has not read her account of feeling completely shunned after giving a speech to that effect in the early 1990s?

> when the word 'material' came out of my mouth it was as though I had farted in public. This is no exaggeration. I felt the atmosphere in the room shift palpably, as those who had been comfortable in the assurance that I was a right-minded person . . . all at once felt something unexpected and foul enter the room.
>
> (Bordo, 1998, p. 88)

Feminism had a problem with the re-emergence of the importance of the body in philosophy and psychology. Bodies at that point were seen as constructed in discourse, mediated and regulated by cultural and political circumstances, which also influenced how bodies were read, what meanings they conveyed in a certain culture/society. The gender differences that were used as justifications for a multitude of inequalities had been exposed as social/discursive constructions, and could thus be challenged. What seemed like a move back to the material body could mean a loss of these founda-tions on which postmodern feminism fought its battles for equality. However, acknowledging the material body does not mean denying its regulation and shaping through discourse, its role in and as a site of power struggles. Rather than denying any connection with the body, and rejecting anything material, the return to the body signifies a critical engagement with the epistemologies grounded in the biological and material. Rather than more or less ignoring the materiality of the body, it means challenging what it signifies, and reconceptualising the body as not (necessarily) distinct and separate from, and not inferior to, the mind: body–mind as dynamic and shifting, constituted and regulated by discourses contingent on history, location, culture, and so forth. This increased interest in the body also opens up opportunities to explore the positive in women's embodiment, particularly in matters like sport and exercise and fat embodiment, which have been kidnapped by the obesity discourses of weight loss and measurable, quantifiable health.

This, of course, does not mean that we need to abandon poststructuralist notions of the regulated, disciplinary body. As laid out above, for Foucault power was everywhere, rather than concentrated in one agent, and (unequal) power relation-ships were constituted and maintained in discourse through regimes of knowledge/ truth and disciplinarity. Disciplinarity is achieved through the microprocesses of self-surveillance and self-regulation, with the body acting as a 'surface of power' (Hook, 2007, p. 22) towards which the disciplinary gaze is directed, and the technologies of the self are active on. This link between macropolitical governance and micropolitical self-governance of bodies and selves is what makes the 'personal political' (Saukko and Reed, 2010) and which thus (still) links Foucauldian poststructuralism with feminist theory and embodiment. The material body, and its theorisation, has a valid place in this, as it is 'real' bodies which are experienced and regulated, and which above all form the site of power struggles. But, to borrow some words from Steven Brown and colleagues (2009), '[r]ather than being interested in the individual or the individual's body, what is interesting lies in the spaces between – in the interaction, between people and people and their world through their embodied being' (p. 214). The body is both material and also socially/discursively constructed, and embodiment is thus both discursive and non-discursive (Gillies *et al.*, 2004); one should not completely eclipse the other, just as a poststructuralist approach should not completely exclude embodiment. How to join them methodologically and effectively is a matter that is still left to be struggled with (Braun, 2000; Brown *et al.*, 2009).

The data for the research presented in this book has been collected in a purely verbal way. I have thus taken Thomas Csordas' (1994: cited in Gillies *et al.*, 2004, p. 101) advice in paying 'attention to bodiliness' in my poststructuralist discourse analysis which is broadly based on Michel Foucault's theories, and Ian Parker's (1992) and Carla Willig's (2004, 2008) guidelines.

Methodology and method applied in the exploration of fat lives

My aim was to explore the discourses my participants had available to them, and articulated in the management of their fat-embodied identities; the various subject positions these discourses made possible and whether/how these were taken up or rejected. I further wanted to explore the discursive constitutions and regulation of my participants' lifestyles and subjectivities, and whether and how the women and men in my study challenged or reinforced dominant discourses, institutions and practices. The social and political structures and cultural conditions in which 'large' people positioned themselves (and/or are positioned in) and thus experience, as well as possibilities for change in current and future health policies and health ideologies were another concern. Based on the theories discussed in this chapter, these multilayered and complex areas, I found, were best explored with a poststructuralist discourse analytic approach.

There are many versions of discourse analysis, with varying degrees of emphasis on an investigation of microinteractions (investigating interpretative repertoires in everyday conversation and interpersonal interaction) at one end, and a focus on broader discursive practices and potential political critique at the other end of the scale, here referred to as discursive psychology (DP) and Foucauldian discourse analysis (FDA) (Willig, 2008), respectively. Both discursive approaches share what many have called psychology's turn to language (Harre and Secord, 1972) in that the focus in both types of analysis is on the language used in texts. They are both grounded in the poststructuralist notion that language does not reflect or transparently represent social reality, but that dynamic and ever-changing versions of social reality are constructed through language (Gergen, 2009). Language, then, is seen as productive, producing or constructing objects, subjects, experiences and events, achieving social objectives and creating and negotiating meanings (Widdicombe, 1993; Willig, 2008). However, the two versions of analysis of discourse are used to answer different types of research questions and are based on different research perspectives.

Discursive psychology

DP is 'focused on discourse because it is the primary arena for action, understanding and intersubjectivity' (Wiggins and Potter, 2008, p. 73). As such it sees people as using language in order to achieve certain social actions, which include concepts such as identity, prejudices, memory, and so forth (Willig, 2008). This action orientation of language is not necessarily intentional but language is very much seen as performative, whether it be with or without the speaker's conscious intention, and it is the discursive psychologist's aim to elucidate what was achieved with the use of the particular discursive features (interpretative repertoires and rhetorical devices) used in a specific interpersonal interaction or piece of text. DP looks at interaction in both language and practice, that is, a discursive psychological investigation includes a consideration of the structure of the text, including features such as turn-taking and breaks, as well as an investigation of how non-textual interactions produce reality (Hepburn and Wiggins, 2005; Widdicombe, 1993). This kind of analysis is based on the belief that every participant in a conversation or interaction, every creator of text, has a stake in the text, and it is for the analyst to find out how this stake and the speaker's/writer's interests were managed (Willig, 2008). DP is looking at people's construction of reality in and through day-to-day interactions, and as such it is not surprising that discursive psychologists prefer to analyse naturally occurring text, rather than interviews (Potter and Hepburn, 2005, 2007), as the stake and the orientation towards any action in an interview would be located within or oriented towards the interview situation, rather than the research topic of interest.

In mentioning the two 'camps' of discourse analysis, and that DP and FDA were forming two 'poles' on a scale of different types of discourse analyses; I made the division between these two approaches sound more oppositional than they are in reality. Both methods have developed out of a growing interest in the role of language in psychology, but DP has developed from within and, after a 25-year-long struggle, is arguably more accepted by and comfortable within (social) psychology (Parker, 2011). FDA on the other hand was developing first outside psychology, and later introduced into it (Parker, 1997). The two types of discourse analysis also focus on slightly different functions of language, or rather, discourse. Language is not synonymous with discourse, in as much as language is very much defined in a Saussurian sense (who used '*langue*') as a homogeneous collection of symbols and codes that are used within a particular society for communication. In contrast to this, the *use* of language was termed '*parole*' by Saussure, to distinguish it from the actual collection of codes (language or *langue*) (Fairclough, 2001). In order to distinguish this theory of unitary language use from the notion that language is a form of social practice, constructive of as well as constructed in social interaction, the term 'discourse' was adopted to signify patterns of meaning constituted in language use (Fairclough, 2001; Parker, 1997).

Both DP and FDA consider discourses as inconsistent and variable, and as constructed in social interaction as well as constructive of objects, subjects and realities. However, while DP focuses and locates this construction within discrete events of interaction, within which versions of the world are actively created between the respective individuals involved (Wiggins and Potter, 2008), FDA turns its focus to the issue of which discourses are available to individuals within certain societal, political and cultural structures and institutions. As such, DP is considered by some as less political and ideologically concerned than FDA (Parker, 1997), as it considers the constructive nature of discourse as situated and hence its focus remains within the context of a specific event, rather than looking at the wider societal and political context (Parker, 1997; Wiggins and Potter, 2008), which is where FDA's focus lies.

Foucauldian discourse analysis

FDA is based on Michel Foucault's conceptualisation of discourse and his method of analysing discursive fields and their consequences. For Foucault, discourses are historically and culturally located dynamic webs of statements, which are interrelated with other statements (Foucault, 1972). Within these discursive fields knowledges and realities are constructed, and the types of discourses available determine what can be said (and by whom), and what types of objects, subjects, realities and ways of being are constructed (Parker, 1992). As described above, Foucault closely links knowledge with power, which he sees as joined in discourse. Knowledges, or 'regimes of truth', are constituted in discourse, which in turn creates fields of possibilities – of acting, being and knowing. There is a reciprocal relationship between power and knowledge, and this power/knowledge permeates all aspects of life (Hollway, 1989; Malson, 1998). It is the critical discourse analyst's aim to explore how these 'regimes of truth' have come into being, what were the cultural and societal conditions that have made them possible, and what are the discursive fields they have been constituted in; or, in Foucault's own words, exploring 'on what type of assumptions, of familiar notions, of established, unexamined ways of thinking the accepted practices are based' (Foucault, 2002a, p. 456).

However, power in and of itself was not the main theme of Foucault's research: rather it was the human subject and how she/he is constituted and positioned within the prevailing discourses and the power/knowledge relationships produced therein (Foucault, 2002b). The subject in poststructuralist theory, as outlined above, is constituted and regulated in discourse, and through dynamic and 'power-infused processes of embodied subjectification' (Papadopoulos, 2008, p. 143). This means that, while the availability of certain discourses produces particular possibilities of 'doing' and 'being', subjectivities are not only imposed and either accepted or rejected, but produced and reproduced through embodied experiences within these fields of possibilities (Papadopoulos, 2008; Smith, 1990). In FDA we thus not only investigate what discourses are available and deployed by individuals but also look at what Ian Parker calls the micro-level, that is, how these discourses are used and how subjectivities are produced within them, in order to be 'able to identify the ways in which processes of ideology and power find their way into the little stories of everyday life' (Parker, 1997, p. 293) and our embodied subjectivities.

The discourses FDA examines are not to be understood in the same way as the statements DP analyses. FDA's discourses occur or exist through the articulation and the relationships between a number of statements, but no direct interaction between speakers is necessary. As Foucault (1972) puts it, the respective authors of the statements need not be aware of the relations between her and other authors' statements; neither do the authors need to know each other, or even be aware of each other's existence. As such the pieces of discourse we investigate will always only be a fragment of the discursive field to which they belong (see Foucault's take on the *oeuvre* in Appendix 1, p. 136). The relations that form the discursive field are always shifting and dynamic, and as such always only provisional, never fixed. The aim is to locate statements within discursive fields and explore their relations with other statements, the knowledges, regimes of truth and power relations that are constituted within their discursive fields and consequently what subject positions and ways of being are constructed and made available within them

(Malson, 1998; Malson *et al.*, 2006). To summarise, psychologists (as well as sociologists and other scholars) using FDA are interested in issues of subjectivity and power/knowledge and in challenging social inequalities and injustice. However, as mentioned before, there is no one agreed way of 'doing' FDA.

In *Discourse Dynamics*, Ian Parker (1992) sets out 20 steps for discourse analysis which begin with the very basic recommendation to treat the object of study as text, which he defines as 'tissues of meaning reproduced in any form that can be given an interpretative gloss' (Parker, 1992, p. 6). Parker leads us through to step 20, which is a political and ideological interpretation of the discourses employed by dominant groups and their function in oppression. Carla Willig (2008) limits herself to six steps, and in her application of FDA seems less overtly political than Parker, and more person-oriented. While she explores the regulation of subjects through their positioning in discourse, she does not proceed to investigate overtly and explicitly ideological or political processes at a societal level. Willig focuses more on the positioning of individuals (or groups within society) within discourses, the different subjectivities that are made available to people within the discourses identified, and the actions made possible or closed down through the respective positionings.

While both authors neatly structure their instructions in distinct steps, neither of them will maintain that any FDA in practice will follow these in an orderly and prescribed fashion. The type of FDA I have employed in this research may be seen as borrowing from both Parker and Willig's instructions, and I would like to outline briefly the principles and characteristics of FDA I adhered to here.

The construction of reality, knowledges, objects and subjects in discourse

Based on social constructionist, poststructuralist and feminist theory, objects, subjects, knowledges and reality are constructed through language and interaction (Gergen, 2009) and one of the first and principal aims in the application of FDA is to explore what and how objects and subjects are constituted within the data analysed (Parker, 1992).

A focus on global discursive fields rather than local discursive interaction

My objective was to identify the discourses deployed by my participants and explore their connections and interrelatedness with existing or elsewhere described discursive fields (Foucault, 1972; Parker, 1997).

Subjectivities and subject positions are made available and produced in discourses

I explore the subject positions that were made available to and produced by my participants and fat individuals generally in the social, institutional and official discourses they employed (Papadopoulos, 2008; Smith, 1990; Willig, 2008).

Discourses regulate practice and dis/empower groups of people and institutions

The types of positions that are made available in discourses make certain practices and ways of being possible or impossible for people. They determine what can be said and done, where, how and by whom. Power structures are implicated in discourses which determine whose constructions of 'reality' will gain 'truth' status; this, in turn, has an impact on the regulation of practices, as mentioned above. It was my aim to explore what power relations and regimes of truth were at play within my data and how these positioned fat individuals (Foucault, 2002b; Malson, 1998; Parker, 1992).

Discourses are historically and culturally specific

In identifying discourses I considered and explored whether other discourses would have been possible in our particular time and culture, and how above all the neoliberal values that are currently predominant in Western industrial nations impacted on the discourses that were possible in relation to being fat (Davies *et al.*, 2006; Parker, 1997).

An attention to bodiliness

While not part of Ian Parker's or Carla Willig's versions of FDA, the body is a crucial element in Foucault's as well as feminist theories. Disciplinarity is played out on and through subjects' bodies in microtechnologies such as self-surveillance, self-monitoring and self-regulation, and in their signification of difference they become the site of power struggles. And, while my aim is to deconstruct the cultural, scientific and discursive basis on which the current war on obesity is fought in western industrial nations generally, and the UK in particular, at the heart of this book lies lived fat embodiment.

From a critical psychological and feminist perspective, research (of any kind) does not happen in a cultural or political vacuum, and both the research process and the researcher are products of their times, their cultural contexts and the prevailing discourses, thus objectivity is impossible (Gough and McFadden, 2001; Willig, 2008). As such, the researcher is not a neutral observer of the event but an active contributor, located within the same discourses as the participant. Our own subjectivities and subject positions, prevailing power relationships and relative positioning to and relationship with the participants will influence the data as well as the analysis that is produced (Ryan-Flood and Gill, 2010). In consideration of the above, feminist and other critical psychological research calls for the researcher to engage in reflexive practice at all stages of the research process (Burns, 2003).

The term 'reflexivity' encompasses an array of different ways and issues to reflect on as a researcher, and the process itself can seem rather woolly. One distinction that can be made, however, and which may lend some clarity to the concept, is between epistemological and personal reflexivity (Willig, 2008). For both types of reflexivity, the objective is to reflect on or think about how personal and epistemological factors in a study impacted on the research, and in particular on the knowledges produced and interpretations made within it. Epistemological reflexivity has the research itself at its centre and what knowledge production was made possible by the way it was carried out, i.e. what is the status of the data drawn from my research? In more practical terms, we are looking at factors such as recruitment strategies and the specific population reached by it; we reflect on the research question and the design and the motivations behind choosing the questions we have posed in the interviews (Gough and McFadden, 2001; Willig, 2008). One of the issues I was continuously struggling with was a linguistic or discursive one. In my recruitment materials I had used the word 'large' instead of 'fat', 'overweight', 'obese', or any other descriptive terms signifying different body sizes available. I wondered whether, or rather was fairly certain that, I had attracted a very specific 'type' of participants to my research with this choice, which would have consequences for the data produced. My reflections on these consequences also inspired me to ask participants about the various terms used to describe their body size, which led to interesting discussions.

Of course the issue of interviewing as a data collection method, and what type of data we are producing with self-selected participants in an artificially created situation, is in itself a controversial topic. The debates around the status of the data, and whether 'naturalistic' data recorded outside an interview situation, in 'real life', would be more useful, have been well recorded (see, for example, the discussions between Chris Griffin (2007a, b) and Jonathan Potter and Alex Hepburn (2005, 2007)). I would certainly agree with the benefits of 'naturalistic' data for the purposes of DP, as advocated by Potter and Hepburn, particularly as the focus here is on analysing the discourses used in a specific context. I do not see the same applying to FDA to quite such an extent and still consider interviewing a valuable way to collect data for research exploring more global or macro discourses. Nonetheless, while books could be (and have been) written about the issues of collecting good-quality data for qualitative research, I would now like to concentrate on issues of power and ethics during the interview process, which are also associated with the second, in my mind, more complex, type of reflexivity: personal reflexivity.

As the term suggests, this type of reflexivity focuses on the researcher's person, her embodied subjectivity as well as the subject positions available to her during the research process (Burns, 2003). Important here is the consideration of the researcher's own social status, and how this influences her part in the researcher–participant interaction and also how the interviewee will relate to her. By social status I mean factors such as 'life' history, age, ethnic background, class, occupation, 'gender', sexual orientation (Wilkinson *et al.*, 2004), and, in respect to my research in particular, body size and appearance (Burns, 2003). Generally, the assumption would be that a similarity between interviewer and interviewee in many of the above aspects was advantageous for the interview process, the rapport and the level of understanding between the two individuals involved (Willig, 2008). However, being 'close' in social attributes to one's participants can potentially also mean that certain issues are not raised, as the interviewee assumes that the interviewer knows about them already – they are taken as said. An example from my research may be the issue of gender, which was raised by all the participating men but hardly talked about by any of the women. Equally, it may sometimes be better not to disclose one's motivations for carrying out the research, or any knowledge one might have about certain issues in too much detail before the interview. Being seen as not too knowledgeable about the experiences in question may elicit more talk from the participants and it can be easier to ask for explanations and expansions on a topic (Burman, 1994; Ryan-Flood and Gill, 2010).

The already-mentioned issue around the language used in recruitment materials plays an important role here, particularly in a divisive and (health) political issue like fat; depending on the terms used we may attract certain 'types' of participants, but not others. I probably would not have attracted fat acceptance activists had I written my recruitment material using medicalised language and terms such as 'obesity' and 'overweight', but I may have still lost out on those women who object to the term 'large', which I decided to use in my leaflets. While I was very pleased with the broad diversity (in terms of class/socioeconomic status, take on fat, and able-bodiedness) in my group of participants, I cannot be certain that each participant was happy with me as their interviewer, and they may well have been disappointed or even annoyed when first setting eyes on me, a 'normatively' sized, white, female researcher. Like other researchers in the field of body size I heard questions like 'what can *you*, considering *your own* size, say about the experience of being fat?', and of course the issue of researching 'the other' has long troubled the feminist research community (Rice, 2009b). Can or should I, as a normatively sized woman, really research a group of people I do not belong to – and quite visibly so? It seems somewhat patronising to research 'the other', objectifying groups in society one doesn't belong to in research – but then is that not the case as soon as we take on the position of 'researcher' who allegedly has the right expertise and institution behind her to explore those 'out there', who do not? Does that, on the other hand, mean that only 'insiders' can research each other, that women can only work with women, black researchers with black respondents and Muslim participants be interviewed by Muslim academics, and so forth? What I am talking about here is the familiar insider/outsider problematic, which in my view cannot be decided on in a broad-brush fashion, but will depend on the research in question on various levels. I believed I could make a valuable contribution to the field of fat studies, particularly as I was not trying to represent the participants' experiences but was interested in the discourses available to them, and the positionings these were offering them. Besides, as mentioned above and as others have observed before me, being an 'insider' can also have its drawbacks for research in terms of the assumptions made by the participants (Ryan-Flood and Gill, 2010).

I would say I was lucky to recruit a very diverse, heterogeneous group of participants which permitted me to collect a good level of data, but also enabled me to experience and reflect on my own reactions to different views on fat. I had to be careful not to get too carried away in positive fat-acceptance discussions with some of my participants; equally, I had to be on guard not to discourage, with my disagreement, those women who believed in the benefits of, and were engaged in, weight loss practices from expressing their views. Similarly to what Paula Saukko (2000) describes, I felt a dilemma between two important feminist commitments: to give women and women's experience a voice through research (including those women who did not share my critical take on the 'war on obesity'), on the one hand, and to be critical of the predominant, damaging discourses on fat on the other hand. And, of course, the withholding or offering of information not only has an effect on the research outcome (Ryan-Flood and Gill, 2010), but also immediately raises the ethical issue of power inequality, which is one of the feminist critiques of interviewing (Oakley, 2005). This is particularly apparent if I – intentionally or not – position myself and my critical (informed?) perspective on fat as 'superior' to the women who 'stick to the mainstream' – the popular or common discourses – which may position them as naïve. Simply by voicing my dilemma in how to deal with those participants who do not reflect my opinions I construct them as 'other' as potentially wrong in their opinion, or as not critical enough. At the same time, by holding back information myself whilst requesting as much information as possible from interviewees, who end up exclusively giving while I am taking/receiving, I also create an exploitative relationship, with me as the beneficiary.

The above presents the researcher as the all-powerful potential exploiter of the interview situation. Others, of course, may argue that participants are not as powerless and disadvantaged as this may seem, as they are disclosing as little or as much as they please, thereby also holding some power over the researcher and the success or otherwise of the project. Young and/or new researchers may certainly not feel very powerful when faced with the prospect of interviews, and within the interview process, particularly so if the research topic is associated with strong emotions, controversial or (overtly) political; all these scenarios bring higher personal investments on both sides with them, which have to be managed in the interview situation by the researcher.

I am (again) using my own experiences above, and, without wanting to generalise from these, the general problematic will be similar across many research projects, as there is no such thing as an impartial researcher or research that is not at least in part structured by the researcher's assumptions. Every project is to some extent carried out to advance the researcher's career (and/or the company she works for), and she will have based her decision to carry out the research on certain theories and perspectives, or political agendas. This personal engagement is even more prevalent and potentially shifting and overwhelming in qualitative studies generally, and those with a political angle in particular (Parker, 1994b). This not only has an impact on the research, the data and knowledge produced, but also carries with it certain power dynamics. The simple requirement for 'personal reflection' somewhat obscures the intricate power relationships present and active during the recruitment, interview and analysis stages of the research process. These dynamically position and reposition, restrict and empower the researcher as well as the participant to varying degrees at and within these different stages. The feminist statement that the 'personal is political' is very apt here; it expresses the interconnectedness of interpersonal with more global power structures. At its most basic, it means that any private interaction or situation (e.g. household roles in the nuclear family) is both impacted on and productive of the more global, societal power relations around gender, class and 'race'. However, in relation to research practice it also means that the researcher herself, her personal history, background and positioning in society will influence the research process, analysis, and the interaction with each individual respondent. This applies not only to the mostly invisible characteristics listed above, but also to the physical, and very visible, body of the researcher, which introduces further power dynamics to the research process (Del Busso, 2007). Slim bodies are positioned as privileged and (morally) 'better' in current fattist UK society, so my visibly non-fat body will position me in relation to the participant in a certain way, and will be read by my participants in ways I cannot influence. Depending on each individual interview interaction, I may be positioned as more powerful, but equally as incompetent due to my visible lack of experience of being fat. As Lilliana Del Busso points out, 'embodied power dynamics have the potential to dis/empower both researcher and participant in the interviewing interaction' (Del Busso, 2007, p. 310).

The researcher also is not the only participant coming to the interview with certain assumptions and potentially an agenda. The interviewee will have her/his reasons for taking part, whether it is to help other people affected by the issue researched (here, other fat individuals), viewing research generally as important and worth supporting, hoping to gain some benefit from the interviewing process, or any other of many possible reasons (Peel *et al.*, 2006). This motivational factor needs to be considered at every stage of the research process, including when drawing up recruitment material. Care must be taken with the language used in these materials in order to manage expectations, particularly in psychological research. In popular culture, 'psychology' can be read as 'therapy' or 'counselling' and the prospect of talking to a 'psychologist' may raise an expectation of such 'treatment' and thus help with any personal issues. Whilst some may argue that the interview process can be of a quasi-therapeutic benefit to participants (Peel *et al.*, 2006), both the interviewer and interviewee are vulnerable to abuse here, and a close eye has to be kept on boundaries. The interviewees must not be coerced – even with empathy – into disclosing more than they are comfortable with; equally, the interviewer needs to set boundaries as to how much disclosure she can accept without feeling uncomfortable or burdened with the participants' problems.

While we do not analyse personal interactions when using FDA, these embodied interview dynamics and shifting power relations need careful reflection on and consideration during the analysis process. I have focused on body size above, but equally and simultaneously important are other strata of power (e.g. gender, ethnicity, class, socioeconomic status) which will intersect and interplay in each participant and her/his interaction with the researcher. Most feminist research these days tries to incorporate as many different power dimensions as possible with the aim of representing and encouraging equality and preventing oppression (Ryan-Flood and Gill, 2010).

My embodied subjectivity as a formerly 'large' female researcher, interviewing self-identified 'large' men and women, and my resulting reactions to what was discussed during the interviews no doubt influenced my interpretations to some degree (Burns, 2003). And, equally, while I do not fall into the same body size bracket as my participants, discourses on weight, health and lifestyle issues still converge on me and no doubt regulate my behaviour. In fact, interestingly, being immersed in the literature on body size, as well as in my data, made me more weight-conscious in reference to my own body, rather than less. This surprised me as my 'rational' thoughts on the topic did become more and more critical about the weight focus in our society. It was therefore enlightening about discursive productions of truths and subjectivities, to experience that despite this 'critical head' I could not (and still cannot) extract myself from the global discourses and worries about weight, where my own body was concerned.

The above are experiences from one research project, and whilst set in relation to the literature on the interview process and inherent power relations, they can only ever present a snapshot of the power dynamics present in one study. As feminist researchers before me have well documented, 'far from being a straight-forward, clinical, easily manageable process, research inevitably presents numerous challenges at ontological, epistemological, political, ethical and personal levels' – it is messy (Ryan-Flood and Gill, 2010, p. 2). Like any other social interaction, research relationships are sites of complex and ever-shifting power relations, and, true to Foucault's take on power being everywhere, it cannot be located in one institution or person, e.g. the researcher. However, in my mind, the onus (and to a certain extent, the power) to address and influence these power relationships towards a more equitable process lies with the researcher, as she designs the project, the agenda and location. Notwithstanding the participants' control over certain aspects of the interview, the researcher still regulates the interview process to a greater degree, as well as more consciously and intentionally, than the participant.

Feminist research practice addresses the power dynamics present in qualitative research interviews with a number of strategies. A reflexive approach throughout the project, as illustrated above, whilst not eliminating the power relations, will alleviate their negative impact by making them, and their influence on the research outcome, more transparent (Ramazanoglu and Holland, 2002). Reflection will also assist us in taking steps in our interview interactions to redress any potential power imbalance. Keeping the interview questions open and less structured gives the participant more choice in what and how much to disclose and discuss. On a pragmatic basis, simple measures may include a casual, non-intimidating dress code, giving the participant the control over meeting place and time and, during the interview itself, over the recording device.

In the exploration of the theories, methodology and methods my research was based on, I have merged theoretical insights with personal reflections of mine, in the hope of making my own positioning as well as my research more transparent. Epistemologies, and the theories and methodologies they are based on or inspire, are never neutral and are always interpreted by the researcher who draws on them. They cannot be used or applied innocently and objectively, as mere tools to carry out a task. Feminist research, in requiring reflexive practice, is asking that 'the unseen and unacknowledged be made visible' (Ryan-Flood and Gill, 2010, p. 1) in order to address any ethical issues, but also to situate the research and thus the conclusions drawn from it. With the discussions in this chapter, I hope I have done this requirement justice, in relation to the following four chapters where I am exploring four aspects of 'fat lives' that were particularly prominent in my conversations with 'large' individuals: in/visibility and surveillance, clothing, health and gender.

3 Women's in/visible 'large bodies'

Always visible but rarely seen[2]

Victor Burgin once wrote: 'Looking is not indifferent. There can never be any question of "just looking"' (Burgin, 1982; cited by Chandler, 1998), which goes a long way to express the notion on which this chapter is based: the active and constructive nature of both seeing and being seen, or what one may call the discursive nature of in/visibility. An exploration of this will form the first part of this section. Chapters 4–6 will cover explorations of themes with the broad headings of clothing, health and responsibility, and finally 'gender'. The fact that I have included a separate chapter on 'gender' does not mean that it will not feature in the remaining analysis or that I perceive the other issues as gender-neutral. Body size and weight are highly gendered issues (Bordo, 1993; Chernin, 1983; Malson, 1998; Wolf, 1991) and the themes I have chosen to explore further in this book are all inflected with gender (as well as other axes of power). I was thus very surprised to find that the women hardly ever talked directly or even indirectly about gendered pressures, especially in comparison with the men I had interviewed. The reasons for this may lie in my own gendered embodiment. As explored in the previous chapter, interviewing is an embodied practice and my visible insider status as a woman may have led to the women participants not talking about issues I, as a woman, would surely already know about. Of course, this is something I will never be able to verify, but in order to explore the role gender plays in the discursive construction and embodied experience of being fat or 'large', I discussed the topic with participants in unisex focus groups, giving both men and women a say in the matter. As a result, the 'gendering of fat' is addressed in greater detail in Chapter 6, drawing on focus groups as well as interviews with women and men.

Deconstructing in/visibility

Visibility can be considered a social process in itself (Brighenti, 2007), as how and what we are seeing is socially and interactionally constructed, and several strands of our social identities, particularly gender and race, but also sexuality and religion, have a clear visual dimension (Alcoff, 2006; Medina, 2011). As a number of writers like Linda Alcoff, Merleau-Ponty and Michel Foucault have pointed out, complex political and social relationships exist between visibility and power, the gendered and other social asymmetries produced in seeing and being seen.

In fact, in *Discipline and Punish,* Foucault (1977) concludes that 'visibility is a trap'. A trap because, while light and being visible at first sight seem positive and benign aspects of life, and better than darkness or, for example, being locked away in a dungeon, darkness in fact may also offer the positive aspects of privacy and protection. Visibility on the other hand is closely linked to discipline and power. Foucault (1977) uses Bentham's conception of the Panopticon as a model for how being continuously visible – or the ever-present potential of being watched, i.e. under surveillance – creates power inequalities and acts as a 'discipline-mechanism' (p. 209) of normalisation. Bentham's Panopticon was the plan for a prison constructed in a way that allowed prison guards in a watch tower to observe the inmates in their cells constantly (but without being seen themselves). This creates a visibility and power asymmetry, with the power lying with the invisible but monitoring prison guards. Expanding this idea to society more generally, Foucault talks about a normalising and regulating gaze, as when there is a constant possibility that people are being watched, individuals start watching or disciplining themselves. They are making sure they do not step out of line (i.e. that they fit the culturally constructed normative rules of appearance, behaviour, and so forth) as someone may see them, judge them or even punish them.

Permanent visibility goes together with an increasing individualisation within a disciplinary system. While power in itself becomes invisible (like the prison guards in the Panopticon), those subjected to the power become more and more visible, not only in person but also in terms of any personal information (medical, educational, jurisdictional, financial, and so forth) about them. This knowledge about each and every individual makes it possible to measure, compare and judge them, and consequently subject them to correction or exclusion (Foucault, 1977). As a result subjects 'assume[s] responsibility for the constraints of power' (Foucault, 1977, p. 202), monitor and regulate themselves, becoming 'docile bodies'.

These can also be seen as products of the discourses and the economic atmosphere of capitalism; 'docile bodies' or workers benefit the economic machinery, which runs most smoothly if each cog in the system is the same and functions according to set standards, rules and regulations, without requiring much direct management. Visibility is thus a prerequisite for discipline and the development of a society where each person scrutinises her- or himself according to societal regulations and norms, to be seen and function as good neoliberal citizens, for the good of the nation's wealth and welfare.

In relation to capitalist, disciplinary societal structures, visibility takes on another meaning for fat individuals. In contemporary neoliberal healthist society, the good citizen is a healthy citizen and this health is achieved through a biomedically sanctioned 'healthy' and above all lean lifestyle, comprising a low-fat, low-sugar diet, and lots of fruit, vegetables and physical exercise. And, as discussed in Chapter 1, the lifestyle and health of individuals are read off their body size, not only by the 'person on the street', but also by health 'experts'. Slim equals health and fat equals pathological, and the notion that being fat is bad for your health is taken as commonsensical truth to such an extent that it does not even require evidence in academic articles any more (Aphramor, 2010; for an example, see Wang *et al.,*

2011). The link to the cost incurred by health services is quickly made and fat individuals thus become responsible not only for their own health but also for the financial health of the nation's health services. This, admittedly, applies not only to fat individuals, but in relation to health in theory equally to smokers and alcoholics. There is a clear bias towards a fat-blaming culture, however, as illustrated earlier with a recent Sky News article entitled 'Cancer "caused by obesity and bad diet"' (Brady, 2011). Apart from the current focus on fat in the media, the difference for fat individuals also lies in the ability (or otherwise) of certain stigmatised groups to 'pass' more easily as non-stigmatised and 'normal' than others (Medina, 2011). Cigarettes or alcoholic drinks can be hidden in the majority of our lives, but other signifiers of a stigmatised identity, such as skin colour or body weight, cannot (and others, like religious symbols or dress codes, may be too important to us to relinquish in order to conform). Thus, unlike the smoker or drinker, the fat individual cannot 'pass' as a 'healthy' good citizen in a society that reads 'health' off people's physical appearance and particularly their body size.

The politics of visibility with all its associated power relations is an important issue in gender studies and feminism. The concept of 'the male gaze' was introduced by Laura Mulvey in her essay 'Visual pleasure and narrative cinema' (reprinted in Mulvey, 1999), which is grounded in media and film studies but can be and has been applied to society as a whole. It refers to the construction of women as passive, objectified bodies and men as active, powerful agents and viewers (Bordo, 1993; Ussher, 1997): the activity/passivity duality that John Berger (1972) expresses with the phrase 'men act and women appear' (p. 47). However, one of Mulvey's most important points, and one that we get back to later in reference to the object/subject relations in the disciplinary gaze on fat individuals (Chapter 6), is that women also view themselves through the male gaze (Sassatelli, 2011), rather than being simply the objects of a unidirectional gaze. Some theorists (Gill, 2008a) have argued that the gender balance within this 'unwritten law' (Gill, 2008a, p. 102) of passivity/ activity and object/subject has shifted in recent years with the increasing objectification of men's bodies through the emergence of more and more men on billboards and male bodies in the media generally. However, this gendered dualism, particularly in respect of women's and men's bodies, is so heavily entrenched in contemporary Western culture, and evident in day-to-day life in films, medical texts and merchandise (Bordo, 1993), that women are still more the objects of an appearance-related disciplinary gaze than men are. According to Mulvey (Sassatelli, 2011), the issue of 'the gaze' has not disappeared but is nowadays more strongly associated with the dynamics of sexuality; and rather than overtly objectifying women, it is often disguised within discourses of female sexual agency, particularly in contemporary, postfeminist 'midriff' advertising (Gill, 2008b; Halliwell *et al.*, 2011; Malson *et al.*, 2011).

Expanding this dualism to power asymmetries more generally, the representation of women as passive recipients of men's actions reflects stereotypical constructions of femininity as passive and masculinity as active generally (Nicolson, 2002). From a Foucauldian (Foucault, 1977) stance, however, we see that power systems are not simple dualistic and unilateral processes any more where, for example, one omnipotent sovereign is ruling over the mass of subordinate individuals. In relation to gender this has been described by Sandra Bartky (1988) as follows:

> The disciplinary power that inscribes femininity in the female body is everywhere and it is nowhere; the disciplinarian is everyone and yet no one in particular.
>
> (Bartky, 1988, p. 74)

In other words, power is not held by one individual, group or indeed 'gender', but rather is a dynamic of non-centralised forces within society. Certain social 'standards' of femininity (and masculinity) are constituted and reconstituted in discourse, which includes talk and text, media representations as well as women's embodied 'performances' of normative femininity. Through the centuries these 'doctrines of femininity' (Smith, 1990, p. 171) have changed but the more powerful women have become in terms of their legal standing in society and career prospects, the more limiting these socially constructed 'norms of femininity' have become in relation to appearance (Wolf, 1991; see Chapter 1), with the maintenance of a slim and taut body currently being one of the prime signifiers of 'femininity' (Bordo, 1993; Wolf, 1991). The consequent self-scrutiny and self-regulation engaged in by many women robs them, according to Naomi Wolf (1991), of the energies and other resources necessary to advance in a male-dominated society. As such, the de-individualisation of power, the notion that it is not individual men holding power over individual women, does not mean all good news for women, as the normalising network of gazes and subsequent self-surveillance and self-correction to norms still contributes to the maintenance of the prevailing societal patterns of domination. Bartky expresses this most powerfully in the following quote:

> The woman who checks her makeup half a dozen times a day to see if her foundation has caked or her mascara has run, who worries that the wind or the rain may spoil her hairdo, who looks frequently to see if her stockings have bagged at the ankle or who, feeling fat, monitors everything she eats, has become, just as surely as the inmate of the Panopticon, a self-policing subject, a self committed to a relentless self-surveillance. This self-surveillance is a form of obedience to patriarchy.
>
> (Bartky, 1988, p. 81)

Sadly, although written in 1988, this quote and Bartky's and Wolf's writing generally still ring terrifyingly true, and the focus on women's bodies and their oppression through doctrines of beautification and femininity still continue, albeit now under the guise of agency and free choice (Gill, 2007). Appearance, and its significance in the performance of 'femininity' (which will be further explored in Chapter 6) is not the only issue implicated in the politics of the in/visibility of 'large' women's bodies, however. One major theme in my interviews with fat women, which brings us back to Foucault's concept of the Panopticon, was surveillance and ways of hiding from it; closely associated with surveillance are the constructions of marginalisation and dis/empowerment through and within it.

Surveillance

The theme of being under constant surveillance was present in most of the interviews conducted. Participants talked about feeling monitored when eating in public and how they noticed people inspecting their supermarket trolley when they went food shopping.

> Scrumpz[3]: I suppose (.) just sit there and eat all day (.) that's what people think / I: hmm / so, which isn't true / I: hmm / (.) which then gives you a complex when you go out, if you *do* go out to eat, it sort of, well me personally I sit there and I'm looking around, 'who's looking at me, who's looking at me' / I: hmmm / uhm, I sort of avoid eating in front of people.

> Blade: it's like if you're uhm, I could take you shopping now and if we went up to uhm a a queue with all slim people in, and I come up with my trolley, they would actually see what I was buying / I: hmm / to prove to theirselves 'that's why she's fat' / I: mhm / and you know that that do, you know, nobody up to now said anything / I: mhm / uhm but you can tell that they're doing that look.

Being watched and judged by others is construed as a common experience in the two extracts above, especially in relation to food and eating. Scrumpz constructs the experience of going out for a meal as affecting her psychologically and practically, as other people's opinions of fat individuals 'give you a complex', which she sees as stopping her from eating out.

Foucault's concept of Panopticism and its regulatory and disciplinary effect (as outlined above) seems a particularly apt framework for the interpretation of the above accounts. In Scrumpz's and Blade's narratives, they and fat women generally are constituted as being monitored and watched in and by society, re-articulating the production of unequal power relations in panoptic systems whereby the individual or group 'under surveillance' are construed and construe themselves as marginalised and not fitting normative rules. They position themselves as objects of stares and judgement and as regulated in their action through it, in terms of eating out 'sort of avoid[ing] eating in front of people'.

As outlined above, Foucault (1977) sees the Panopticon mainly as a disciplinary and regulatory system, which, by extension to society in general, leads to self-scrutiny and self-regulation by individuals, according to societal standards or norms. This self-adjustment to what is socially constructed and disseminated as desirable, as well as the awareness of being judged by others according to these 'norms', was also evident in my data. In the context of this research a 'healthy' lifestyle and acceptable body size were main features of the socially constructed norms that need to be adhered to.

> I: What are your reactions when you, personal reactions when you see those programmes [e.g. reality TV shows on weight loss] or read about the so-called obesity epidemic?

Jacqueline: (.) uhm it's an immediate uh, I should, if I'm eating then I have to stop eating / I: hmm / you know if I'm you know, thinking about going shopping that day then (.) the shopping I bring back is is fruit and vegetables and make sure that kind of, cause I think when I *see* things I become even more conscious of eating or buying food or anything and what people might think of what I'm buying, what I'm eating.

Jacqueline construes herself as immediately receptive and affected by the media coverage of the alleged 'obesity epidemic', positioning herself as one of the target group, as regulated in her behaviour by society's rules and norms in terms of food and eating. Fruit and vegetables are constructed as 'good' whilst eating generally for a fat person is prohibited, as Jacqueline positions herself, as a fat person, as someone who has 'to stop eating' and equally as somebody whom other people watch and judge depending on what food she buys or eats.

The theme of surveillance is not only about direct observation and not/fitting into normative rules, however, but also about not/fitting the environment: about the constant reminders of one's size through the physical environment.

Emily: I couldn't [laughing] fit between the arm chairs / I: hmm / and I'm thinking what am I supposed to do because people, as I went to walk in, people saw (.) and I walked out again / I: hmm / and we looked, we went to another carriage where there was nobody (.) and (.) I, I went in where I could actually try and see if I could *squeeze* in without it being obvious to the other people.

Scrumpz: I'm very much into football / I: hmm / I got stuck in a turnstile / I: hmm / and it was the most, it's, *embarrassing* experience I've ever, ever / I: hmm / and it was (.) I sort of tried to laugh it off at the time, got the comments / I: hmm / I mean I even made it into the national papers and everything / I: Did you? / yeah and magazines and (.) I was like, yeah, yeah, yeah laughing about it but soon as I got in the door I cried / I: hmm / and cried, and cried / I: hmm / because I was so humili, humiliated.

In Emily's and Scrumpz's accounts above, being watched as one struggles with the physical environment is experienced as embarrassing and humiliating. Emily avoids being seen by others by trying to get on the train at another carriage and people seeing her is construed as one of the major concerns. 'People saw' that she did not fit, which positioned her discursively and practically outside normative society, that is outside that part of society who are 'normatively' sized and thus can fit into train carriages or walk through turnstiles. While not wanting to equate 'large' individuals with people with disabilities, this construction and positioning as an outsider through the built environment is not unlike the positioning to which individuals with disabilities are subjected. In the social model of disability (Oliver, 1990), the built environment which restricts the mobility of individuals with disabilities is seen as one of the major factors that construct these individuals as disabled. It is not the individual's impairment in itself that stops her or him from entering certain buildings, for example, but the lack of a ramp, the narrow construction of the entrance, and so forth. Similarly, it is not only the language used and people watching them that construct fat people as outsiders in the above excerpts. They are also constructed and positioned as such through the physical environment. As a cultural signifier, the built environment can be read as text and thus represents a form of discursive regulation in relation to body size.

There is another element to Scrumpz's account, however, which reflects Sandra Lee Bartky's (1990) philosophical writing about domination and oppression, and the role objectification plays in this. According to Bartky, domination requires not only the objectification of the dominated person but also that the person be made aware of being objectified, and she uses an example of being whistled at by men, to illustrate this.

> I freeze. As Sartre would say, I have been petrified by the gaze of the Other. My face flushes and my motions become stiff and self-conscious. The body which only a moment before I inhabited with such ease now floods my consciousness. I have been made an object. [. . .] They could [. . .] have enjoyed me in silence. [. . .] But I must be *made* to know that I am a 'nice piece of ass': I must be made to see myself as they see me.
>
> (Bartky, 1990, p. 27, original emphasis)

Had she been unknowingly watched and objectified by the men, she would have not been made aware of her objectification and it would not have had any negative effect on her. Being aware of this objectification, however, subjectifies her in the experience, and humiliates and denigrates her. It reduces her body, and by extension herself, to a 'nice piece of ass'. Bartky interprets this wolf-whistling, and what she calls the compulsive nature of men's behaviour, as part of a ritual of subjugation of women. Scrumpz's experience of not only getting stuck in a turnstile but her photograph and story being published in newspapers can be interpreted in the same light. Scrumpz would not have drawn attention to herself had she got stuck in the turnstile with a rucksack or similar, but having got stuck due to her size seemed to warrant her (deliberate) humiliation. Obviously, Scrumpz was aware of being watched by other football fans on the day, but she is further objectified in the gaze of the nation, as an example of a fat woman, and she is 'made to know' that she does not fit. As Samantha in another interview summed up, 'you know, the world is very firmly there to tell you that you don't fit'.

Being in the watch tower and the cell

The women in the study generally constituted themselves as targets of observation and judgements, as being singled out and marginalised within society, and they construed their lifestyle as controlled by it.

> Emily: If, if *I* didn't feel other people looking at me and thinking 'yuk' (.) then I would go [laughing] swimming / I: hmm / yes, it is that simple actually, isn't it?

Being policed in this way was constituted by these participants, not surprisingly, as something negative. Their imposed, but resisted, subject position is constructed as that of a passive object of a judgemental gaze and as excluded from the norm within that gaze. In other places, however, women positioned themselves and fat women generally as active agents in this politics of visibility. This is illustrated in the two quotes below, where the politics of the regulating gaze on fat women remain constant, but Emily and Jenny are now active and included in the process of its regulatory deployment. In terms of Panopticon architecture (see explanation above, and Foucault, 1977), they are now in the watch tower as well as the cell:

> Emily: I *know* people go into, wear swimming costumes on the beach when they are my size, but [laughing] they shouldn't. Uh, you see, I'm, I'm fat and I can look at other people and say 'oh, no, you shouldn't. . .', uhm, so it's not just thin people [laughing] who do that / I: hmm / it's fat people as well.

> Jenny: I think that a fat person walking down the road eating a doughnut (.) gets more attention than a thin person walking down the road eating a doughnut /I: mm/ um, and (.) and and and would get more attention from *me* as well and that's where I feel so conflicted because I, I feel fat and happy or whatever (.) but I would (.) I guess I wouldn't ever want to be smaller than a size 16, I can't see /I: mm/ I can't really see see that (.) but I'd I'd quite like to be maybe maybe I just want to be a size 18 because then I'd still be able to shop in most shops /I: mm/ I don't know if if all shops went up to size 30 maybe I'd put on weight um (..) but you know I still I *do* ha- make those automatic judgements of people when I see them.

Germov and Williams (1999), drawing on Foucault's Panopticism, refer to this constant monitoring of one's own and other women's size as the 'body Panopticon' (p. 126). Both Emily and Jenny are positioning themselves as active viewers in the above quotes but construe their motivations completely differently. Jenny construes herself as conflicted, as being aware that her thoughts on the issue of weight and size contradict her immediate judgement of 'large' people eating in the street. Jenny is positioning herself as a happy fat person whose body size does not affect her negatively, were it not for the lack of clothes to buy in her size. At the same time, however, she also constitutes other 'large' persons as standing out and herself as automatically, that is to an extent involuntarily, judging them – (other) fat people are thus positioned as naturally attracting judgement. Emily on the other hand construes herself in her two accounts above as intentionally hiding from the gaze of others, and the judgements passed on 'large' individuals by herself and others – contrary to Jenny's construction – as equally intentional and as justified.

Hiding and being hidden

The theme of hiding, or avoiding a judgemental gaze, can also be found in other quotes. Ali, for example, spoke about using colour to hide behind: 'traditionally you always see a larger person wearing black (.) they [laughing] wouldn't really go for a nice cerise dress or something / I: hmm / usually try and hide away behind a black (Ali)'. Not wanting to stand out is constructed as normal, or traditional, for 'large' persons, and wearing bright colours like a 'cerise dress' would draw attention to them. 'Large' people, then, are positioned as hiding away, as not wanting to be seen in public as putting themselves on the margins of society. However, similarly to the issues discussed above, the theme of hiding and the politics and power relations constituted within it are dynamic and shifting. Whilst the invisibility of the fat person appears as desired by fat individuals themselves in some accounts, it is also present as an imposed subject position, something that is being done to the fat woman. For example:

> Jacqueline: I don't know it's probably a stroke of paranoia and also *maybe* it is happening, but I always feel that when I go in a restaurant, my partner who is also big that we get put nearer the back so we are not seen near the front of the restaurant to be eating food as two big people / I: hmm / and that seems to have happened quite a lot you know.

Being placed at the back of a restaurant signifies the direct and physical marginalisation of individuals, that is, their being placed at the margins of a certain defined space. By drawing on discourses of mental health, and paranoia in particular, Jacqueline construes herself as conscious of being a target of judgement and discrimination, but at the same time she positions herself as ambiguous as to the extent and intentionality of it, and as to how serious an issue it really presents.

The issues discussed so far are all grounded in the theme of surveillance. Fat women were constituted as targets of stares, judgements and marginalisation, and their lives as regulated in and by the societal normalising gaze. The power relations implicated in this regulating Panopticon network were not unidirectional, however, with fat women positioned only as the objects of the normalising gaze. Rather, subject positions of the viewing and judging subject as well as the regulated object and self-regulating subject were dynamically and interchangeably taken up, accepted and rejected.

Wanting to be seen?

Visibility is not always synonymous with surveillance and oppression, of course. Being *in*visible can equally be disempowering and marginalising (Frith, 2003; Zitzelsberger, 2005) and making oneself visible can have empowering effects – 'visibility is a double-edged sword' (Brighenti, 2007, p. 335) in relation to power and oppression. As such it was not surprising that visibility, being seen and looked at, was not exclusively construed negatively in my interviews either. Certain looks and a certain kind of visibility seemed welcome or desirable, but were also sometimes construed as unachievable for fat women.

> Eileen: There was two managers, male managers in the cash safe, doing something and obviously I walked past without them seeing and they were

talking about the fit birds in the office [. . .] and um then he said yeah well what do you reckon about Eileen then /I: mm hmm/ and he said yeah she's a yeah she's nice yeah bit of alright, shame she's so fat though /I: mm hmm/ and uh and the other one said yeah no I wouldn't give her one she's too fat [. . .] that made me feel absolutely dreadful /I: mm mm/ 'cause you think well hang on a minute, um, does that mean that because I, and I wasn't anywhere near as big as I am now /I: mm/ does that mean that because I am big I'm not worth being looked at /I: mm/, I'm not worth having any feelings over, I'm not fanciable, no one's gonna love me, you know /I: mm/ no one's gonna want me /I: mm/ all those things which, you know, luckily enough on my part, I already had a partner I knew I was loved I knew I, you know, I knew I was wanted but looking at you about the way you are perceived sexually as well /I: mm/ if you're fat, no one's gonna wanna go near you /I: mm/ or touch you and that because it's revolting.

Yvonne: I'd like to say, I've got complete freedom /I: mm/ but there is a societal pressure to conform to that image [. . .] I do, at the back of my mind think, look at yourself you know, is this what your husband really wants to wake up to in the morning?

In the above extracts, fat women are constituted as not what one (men) necessarily wants to look at. As outlined in the introduction to this chapter, the construction of women as passive objects (to be looked at) and men as active subjects of the gaze (the viewers) is often seen as a factor in the oppression of women in patriarchal society (Bordo, 1993; Wolf, 1991). This does not mean that women are just passive dupes of the production of these power relations, however. Women are actively (but not necessarily completely agentically) involved in the constitution and reconstitution of the 'doctrines of femininity' (Smith, 1990) and the power relations implicated in the normalising gaze of a Panopticon society, for example by participating in certain beautification practices. The notion of women's free choice in this and any other area of life is frequently drawn on in assertions of a postfeminist era. However, as laid out earlier, women's oppression through means of beauti-fication and feminising practices has simply become more subtle, and, as Stuart and Donaghue (2012) observe, 'women can embrace their liberated social status, as long as it is not at the "expense" of their femininity' (p. 3), and femininity is still very much tied to appearance or beauty. The importance of women's 'beauty' in attracting men is also entrenched in (heterosexual) romantic discourses (Malson, 1998; Ussher, 1997). Within romantic narratives, women get and keep their men to a great part through their 'beauty' or appearance (Ussher, 1997), and being sexually attractive in this context is also part of 'doing woman' (Ussher, 1997). In this context, being slim is a socially constructed signifier of feminine beauty and of being heterosexually attractive as a woman in contemporary society (Bordo, 1993; Germov and Williams, 1999; Malson, 1998), which in reverse disqualifies fat women from feminine sexual attractiveness.

Drawing on heterosexual romantic discourses, Eileen construes a certain visibility, namely looks of male admiration, as desirable and attracting men's admiring looks is equated with being worthy of love in the above excerpt. The imposed subject position of the unlovable fat woman is rejected by questioning the implied consequences of being 'big', that is, not to be worth being looked at, having any feelings over or not being fanciable, in Eileen's words 'no one's gonna love me, you know /I: mm/ no one's gonna want me'. Eileen construes these assumptions as invalid as she had found a husband, despite her size. However, at the same time, Eileen also imposes boundaries on a 'lovable' body size by stating that she 'wasn't anywhere near as big as [she was] now' at the time of the described episode. She thus construes it as potentially understandable if men talked about her in the way described above now, at her bigger size. Similarly, Yvonne construes a certain body size in women as disqualifying them from attracting affectionate looks by men, with the benchmark image being socially determined, and the pressure this puts on her as at odds with the freedom Yvonne positions herself to have in life generally.

While the politics of visibility are different in the above excerpts as certain types of visibility are construed as desirable and empowering for women, fat women are positioned as disqualified from this positive visibility. It seems that, despite rejecting certain subject positions of the stereotypical fat woman as unattractive and unlovable, Eileen and other women in my study still employ romantic discourses that position them and other 'large' women on the margins of femininity and romance.

Fat efficacy

Another theme where 'being seen' is construed positively reverses the politics of visibility. Leaning very slightly on Bandura's (1994) concept of self-efficacy, eschewing the individualising factors and moving it outside of the individual, into the interactionary space of society, I would like to term the process referred to here 'fat efficacy'. Within the interviews, choosing to be seen in – for 'large' individuals – exceptional ways, and seeing other 'large' people achieving in areas that are often socially constructed as reserved for 'slim' people, was constructed as empowering and supportive. Eileen spoke about wearing shorts in public, for example, and Charlotte talked about her dancing and orienteering friends.

> Eileen: I mean I personally haven't got a problem with wearing things like shorts /I: mm/ um, but I'm, I've got big friends and I've got friends that wouldn't wear sleeveless tops [. . .] and I've even had people stop me in the street and say oh I've always wanted to wear shorts, I just wanted to say 'oh God you've just made my day /I: mm hmm/ seeing you in a pair of shorts'.

> Charlotte: I guess I *do* carry these internalised notions of what a fat person can do / I: hmm / and it's important to me to be around people that that kind of buck those notions / I: hmm / like (.) my friend [name] is a dancer she's just an incredible dancer / I: hmm / and you know, uh and not just like (.) a [laughing] crappy dancer, she's like a da, a prop, a proper professional dancer

and she's fat and my friend [name] in Norway does orienteering and / I: hmm / you know, she runs around in the woods with a map and she's my size, and you know I find that (.) just amazing and and kind of nearly nourishing to be around people like that.

Being visible and watched by others takes on a different significance, as it is constructed by both Eileen and Charlotte in the above extracts as having a productive rather than constraining power. There is in these accounts a similar emphasis on the *visibility* of women's large bodies but the power relations that are constituted in Eileen's and Charlotte's accounts are normalising of bigger women's bodies and enabling rather than excluding and disabling. While visibility appears here, as in previous quotes, as a highly significant field of regulation and sub-jectification, the (gendered) politics of these fields of visibility are very different. The similarity to 'self-efficacy' is limited, however. While self-efficacy is (partly) developed through social modelling on an individual basis, the positive effects that 'being seen' and 'seeing other "large" individuals' achieve here are not just restricted to one person learning from another. The empowering effect of visibility was also constructed as an empowering dynamics within society generally, the outcome of which would be the normalisation of the visibility and physical capability of 'large' people.

What does this mean for fat women?

Seeing and being seen, and avoiding either or both – in/visibility – were themes and issues that emerged in various places throughout the interview transcripts. Amongst these themes, 'surveillance' was a prominent one. On the one hand being seen, monitored and judged as a 'large' person by society and through the physical environment was constructed as oppressive and lifestyle-controlling. Parallels can be drawn to what Foucault (1977) describes as a principle of panopticism where constant surveillance creates a culture where individuals, in continuous anticipation of being monitored and judged, turn their gaze on to themselves and self-monitor and self-discipline according to the prevailing order.

In the present research, this was not the only way the theme of surveillance emerged, however. A number of subject positions, linked to the in/visibility of 'large' bodies, were taken up or rejected. Participants constructed themselves as targets of stares and comments, and as such as being on the outskirts of society, and being controlled in terms of their lifestyles, in relation to what they should and should not do. Fat women's bodies were construed as excluded from romance in the heterosexual male gaze. While an inclusion within this gaze is not necessarily constituted as a good thing from a feminist point of view (cf. above excerpt from Bartky, 1990), being excluded was construed as denigrating in my data and the positioning of the unlovable fat woman was both accepted and rejected. Other imposed denigrating subject positions were also rejected, for example, that of the lazy glutton who 'just sit[s] there and eat[s] all day' (Scrumpz). In other places, participants constructed themselves as part of the surveying or monitoring society

– 'so it's not just thin people [laughing] who do that, it's fat people as well' (Emily)
– and as such perhaps as less marginalised, as active participants in this social process of positioning fat bodies.

Yet, as we have seen above, being seen and seeing other 'large' individuals was also constructed as positive and empowering, and seemed to offer the subject positions of a member of a capable community, being nourished and accepted, rather than stigmatised and downgraded, as well as being an advocate for this community. This construction of visibility I have termed 'fat efficacy': Through an increased visibility of fat people in positively valued situations and positions in society, large individuals are empowered and enabled, and being 'large' is normalised, which has the potential to reduce stigma and discrimination. Of course it is not quite that simple. The multiple discourses converging on fat women and the power relationships and oppression and discrimination produced within them are not solely linked to representations – to the in/visibility of fat. Issues of ethnicity, geo-location and class (although the latter can also be signified in appearance) are inextricably linked to the processes of power inequalities, and fat women's bodies are not lived and experienced outside of these (Probyn, 2009).

In a society where the fat body is inscribed with negative meanings of pathology, irresponsibility and immorality, however, the unavoidable visibility of fat will play a major part in its experience and sociopolitical consequences. The politics of visibility in terms of 'being fat' seem to be highly dynamic and shifting, and a number of subject positions are frequently and interchangeably being taken up, imposed, accepted and rejected. Despite there being resistances to cultural constructions of 'the large individual' and notions of what 'they' should or should not do, the prominent theme of surveillance is that of oppression and control, and of the fat body being constructed as better hidden/not to be seen. I would thus assert that Foucault's (1977) notion that 'visibility is a trap' still holds true in many ways for the community of fat women. What we wear plays another major part in the politics of visibility or appearance, and it is to clothes and the issues around wearing and buying clothes for fat women that I turn next.

4 'I just wear clothes to keep me warm'

My favourite singer-songwriter is Konstantin Wecker, who in one of his songs sings about the beautiful people who get obsessed about what to wear, as they seem only to exist if we actually look at them, see them. He continues by singing about those who do not fit the normative standards of beauty; how they do not feature in the world and instead sit quietly in the corner and feel marginalised and alone (Wecker, 1989). The marginalisation of those not fulfilling the societal prescriptions of appearance was also one of the prominent topics in my interviews with fat women. Clothes, and not being able to buy clothes that fitted and were deemed attractive, played a big part in this matter. What we wear can have a significant impact on how we experience life. In addition to body size and shape, clothes are a major part of our appearance, and thus of what others initially see on meeting us. Perhaps it is not very surprising then that quite a substantive amount of literature, from various disciplines, can be found on the history, use and meaning of clothes and fashion. According to Joanne Entwistle (2001; citing Polhemus, 1988), all known human cultures have in some ways been 'decorating' or 'dressing' the body – through make-up, body painting, tattooing or clothing. Dressing the body not only fulfils practical functions of warming and protecting the body, but certain conventions of dress are recognised and mean something to certain cultures and subcultures. They are 'adding a whole array of meanings to the body that would otherwise not be there' (Entwistle, 2001, p. 33).

As a signifier of a person's age, social class and standing, group identity, religion and sexuality, clothing could be deemed a cultural category (Abbott and Sapsford, 2001; Clarke and Turner, 2007; Craik, 1994). A concern with this category has long been considered a predominantly feminine domain, however. Jennifer Craik (1994) provides a detailed history of how this 'meaning' of fashion/dress, and the 'fashioning of women' in particular, developed from the eighteenth century, when fashion was starting to be considered an unavoidable weakness of women (Hollander, 1980). The framing of fashion as a feminine concern can be understood in the context of shifts in gender ideologies that accompanied Western industrialisation, in particular the division of labour and the rise of consumer culture. During this period, women became associated with domesticity and managing the household (and related purchasing activities), which developed into a general 'feminisation of consumerism' (Craik, 1994, p. 70). Men became associated with earning, while women became 'shoppers'. And while consumer culture and shopping generally became gendered, there was also a growing fragmentation noticeable within the sector of consumer products geared towards women.

In the late nineteenth century, the number of women's magazines grew rapidly and with it the specialisation of each individual journal/magazine towards a certain readership. Depending on the wealth/class, generation and status of their target group, each associated with certain moral and value systems, different ways of 'being a woman' were advocated. An advance in visual technology also meant that the focus was more and more on appearance, including clothes and make-up, which in turn now reflected the various ways of 'doing femininity' (Craik, 1994). While clothes had carried meaning in relation to social class and standing for a long time previously, now a person's individual identity, moral attributes and worth were seen as being signified in their appearance and clothes (Craik, 1994; Soper, 2001).

The signifying function of appearance and clothes is continuing in today's societies (Frith, 2003). Clothes have the potential of 'marking' somebody as belonging to a certain social group, and can thus also function as aids to oppression. One of the best examples here is the hijab, a headscarf worn by some Muslim women. It serves as an example of marginalisation and oppression not because of the commonly held (and erroneous) assumption that all women wearing it have been forced to do so, but because it marks the wearer out as a Muslim woman, and thus belonging to a religious group that post 9/11 is associated with terrorism, hatred and fear (Medina, 2011). Jameelah Medina provides an illuminating account of the reactions to her clothing she encounters on a daily basis, ranging from verbal abuse to well-meaning but misguided attempts by Western feminists to 'liberate' her from her alleged oppression (i.e. the hijab). Unless she denounces her beliefs and associated dress standards, she cannot 'pass' as the mainstream within Western 'judeo-christonormativity' (Medina, 2011, p. 140) and is thus immediately vulnerable to marginalisation, discrimination and oppression.

But clothes are markers of difference, of otherness, within as much as between cultural groups. Similarly to the past, when the lavish clothes of the aristocracy signified their superior standing in comparison to the peasants, a very well and expensively dressed person may inspire awe and a feeling of inferiority in those who cannot afford such clothes today (McDowell, 1984). Then and now, power relations between the more or less well off are constructed and perpetuated through clothes and appearance generally. In the eighteenth century physically restrictive clothes signalled that one was well off enough to employ others for hard, manual labour (McDowell, 1992). Today people are generally categorised and judged by their appearance, a process Young (1998/1990, cited by Frith, 2003) refers to as the 'aesthetic scaling of bodies'.

Fashion and clothes can function as an expression of the self, but always linked to the cultural background an individual is moving in. As such, dress orientates a person towards a certain culture and position in society (Entwistle, 2000; Soper, 2001). Clothes and fashion could thus also be called a type of language which is not only read off our bodies, based on a shared societal code, but through which individuals can express themselves. However, dress constitutes a very restrictive language, as there is no facility within it to express entirely new things, due to consisting of prefabricated codes, or, as McCracken expresses it:

> [T]he code has no generative capacity. Its users enjoy no combinatorial freedom . . . The code specified not only the components of the message, but also the messages themselves. These messages come, as it were, pre-fabricated. Because the wearer does not have this combinatorial freedom, the interpreter of clothing examines an outfit not for a new message but for an old one fixed by convention.
>
> (McCracken, 1990, cited by Craik, 1994, p. 10)

The limits imposed on the individual's expression through this impoverished language of prefabricated (dress) codes are not the only way one's expression through clothes is restricted. As Holliday (1999) reminds us, in particular referring to the ability to 'power-dress' for one's job, not everybody is able to use the codes of fashion language equally, as not everyone has the appropriate financial means or access to the relevant retail outlets. For many 'large' individuals, the necessary clothes or quality of material are simply not provided in the size needed for their body shape (Adam, 2001). As in the eighteenth century, and outlined above, one's means dictate the extent of self-expression that is possible through one's clothes and in reverse one's social standing, status and thus power are not only signified but partially also constituted by one's clothes.

This is particularly true for the constitution of gendered subjectivities and sexualities. Craik (1994) calls the clothing of our bodies a 'tool of self-management', as identity, sexuality and social position are being constituted in the way women are 'fashioning' their bodies. So clothes, or rather fashion, as one would have to include make-up, certain items of jewellery, and things like haircuts in this toolbox of self-management, can not only be used to express an individual's social position in the widest sense (including class, age, political views), but identity and femininity are also constituted through these practices (Smith, 1990). Women create themselves with their appearance, including clothes, but this work and their skills are closely associated with, and in parts regulated by, the market for the consumer goods (clothes, accessories, make-up) applied in their self-creation work (Smith, 1990). As such, despite women's active engagement in this process, the issue of choice is a contested one. While Giddens (1991, cited in Frost, 2005) sees the individual as an agentic creator of his or her own identity, other theorists (Craik, 1994; Frost, 2005) point to the limitations of choice, not only in regard to one's financial means but also in relation to certain societal rules, the transgression of which may come at a cost. This also links to Chapter 3, where I discuss how 'large' women construe themselves as marginalised and restricted in their practices through the normalising and disciplining politics of the fat body's in/visibility.

The potential cost incurred by women for disregarding societal fashion and appearance rules would, in the majority of cases, not take the form of physical punishment or otherwise overt displays of power and domination by another individual in Western cultures today. It can manifest itself, however, in the exclusion from or marginalisation within society (Frith, 2003; Frost, 2005). This shift in the way women are being controlled, away from the direct individual domination by a singular (sovereign) power, to a complex, multidimensional and dynamic power system, is a reflection of the changes within the power relations in society generally. Bartky's (1988) uses Foucault's (1977) theories on discipline and power, and his concept of panopticism (see Chapter 3 on in/visibility) to explain her theory on how women and their bodies are being objectified and dominated by a generalised gaze of normalisation, and how they consequently self-discipline and self-police themselves. She also gives us her answer to the question why it is so difficult for women to resist this domination, or in her words: 'Why isn't every woman a feminist?' (Foucault, 1977, p. 77). In short, nowadays, women have incorporated cultural requirements for being a woman, including body disciplines such as dieting (to slim the body), exercise (to resculpture the body), make-up, high heels, certain hairstyles, clothes and demeanours, into their 'selves' to the extent that they constantly scrutinise and discipline themselves in order to fit and perform normative femininity (Bartky, 1988; Smith, 1990; Wolf, 1991). Transgression of these rules or norms, i.e. not being able or willing to conform to them, may, according to Bartky (1988), result in potential punishment in the form of not being able to find a (heterosexual) partner and thus having to live without heterosexual intimacy in one's life, and generally being marginalised within society.

However, Bartky (1988) also maintains that, despite the fact that a concern with one's (ideally well-groomed) appearance leads to objectification and domination, and that it does not earn a woman any real respect (simply because it falls within the remit of what *women* do), the proficiency in the above body disciplines gives women a sense of accomplishment or mastery (Bartky, 1988, p. 77). As a consequence, an absence of these proficiencies may mean a certain feeling of deskilling, which is something people generally seek to avoid. Now some may argue that things have changed since Bartky, Smith and Wolf (and others) warned of this backlash against feminism and may want to point to women's empowerment and greater influence in contemporary, postfeminist, Western society. Some studies suggest that young women believe feminism is no longer necessary (Rudolfsdottir and Jolliffe, 2008), and few women would want to say of themselves that they are dressing up or engaging in beautification activities 'for men'; rather, these 'innocent' behaviours of make-up, body hair removal and cosmetic surgery are pleasures which we carry out for ourselves, and we should be allowed to do so without feeling guilty for letting womanhood or feminism down. As free, powerful agents we should be allowed to choose to do whatever we want – including the beautification or modification of our bodies with whatever means available (Braun, 2009; Gill, 2007; Malson *et al.*, 2011; Stuart and Donaghue, 2012). Yet, as writers like Ros Gill, Helen Malson and colleagues, and Virginia Braun demonstrate, the shift has not been to more equality but towards a greater sexualisation of women (and girls); however now, dangerously, under the guise of free choice – the choice to self-scrutinise and self-regulate, in essence to conform, in order to be able to live out one's sexual liberation, which in the end is only available to the owner of a flawless and hairless, and above all, a lean, fatless body. A shift *has* occurred since Bartky and Wolf (*et al.*) published their seminal works – but it is a shift towards greater sexualisation, and from objectification to subjectification; not towards gender (power) equality.

In summary, clothes seem to play a noteworthy role in contemporary society, not only in signifying our social standing, class and sexuality but also as aids in the constitution of our (gendered) subjectivities. Considering this together with the significance of issues of in/visibility (see Chapter 3) for 'large' women, it seemed apt to explore the topic of clothes in relation to the experience of 'being large' in more detail. The unavailability of desirable clothes for 'large' women, a lack of choice and, consequently, a lack of resources to express their individuality and femininity were all frequently raised topics during the interviews.

Our bodies are not the problem

The importance of clothes could be gleaned in several places, where my participants constituted their bodies as not being the problem; rather the issue was how their embodied interactions with society, the physical environment (see Chapter 3) and commodities such as clothes made them feel.

> Jenny: I have in common with *a lot* of my fat friends is it's the the reason you *don't* feel attractive is just because you can't get the clothes /I: mm/ that you want , and I know, I've got two other friends who've admitted to me that they feel most attractive and most comfortable when they're naked /I: mm/ and I, I certainly I've *never* had any problems like I've never been a oh, got to have the lights out /I: mm/ and get undressed in the dark, and it's when you have to come and put clothes on, and you can't find clothes that you really want to wear /I: mm/ that's when you feel unattractive.

> Eileen: When I go to shop for clothes I am (.) I don't *ever* look at what I like first thing I do is look whether they've got the size for me /I: mm/ and then you narrow down what you like and then you narrow it down again to what is actually not going to make you look too fat /I: yeah/ um, you know (.) so, it's not as easy as just /I: mm/ sort of going out and thinking right okay I'm just gonna buy this particular outfit, you are very aware of what other people, uhm (.) how, how they perceive you.

Jenny, in the above extract, positions herself and her fat friends as women who feel comfortable and positive about and in their naked bodies, which only become a problem once they 'have to come and put clothes on'. Through the unavailability of clothes they want to wear, fat women are being positioned as intrinsically unattractive and scruffy, uninterested in clothes and their appearance generally. Discourses are not limited to texts, but clothes – as well as, for example, the built environment (see Chapter 3) or images – constitute non-textual discursive tools that are expressive and constructive of meaning, and read and interpreted by others

(Foucault, 1972, 1977). This being judged and read by others is articulated in Eileen's narrative above: Eileen construes herself as regulated in the choice of clothing by the resources available to her but also by the gaze of others. Not being able to find clothes that they would construe as attractive or as expressing their identity and their happiness in their bodies, and having to wear clothes they 'do not really want to wear' constitutes 'large' women as unattractive. The 'texts' inscribed on them through these clothes, and not their bodies in themselves, signify this perceived unattractiveness in the gaze of others.

Kate Soper (2001) refers to Kant and his concept of how we judge people's inner (read moral) and outer beauty by their appearance, when she writes about clothes as a form of self-expression. Based on the assumption that clothes are chosen voluntarily – which in the 'large' person's case is not entirely the case – people draw conclusions from the aesthetics of the clothes to the 'aesthetics' of the moral make-up of a person (Frith, 2003; Soper, 2001). Of course, considering our current neoliberal societies with an emphasis on individual responsibility for one's life in all aspects (Rose, 1996; Throsby, 2007), this will also apply to people's clothed and unclothed bodies, as an individual's body size and shape can also be considered a manifestation of her or his lifestyle and as such as voluntarily chosen. This has further implications for the construction of the fat person as a health offender, which I will explore in the next chapter; the point Soper (2001) makes, however, strikes a chord with Jenny's constitution of clothes as the problem. Jenny's 'feel[ing] unattractive' is portrayed as the way she thinks other people perceive her, or as Levene and Gleeson (2003, p. 18) put it: 'body size is important to identity . . . because it is important to others'. The clothes they are confined to wearing because of their size further discursively construct and signify fat women's unattractiveness to other people.

Containment and regulation

As well as construing the clothes available to fat women, rather than their bodies, as constituting the problem faced by 'large' women, Jenny, in the following quote, constructs the unavailability of fashionable clothes for her and other 'large' women as an intentional strategy employed by the rest of society.

> Jenny: I don't know like what, what's gonna happen the world's not going to stop if if a fat girl gets something from Top Shop.

> Samantha: Over a size, dress size 18, you know, they (.) have an average number of shops, which is like four shops / I: hmm / whereas women who're within a normal range, you know, they have a choice of 20, 30 or something, so, and I've, I found that (.) really restrictive.

In the above, Jenny construes the thought of a fat woman shopping in Top Shop as something society sees as a threat, as something that causes something bad to happen. Generally within the women's narratives on clothing, they construed themselves as restricted and regulated through types or number of shops open to them, as is also articulated in Samantha's quote. Adam (2001) refers to Douglas (1966) when she talks about fat women threatening men and society through their 'transgression of boundaries' (Adam, 2001, p. 41). An orderly world with demarcated categories symbolises safety which is threatened by anything that is perceived as at or outside the margins of these categories. 'Large' women's bodies can be seen as transgressing the boundaries of acceptable body sizes (Orbach, 2006b; Wolf, 1991) and are as such polluting and jeopardising the safe orderliness valued in Western capitalist nations (LeBesco, 2004). As such, the restrictions imposed through the unavailability of appropriate clothes can be construed as attempts to contain these potential 'sources of dangerous power' (Adam, 2001, p. 41).

The theme of containment, or regulation of fat women's subjectivities, movements and practices, was also evident in a more practical sense in the following quote.

> Louise: I mean it affects my life because I don't tend to go and shop with my friends / I: hmm / because my friends are smaller than me and if we go to the shops where they can buy clothes I could buy a bracelet or a bag / I: hmm / you know and the it it's quite it's annoying / I: hmm / more than anything to have to walk around and and not to see anything that I could fit into.

The above and the following, extract constitute fat women as marginalised within and by society through size segregation within shopping centres and individual shops (Adam, 2001). It is remarkable that the thought that her 'smaller' friends could come along to browse in her 'special shops' is completely absent in her talk about 'going shopping with friends'. It is the fat woman who is hanging on to the group of 'normatively sized' women; she is allowed to come along but not to join in. Instead of having fun, her experience is, or appears as, one of annoyance. And the women in my study not only felt marginalised and excluded from and within the shopping experience itself, but also from activities that necessitated certain clothes that were unavailable to them.

> Eileen: there was um, a double-page spread on uhm (.) uh costumes / I: mhm / fancy-dress costumes, I thought, *brilliant* oh isn't that a good idea /I: mm/ there was sort of some Flintstones and Superman, Superwoman, uhm, nurses' outfits uh Elvis all this sort of thing, quite reasonably priced about thirty quid and you think well how much you pay to hire one /I: mm/ when I actually looked at the [laughing] costumes sizes for the women's it was eight to ten and ten to twelve /I: oh right/ and that's where it stopped,

> I: and above that you don't do fancy dress,

> E: No, no, 'cause you'd draw attention to yourself you see /I: mm mm/ uhm, so does that perceive the fact that you can't enjoy yourself if you're fat /I: no mm/ you know you can't join in with other people /I: mm/ because you're fat,

um, you know and I *I couldn't believe* it stopped, [. . .] if you're bigger than a size twelve, you know, you actually can't, or you shouldn't be enjoying yourself.

Similar to my arguments in Chapter 3, fat people are constructed here as better hidden, not seen and certainly not 'draw[ing] attention to yourself' (Eileen). However, the positioning of 'large' women on the margins of society goes further here, through the literal and practical exclusion of individuals above a certain size from social activities through the non-provision of the appropriate items necessary for participation, in this case fancy-dress clothing. Eileen in fact poses the question of whether this is the message to be perceived by fat people that they 'can't enjoy [themselves]' and 'can't join in with other people'. By challenging this implied message, she is rejecting the imposed subject position of the outsider fat woman.

Clothes and their unavailability, then, are construed as marginalising and regulating fat women and their activities, as well as marking fat women as something they reject being – unattractive, not happy with their bodies and not capable of having fun. This constitution of clothes as markers is not surprising, given the significance clothes have in most human cultures, as signifiers of social status, 'gender', sexuality, subjectivities and so forth.

The uniform of fat women

A special category of clothes are uniforms, which are designed to mark people out as belonging to a certain societal group, and to bestow or remove privileges (Joseph and Alex, 1972). The clothes available to 'large' women were construed in a similar fashion in the interviews.

Jenny: it's when you have to come and put clothes on, and you can't find clothes that you really want to wear /I: mm/ that's when you feel unattractive /I: mm/ and you end up you know relegated to this like uniform. [. . .] Maybe fat people look so crap because they don't have any nice clothes to wear, rather than just fat people don't know how to dress /I: mm/ so, you know, maybe we don't actually all want to walk around in leggings and baggy t-shirts /I: mm/ maybe that's just the only clothes we can find.

In the above quotation, Jenny construes leggings and baggy t-shirts as the uniform for fat women – the only clothes they can find, but which make them 'look so crap' and like they 'don't know how to dress'. Uniforms can be required in certain jobs or are mandatory attires for students in schools, or inmates in prisons. The functions of the uniform are manifold, according to Nathan Joseph and Nicholas Alex (1972). Not only do they distinguish between groups, or designate a group, but they signify the attributes (in terms of rules, privileges and duties) that are directly or practically attached to, or socially associated with, the respective group. Uniforms often imply the existence of a hierarchy, consisting of at least two levels: that of the wearer and that of the superior(s) (Joseph and Alex, 1972). It signifies to all others that the wearer of the uniform is part of a group that is being controlled by a set of rules and that a higher instance ensures that wearers adhere to these. By construing their clothes as uniforms, Jenny and others (see quotes below) position themselves as members of society who are being marked and regulated in a hierarchy, taking on a level below the fashion industry and the 'normatively' shaped and clothed parts of society.

The women in my study constituted the clothes available to them as objects that made 'large' women feel 'unattractive' and 'look crap' (Jenny), they were standing out or looking like 'I've got a pimple on my chin' (Charlotte). This imposed subject position of the marked, uniform-wearing outsider also reminds us of Foucault's (1977) description of a hierarchy of ranks within a military school. The ranks were clearly visible through alterations in the uniform and the lowest of the ranks, 'the shameful' class, had to wear sackcloth to make sure they were always separated from the others. The ranks and uniforms signified the moral standing of the wearer, and the clearly visible membership of each rank was intended to motivate pupils to earn a higher rank in the hierarchy, to work to make themselves worthy of belonging to the higher class. Similarly, fat women in Western cultures would be rewarded for their personal 'improvement', that is, weight loss, with accession to a higher societal level; signified not only by slimmer bodies, but by their now available fashionable clothes that would no longer mark them as outsiders, but instead as 'normative' and acceptable.

Although only Jenny refers to the clothes available to fat people literally as a 'uniform', this theme of being marked, regulated and restricted through the limited amount and style of clothes available was evident in several other accounts. The women in my study, and fat women generally, are positioned in these excerpts as 'other', whose clothing is prescribed and who are marked out as inferior by the limited shops and clothes available to them.

> Emily: There is absolutely no point in have (.) in having a a way you want to look if they don't sell clothes anyway.

> Samantha: I didn't, just didn't have the same freedom as she had / I: hmm / to express her personality through her clothes, you know, to express her politics through her clothes / I: mhm / because (.) you know, you're restricted to what you can fit into and what you can fit into is often (.) awful.

> Jenny: it's because if you're fat you're not allowed to wear /I: mm/ nice clothes /I: mm/ everything has to be just the wrong tone for it to be on trend /I: mm/ it's like if apple, apple green is the trend for the season then you'll get pea green, or everything, you can have anything you want as long as it's brown um (.) as long as it's in man-made fibres.

The above excerpts all construct the clothes available to 'large' women as imposed on them – large women are 'not allowed' to choose freely. They are given a uniform which marks them and positions them outside the acceptable norm, outside what a 'good' person should look like. The inferior quality and style of the clothes available to 'large women' also mark the women themselves as inferior, akin to Foucault's 'shameful' class (1977) (see above). Clothes then, together with the women's body shape, take on the function not only of aesthetic but also of moral indices, that are made to signify the moral value of an individual (Soper, 2001).

Being denied the 'right' uniform

However, uniforms were not only construed as undesirable, as in the case of leggings and baggy t-shirts, which were felt to be the disagreeable uniform of the fat woman. Uniforms can also be welcomed by the wearer. They can bestow privileges and status and thus be worn with pride (Joseph and Alex, 1972). Uniforms can also provide some relief from the problems of dressing (Holliday, 1999) and have an inclusive, normalising effect, or as Ruth Holliday (1999) and Clarke and Taylor (2007) found in their studies, they can act as a 'mask' and enable individuals to 'pass' as part of the mainstream. Constructions of work uniforms as normalising and, in reverse, the problem posed by not finding uniforms that fitted were also present in my research. Eileen, for example, commented on her plans to sign up for a course that required her to wear a beauty therapy top.

> Eileen: I just about managed to get one [beauty therapy top] /I: mm hmm/ and I felt so much more, accepted because I could get a top /I: mm/ which would then, make me part of the norm in all honesty if I couldn't have got a top I wouldn't have done the course /I: mm hmm/ I actually would've said no I'm not gonna further my education and I'm not gonna do it.

The unavailability of the appropriate work uniform thus is constructed as restricting Eileen's career choice, and as such her fulfilment in life. It is not her body size *per se* that would have excluded her from the course but having to attend without the appropriate garment. Eileen construes finding a beauty therapy top as the prerequisite for attending this course, without which she would not have furthered her education. The availability of certain clothes is thereby construed as influencing her life course. Yvonne equally associates the non/availability of (well-fitting) work uniforms with problems:

> Yvonne: Certainly uniform's been like it's always been more difficult to get uniforms /I: yeah/ they never fit properly.

So even if they are able to obtain a uniform, this may still not fit properly, which will again mark the women as not fitting the clothes or, in extension, the job role signified by that uniform. The lack of large-size clothing prevents her from properly inhabiting her 'role'.

Related to the topic of uniforms is the paradox of being made to stand out and at the same time forced to conform, as I will outline below.

Branding versus conformity

In my analysis above, I argued that the 'uniform of leggings and baggy t-shirts', the ill-fitting work uniforms and inferior style and make of clothes, framed fat women's bodies as unattractive, and made them stand out and branded as inferior. Seemingly contradictive to my analysis, Adam (2001) noted that large people's clothes are conformist. These two interpretations of 'large' women's clothes are less paradoxical than they may seem, as is evident in the following excerpt from the interview with Scrumpz.

> Scrumpz: To me everybody's the same / I: hm, m / I mean, yeah smaller people *can* dress more fashionable, nice and that but there are (.) there are more um what am I looking for uhm (.) options for larger people now to look / I: hmm / to look smart which is a good thing / I: hmm / and (.) yeah if you dress the right way you can look really smart / I: hmm / you can, I mean (.) I mean I can be as scruffy as you like one day and I can be smart / I: hmm / the next day.

Scrumpz in the above account is drawing on the construction of the scruffy and appearance-illiterate 'large' woman, a subject position which she rejects by construing herself as having a choice in whether she wants to look smart or scruffy, and as being able to tell the difference. However, the option to express oneself through clothes and dress that are 'more fashionable, nice and that' is construed as one way of using clothes that is not open to fat women, who merely have the option to look smart. There is a 'right way' to dress for the 'large' woman, which will make her look smart, according to common cultural rules, but will not make her look nice or fashionable. This construction of a restricted binary choice between 'scruffy' and 'smart' which is imposed on 'large' women leads me to the issue of self-expression generally and the expression of identity and constitution of subjectivities through clothes for fat women in particular.

Identity construction through clothes

Clothes have been described as a means of expressing or constructing one's identity or subjectivity by a number of writers. Joanne Entwistle (2000), for example, links styles of dress to Foucault's 'technologies of the self' (Foucault, 1988) as ways to perform and express one's self. This self-expression is not without constraints, however, since what is and can be read off one's clothes is culturally and historically specific and certain contexts allow for more or less expression of one's 'identity' through clothes (Holliday, 1999). Jennifer Craik and Efrat Tseëlon talk about how clothes can be seen as 'technical means for constructing and presenting a bodily self' (Craik, 1994, p. 1) and, drawing on Gergen's and Gidden's work, how in postmodernity identities are continuously reconstructed out of existing cultural resources, including fashions. Style, thus, becomes 'a substitute for identity' (Tseëlon, 1995, p. 122).

A similar interpretation of the meaning of clothes was also articulated in my interviews with women. To come back to Samantha's earlier quote, where she construes clothes as a way to express one's personality and political views which is not available to 'large' women:

> Samantha: I'd get, I'd get annoyed and frustrated with my friends because they wouldn't understand, they can never get their head round the fact that (..) one friend in particular, that I (.) that I couldn't (.) I didn't, just didn't have the same freedom as she had / I: hmm / to express her personality through her clothes, you know, to express her politics through her clothes / I: mhm / because (.) you know, you're restricted to what you can fit into and what you can fit into is often (.) awful.

Samantha construes clothes as a means of expressing not only one's personality but also one's politics, and to a certain extent to perform activism through her clothes. As such, 'awful' clothes are not only construed as aesthetically unpleasing, but also as not expressing the right sentiment, as not fitting her personality and values. This inability to express 'her politics' may also exclude her from, or marginalise her within, certain subcultures, or a group of friends, she identifies with.

Some subcultures intentionally 'break the rules' or invent their own in order either to signify their resistance or opposition to the dominant culture, and/or as a way of forming a sort of group/subcultural identity (Holliday, 1999). Both Ruth Holliday (1999), and Victoria Clarke and Kevin Turner (2007) carried out research into clothes and the construction of identity within gay, lesbian and bisexual subcultures. They found that clothes as well as other body techniques are used to signal to 'those in the know' (Clarke and Turner, 2007, p. 267) that one belongs to a certain subculture. This is not to say that the appearance pressures in these subcultures are altogether dissimilar from those experienced within the hegemonic heterosexual cultures, however. For example, participants were quoted as saying that they would not be seen on the gay scene in certain clothes, as they didn't have the appropriate body to go with it (Holliday, 1999). Within the lesbian scene not being 'butch' enough can attract derogatory comments and one's authenticity as a lesbian may be questioned. As such a certain pressure on individuals to wear the 'right' clothes in order not to transgress the rules of the sub/culture they see themselves belonging to seems to be present in many societal groups.

Sue Widdicombe (1993) explored the discourses found in respect to appearance and identity authenticity within the 'Gothic' subculture. What seemed to be important to her participants was the recognition of an authentic portrayal of their identity through their clothes. The constitution of an identity through clothes seems to be dynamic and shifting in so far as individuals, through their choice of clothes, can position themselves as individuals who affiliate with a certain subculture, and outside the mainstream. However, at the same time belonging or wanting to belong to a subculture may also impose its own 'dress language' or 'dress codes' on individuals, and non-adherence can thus marginalise individuals within the subculture.

From my interviews with fat women, there also seems to be a third way of cultural signification through clothes: the imposition of a denigrated subculture/identity on a group of people, through the unavailability of good-quality and diverse styles of clothing that would allow them to express themselves and/or their potential membership of a chosen subculture. Similarly, as noted above, 'large' women seem to be restricted in their expression and construction of what is deemed 'feminine'. That is, they have restricted access to the sartorial resources necessary for 'doing femininity' (Craik, 1994; Smith, 1990).

Femininity and feminism

Historically, since the eighteenth century, an interest in fashion has been socially constructed as a 'women's thing', as something intrinsic to being a woman, something women 'couldn't help' (Hollander, 1980, p. 360). Efrat Tseëlon calls it 'a common cliché that the woman cares about appearance' and 'that fashion is a feminine affair' (Tseëlon, 1995, p. 3). As such a devotion to fashion can be considered as 'doing' or performing femininity (Bartky, 1988; Craik, 1994; Young, 1998/1990) through the clothes one wears (Bartky, 1988; Craik, 1994). I will discuss gendered embodiment of fat in more detail in Chapter 6 but the theme of being denied the means to perform femininity 'satisfactorily', particularly through an actively lived interest in fashion and clothing, is also relevant here, for example in the following two excerpts:

> Emily: It, it's just, clothing isn't important to me so I guess that's why I didn't bring it up / I: hmm / clothing to me is something to keep me warm / I: yeah / so, and if (.) I have *no* idea what my style of clothing is because (.) it's whatever fits (.) and I'm, maybe that is me suppressing my female wanting to have my own style and look nice because there is absolutely no point in have (.) in having a a way you want to look if they don't sell the clothes anyway.

> Jenny: Really clothes /I: mm/ really such a big issue, um, so frustrating because I am actually really quite interested in fashion /I: mm/ and um, I I mean I guess I've always said you know I'm interested but not to the point of going on a diet /I: mm/ um, it irritates me but not enough to actually lose weight /I: mm/ um because I I think- I don't see why I should lose weight I think that (.) you know what's the national average 14, 16 /I: mm/ why are high street shops only going up to a 16 /I: mm/ [you know] you're missing out a huge huge amount of the m-, of the market /I: mm/ and um yeah maybe fat people look so crap because they don't have any nice clothes to wear, rather than just fat people don't know how to dress /I: mm/ [so, you know], maybe we don't actually all want to walk around in leggings and baggy t-shirts /I: mm/ maybe that's just the only clothes we can find.

Both the above extracts draw on discourses that construe fat women as not really caring about fashion or about appearance, and therefore as not really being feminine. With fashion being socially constructed as something women 'couldn't help'

(Hollander, 1980, p. 360), not being interested in fashion and clothes in reverse must mean that one is not a 'real' woman; that one is lacking in femininity. As such, in maintaining that she is viewing clothes as merely functional items, Emily initially confirms the often socially held view of fat women as not being interested in their appearance, but goes on to construe this as an imposed subject position that denies her one of the tools of 'doing femininity' (Young, 1998/1990). Equally, in Jenny's quote society's perception of fat people generally is constructed as 'look[ing] crap' and as not wearing nice clothes and not knowing how to dress, questioning this construction of large people in saying: 'maybe fat people look so crap because they don't have any nice clothes to wear, rather than just fat people don't know how to dress'.

Although Jenny talks about 'fat people' generally in a number of places, it is nevertheless clear that she is referring to women in particular, with the comment that they do not all want to wear 'leggings and baggy t-shirts'. This imposed subject position of fat women as fashion-illiterate, voluntarily badly dressed and indifferent to their appearance is rejected in both quotes, however. Fat women are construed instead as being as interested in fashion as the next woman; however, there is 'absolutely no point in having (. . .) a way you want to look if they don't sell clothes anyway' (Emily). Jenny expresses this interest in fashion more directly in saying: 'I am actually really quite interested in fashion', defending herself against common claims of the opposite, and goes on to underline her construction of herself and other fat women as equally devoted to fashion and clothes by saying:

> Jenny: I've started to make my own clothes again and um (.) getting so many people that want me to make clothes for them.

The association of fashion with femininity also has a dark side, however. In contrast to masculinity, femininity and, by extension, women are associated with emotionality, irrationality and an interest in frivolous things such as fashion and appearance (Frith, 2003; Smith, 1990), which in effect construes women as inferior to men in a patriarchal society that values stereotypical masculine characteristics like rationality and unemotional decision making (Bordo, 1998; Malson, 1998; Smith, 1990). Some feminist theorists would also argue that the 'female duty' to be interested in fashion and appearance aids women's subjugation and oppression in patriarchal societies (Wolf, 1991). Clothes can therefore also play a role in the resistance against the social construction of femininity, as is evident from feminist, including lesbian feminist, literature (Craik, 1994; Crawley, 2002). By not following the rules of mainstream heterosexual fashion, by expressing one's own individual style or one's membership of a particular subculture, patriarchal societal systems can be overtly rejected and challenged – an option, however, as I have discussed above, which is not necessarily available to fat women.

While large women are being positioned within and by society as on the margins of society as well as womanhood, the intentional expression of resistance to societal gender norms also seems to be restricted. This is most evident in the following extracts from the interview with Samantha:

because of my (.) kind of feminist values I feel really (.) uncomfortable (..) not just intellectually uncomfortable but *emotionally* uncomfortable looking too feminine / I: hmm / or too kinda girly, uhm (.) [. . .] [I] try to avoid kind of girly jewellery and girly clothes, I feel very uncomfortable in skirts and / I: hmm / and dresses (.) uhm, I kind of try out wearing them, I (.) every now and then I might buy a skirt / I: hmm / and I wear it once and then that's it, it goes back in the cupboard, I feel like I'm in drag and I'm putting on a performance.

An overly feminine look, or looking 'too kinda girly', is here constructed as not expressing feminist values, and in fact opposing them. By drawing on a discourse that positions 'feminism and femininity as almost antithetical' (Rudolfsdottir and Jolliffe, 2008, p. 272), Samantha construes herself as feeling 'intellectually uncomfortable' and inauthentic in feminine clothes like skirts. But this is not constructed as just a conscious and rational decision about what certain clothes portray. Samantha also speaks of feeling '*emotionally* uncomfortable looking too feminine', she says she feels like she is 'in drag', which constructs feminine clothes as camouflaging her chosen identity as a feminist. She construes herself as not being herself in such clothes. The lack of choice in clothes is thus constructed as restricting fat women's ability to express and constitute their subjectivities, particularly so if they form expressions of resistance:

Samantha: Over a size, dress size 18, you know, they (.) have an average number of shops, which is like four shops / I: hmm / whereas women who're within a normal range, you know, they have a choice of 20, 30 or something, so, and I've, I found that (.) really restrictive, a) because (..) I have a different set, you know I have a different set of values determining the kind of clothes that I'm comfortable wearing / I: hmm / and then (.) I'm (.) outsized or *plus* sized, and also I'm tall / I: hmm / so, that mixed together is you know [a lethal cocktail] / I: hmm / in terms of finding clothes. I find it incredibly difficult to find clothes , which (..) to some extent I don't care and to some extent it's a pain in the arse / I: hmm / because I don't get to express my personality through my clothes, I get a limited range of choices and I find that really frustrating.

The ambivalence of both *not* caring and caring about one's appearance – as 'to some extent [Samantha does not] care and to some extent it's a pain in the arse' – also reflects the unavoidability of expressing something with one's appearance. Like everybody else, Samantha has 'no option not to appear' (Frith, 2003, p. 4) and as such has to make decisions on a day-to-day basis as to what to express with her appearance, i.e. what she would like others to read from her clothes. Yet, caring about clothes and dressing in an expressed feminine way jars with Samantha's feminist values. However, at the same time she construes herself as frustrated by the restrictions she encounters in actively expressing these values and her personality.

Being seen and hiding – once more

Not surprisingly, the awareness that they are seen, read and judged by others was evident in most interviews with the women in my study.

> Eileen: When I go to shop for clothes I am (.) I don't *ever* look at what I like first thing I do is look whether they've got the size for me /I: mm/ and then you narrow down what you like and then you narrow it down again to what is actually not going to make you look too fat /I: yeah/ um, you know (.) so, it's not as easy as just /I: mm/ sort of going out and thinking right okay I'm just gonna buy this particular outfit, you are very aware of what other people, uhm (.) how, how they perceive you /I: mm/ you know.

> Emily: I would go [swimming] / I: mhm / if'n, I *didn't* have to creep [laughing] to the side of the swimming pool in a towel and let it (..).

In the above extract, Eileen describes her selection criteria for clothing, and construes the anticipation of others' judgement as a major factor. She draws on a discourse of beauty that constructs 'looking fat' as unattractive and thus best avoided. It is not 'being fat' that Eileen in the above extract construes as the problem, however. It is the lack of clothes available that forces her to narrow it down from the few items that fit to those that will not make her 'look too fat', in order to avoid negative judgement. Similarly, Emily construes the major problem in being fat as being looked at and judged, which affects her behaviour. She would go swimming if it was not for others looking at her, seeing her body.

This brings me back to Foucault's Panopticon (Foucault, 1977; see Chapter 3) and his theory of regulatory systems based on an ever-present potential of being seen and judged by the generalised other, which causes people to scrutinise themselves continuously. With my work with 'large' women and the interpretation of their accounts offered above, I would not want to express that 'slim' women are not subjected to the objectifying and regulating gaze; however, 'large' women in particular seem to constitute a 'free for all' object of judgement and 'corrective' comments. The 'large' individual's body size means that it is difficult for that person not to be seen. So, for large women, Hannah Frith's (2003, p. 4) comment that 'it is not as if women have the option *not* to appear' may be doubly true.

Clothing the fat female body

In the present chapter I have focused on women's accounts of their clothes and clothing practices as fat women. Within my data, the problems inherent in 'being large' were construed as not intrinsic to the fat body but caused by interactions with society and the physical environment and in particular the lack of appropriate clothes available for 'large' women. The women construed themselves as limited in their choices as well as marginalised in and excluded from society, for example by a restricted number of shops that segregated them from normatively sized women. They positioned themselves as excluded from certain activities and careers that required specific clothes or uniforms that were not available in 'large' sizes.

In various places, clothes available to 'large' women were construed as an undesirable uniform, specifically relating to the stereotypical leggings and baggy t-shirts. By being 'relegated to this like uniform' (Jenny), participants construed themselves as branded as inferior and unattractive, as regulated and constrained by and through society. At the same time, an expression of their own style, personality, values or politics seems impossible given the choice of clothes available to them. These do not allow them to constitute and express their (gendered) subjectivities in the same way as 'normatively sized' consumers (Guy and Banim, 2000). With a dedication to fashion construed as a feminine pastime, fat women were also construed as excluded from 'doing femininity' (Smith, 1990; Ussher, 1997) through the restriction in the number of shops and the range of clothes available to them.

Drawing on discourses of the unattractive and appearance-illiterate fat woman, my participants positioned themselves, and fat women generally, at the margins of society, judged as unattractive and barely feminine. While construing fat people as 'looking crap', the negative subject positions described above were rejected by constituting them as imposed on 'large' women through the poor choice and quality of clothes available to them. The women constituted themselves as interested in fashion and appearance, but regulated and hampered by the fashion and retail industry, and a neoliberal society that values self-perfection according to socially constructed standards which equate fat with unattractive, and unhealthy. The issue of health and responsibility, and its discursive interweaving and equation with body size, will be the topic of my next chapter.

5   Health, well-being and the responsible fat woman

One gross but unfortunately ubiquitous generalisation about fat people is that they simply eat too much. This is an all-too-common assumption, voiced within the dominant discourses on fat in day-to-day talk, the media, as well as the medical and health promotion literature. And whilst advocating for women's empowerment, some liberal feminist comments on the issue also base their writing on the assumption that most fat women are compulsive overeaters and thereby construct uncontrolled eating as the main cause of 'obesity' (Orbach, 2006b). In fact, there are numerous theories on the causation of 'obesity' (see Chapter 1) ranging from the simplistic energy balance theory of 'too much in – not enough out/used' to notions that include an obesogenic physiology and environment, sleep deprivation or depression as causal factors (Blaine, 2008; Egger and Swinburn, 1997; Hilbert *et al.*, 2009; Sekine *et al.*, 2002; Well and Cruess, 2006). There seems to be general consent that the causation of 'obesity' is a complex issue and cannot be reduced to one neat causal factor. The discussion around the alleged health risks posed by a body size over the prescribed medical limit, is a lot less diverse and critical, however. The mainstream biomedical perspective which considers obesity as a severe health risk in regard to both morbidity and mortality is generally accepted as a commonsensical truth (Campos, 2004; Cogan and Ernsberger, 1999; Gard and Wright, 2005). As mentioned earlier (see Chapter 1), this 'health truth', i.e. that if you are fat you must be unhealthy and 'diseased', has gained such a fact status that it does not even require evidencing in academic journal articles any more (Aphramor, 2010; Wang *et al.*, 2011). Both dominant medical and cultural discourses on body weight and size are grounded in the dualistic equations of 'fat equals ill health' and 'thin equals healthy'. Body weight is considered a consequence of an individual's lifestyle in respect of dietary intake and exercise, and a simple energy balance approach is often taken, as in 'just eat less and move more' and the 'obesity problem' is solved. Ultimately the main responsibility for body weight and health is assigned to the individual (Saguy and Riley, 2005). Not surprisingly then, weight loss is being promoted as an efficient, if not the only, way to health despite considerable evidence to the contrary (Aphramor, 2008b; Campos, 2004). Lucy Aphramor in fact maintains that the current practice of advising weight loss for cardiac health is at best contestable and probably unethical as it does not fit within the ethical requirements of any health practitioner and dieticians in particular

(Aphramor, 2008a). She suggests a wellness-centred approach or Health at Every Size Approach in supporting individuals to work towards a healthier lifestyle rather than towards weight loss.

Thus, while the importance of lifestyle for health is generally accepted, the connection between weight and health is contested and the evidence used to support the notion that a high body weight *per se* is a risk factor is thin and often based on flawed research (Aphramor, 2008b; Gard and Wright, 2005). Critical voices and counter-discourses struggle to be heard or to be taken seriously, however. As Helen Malson (2008) suggests, body weight has taken on the status of a 'master signifier of health' (Malson, 2008, p. 35), and body shape and weight are seen as 'the proof of health and healthy body management' (Malson, 2008, p. 28) and as 'metonymic of everything' (Malson, 2008, p. 37). Similarly, fat bodies have become metonymic for the whole person; Samantha Murray terms this our 'collective knowingness' about fat individuals, which constitutes them as 'lazy, not willing to commit to change or to the dictates of healthy living' (Murray, 2005a, pp. 154–155) – and consequently as failed neoliberal citizens.

Valuing the individual, autonomous, self-improving and self-regulating self is a characteristic of neoliberal societies, like the UK and other Western industrialised nations. Within neoliberal societies, subjects are 'obliged to be free' (Rose, 1996, p. 17) to choose the right actions, or, in Foucault's terms, to apply appropriate 'technologies of the self' (Foucault, 1988, cited in Rose, 1996) towards self-fulfilment and self-realisation. In other words, we are obliged to be free to take appropriate action 'for understanding and improving ourselves in relation to that which is true, permitted, and desirable' (Rose, 1996, p. 153). What is true, permitted and desirable is culture-specific and, according to poststructuralist theories (Foucault, 1972, 1978; Weedon, 1997), dynamically constructed through discourse. In relation to health and health management in Western industrialised nations, it is predominantly biomedical discourses that construct the cultural 'realities' of health, including the increasing links made between an individual's lifestyle choices and health. Thus optimal health can be achieved by each individual with the right lifestyle choices (Department of Health, 2004a), and the state's and industry's responsibility is reduced to providing the information necessary to make the correct choices. This neoliberal take on health (Ogden *et al.*, 2006) and focus on 'free informed choice' is reflected in health promotion campaigns like Change4Life in the UK, or the initiative that requires high-street restaurant chains to display the calorie count of each food item on their menus (BBC, 2009). The latter tellingly also equates health with the number of calories consumed. The role of the government, as educator rather than provider of health, was also spelt out by Tony Blair (then Prime Minister) in his forward to the UK government's policy statement *Choosing Health* (Department of Health, 2004a):

> Small changes in the choices people make can make a big difference. Taken together, these changes can lead to huge improvements in health across society. But changes need to be based on choices, not direction. We are clear that Government cannot – and should not – pretend it can 'make' the population

healthy. But it can – and should – support people in making better choices for their health and the health of their families. It is for people to make the healthy choice if they wish to.

(Tony Blair, foreword to *Choosing Health*,
Department of Health, 2004a, p. 3)

The responsibility for the nation's health thus lies firmly with each individual and her or his ability to make the right choices for a healthy self; and, where women are concerned, for a healthy self *and* a healthy family (Davies, 1998). The role gender plays in the politics of fat will be explored in more detail in the following chapter. It is important, however, to draw attention to the multiple burdens this neoliberal healthism places on women. Apart from a generally greater emphasis on and scrutiny of women's bodies and pressure to be thin (Bordo, 2009), women are also still more engaged with duties of care for the whole family and made responsible for the health and body size of not only themselves but also their spouses and children (Davies, 1998; Kokkonen, 2009; Raisborough, 2006). This chapter, like the previous two, will thus focus on the women's accounts in my study, concentrating on the discourses of health, lifestyle and responsibility (for health) to explore the positioning of fat individuals, and fat women in particular, within them. I will discuss the constructions of health and lifestyle choices produced by my participants, and the different 'ways of being' the available discourses produce for them.[4]

Constructions of health

Health, as well as 'being healthy', featured strongly in all the interviews. Drawing on various discourses, the women in my study constructed health as an important factor in their lives and something they were taking seriously:

Jemima: I think there is a lot of perception that if you are bigger you can't be healthy / I: hmm / while I know that's that's no I know some people who eahm are are quite big and yet they'll run a couple of miles a day and eham do exercises I mean I walk a lot eehm I've got a little steppy type machine over there [. . .] I mean I can't remember the last time I added salt to anything, probably about 20 years ago because I don't like the taste of / I: mhm / salt [. . .] I try and make sure I have my five plus portions a day fruit and veg like we are like we are told to.

Louise: I think generally it's not it's about healthy lifestyle and that doesn't have to be about you know. I get more exercise than quite a lot of people I know / I: hmm / they're are all smaller than me, fine, I eat lots of fresh food I don't eat processed food / I: hm / and they do.

Sue: I'm sort of *fully* aware of what I need to eat and I *do* on the whole eat a pretty good diet / I: hmm / uhm you know I'm a lot healthier than some people who are *not* obese that I know / I: hmm / you know, I, you know, I have very good resistance to disease, I *don't* get bugs that everybody else gets.

Jemima, Louise and Sue are drawing on medical, and more specifically health promotion, discourses to position themselves as health-conscious and serious about looking after themselves. Within the discourses they employ, health is constructed as achievable by each individual by adhering to a 'healthy' diet (low in salt and fat, and high in fruit and vegetables) and regular exercise. Thus, the dominant neoliberal discourses, assigning the responsibility for their health to the individual, are being kept in place. At the same time, however, drawing on the same discourses, the women in my study position themselves as healthy, and in fact as (at least) equally healthy as 'people who are *not* obese', thus rejecting the imposed subject position of the lazy, health-indifferent fat woman. Sue also defends herself against the ubiquitous assumption that being fat automatically means not being healthy by borrowing from biomedical discourses and constructing (her) health as having a 'good resistance to disease'. The reductionist dualistic construction of 'slim = healthy' and 'fat = unhealthy' is thus rejected for themselves and other fat individuals by these women in offering comparisons between themselves, the health promotion messages available and other, 'non-obese' individuals. Samantha in a way summarises the issue in a more generalised manner:

> Samantha: To me the connection between weight and health isn't necessary straightforward, it's not necessarily the case that someone fat is unhealthy, and someone thin (is), I think it's more complex and I wish to God that (..) the discussion around obesity would be a bit more complicated / I: hmm / that we recognise that (.) you know, someone who is fat (.) or overweight, you know, who doesn't smoke, who doesn't drink that much, who eats a really healthy diet / I: hmm / and takes regular exercise is probably far more healthier than someone who *looks* (.) slim but, you know, is a couch potato who never moves, who smokes 25 a day, drinks loads of beer and eats everything deep fried / I: hmm / but the discussion doesn't seem to acknowledge / I: no / *that* / I: hmm / complexity whatsoever.

In a similar way to the women quoted above, Samantha borrows from health promotion discourses to construct health as linked to lifestyle but not necessarily to body weight. Using extremes of 'good' and 'bad' lifestyles, which she constructs as unrelated to weight and consisting of multiple factors, she construes the simplistic equation of 'fat = unhealthy' as exasperating, 'wish[ing] to God that the discussion around obesity would be a bit more complicated'. In Samantha's narrative, the current debate on 'obesity' is constructed as something that is based on people's looks rather than any convincing health indicators, while the *real* factors underlying health, i.e. a healthy diet, not smoking and exercise, and their inherent complexities are generally ignored. Whilst drawing on different aspects of health promotion and medical discourses, all the accounts above construct health as multifaceted and inherently complex, rejecting the simplistic correlation between weight and health promoted by dominant discourses which constitute fat women as always-already unhealthy.

The expansion of the construction of 'health' is taken further still in the following quote. While all the above excerpts drew from medical and health promotion discourses to construct health as something important and meaningful, Charlotte also construes health as a matter of holistic well-being, exceeding biomedical constructions:

> Charlotte: Creating a lifestyle that is good for, for my health / I: hmm / my mental health which also impacts on my physical health / I: hmm / [. . .] I mean, even not necessarily to do with eating or you know, adopting exercise / I: hmm / anything like that, because those (.) I mean I've exercised throughout my life, you know, I was a very active kid, and uhm (.) I uh (.) was a synchronised swimmer [laughs] when I was a little girl and you know, throughout my teens I was swimming and riding my bicycle and you know, I still do those things, that's been a constant throughout my life / I: hmm / and I love to go out dancing and you know, I'm pretty active / I: hmm / so uhm (.) I don't think about health changes in (.) in those kinda terms / I: mhm / but uhm (.) but, yeah, changes that I've made for my mental health are things like thinking about my future, going to do another masters degree to, you know, invest in my future, my future career (.) I I guess the, the lifestyle things that concern me the most are how to (.) have more of an income, how to, you know, develop my work / I: hmm / those are the things rather than whether I'm eating the right food / I: hmm / or exercising, cause I feel like (.) I eat OK and my exercise life is (.) is alright, too / I: hmm / you know (.) yeah.

Reflecting the current common health advice of keeping active (Department of Health, 2006; Shaw *et al.*, 2006; South Gloucestershire Council, 2006), Charlotte in the above account employs health promotion discourses to position herself as a physically active and thus healthy person. This contrasts with the generally more negative self-constructions within discourses of in/visibility, surveillance and clothing (see Chapters 3 and 4), reflecting poststructuralist notions of dynamic, multiple and at times contradictory subjectivities (Henriques *et al.*, 1984b). Drawing on discourses of health and well-being, Charlotte and other participants now position themselves in a positive light, as broadly enjoying physical well-being. Charlotte in the above quote also construes health as much broader than the generally narrow biomedical definition. Using what I would call a discourse of holistic well-being, Charlotte construes health as encompassing not only a healthy body but also good mental health, which she associates with physical health, as well as with having plans for the future and financial security. In a similar vein, Jenny talks about the importance of feeling safe and calm in her home and constructs her move away from a busy city centre to a country town as beneficial to her health:

> Jenny: I was living right in [city centre area] and [. . .] coming home and finding you know (.) police walking past with machine guns and /I: hmm/ (.) [. . .] and then I kept coming down to [town] to visit my sister and just feeling like much calmer and much happier /I: mm/ so I this is kind of a move for my (.) um a change of health I suppose.

Both the above accounts were responses to my question as to whether they had ever tried to change their lifestyle in relation to health, and both Charlotte and Jenny in their accounts construe health, and what 'lifestyle choices' are beneficial to health, as far wider than the simplistic message of eating a healthy diet and exercising. They construe health as a composite of physical, mental and financial well-being and as associated with societal issues such as personal safety; they position themselves as interconnected parts of a societal system that influences a person's health and well-being, rather than locating health as a discrete function within the individual. This reflects the writing of critical health psychologists (Murray, 2004; Stam, 2004) who call on the discipline of health psychology to take a more critical approach to health. Critical health psychology argues that health and well-being are both social and political issues which have to be seen in a broader light than the currently prevailing functional biomedical approach, with its purpose to keep individuals functioning effectively for the supposed national interest (Kugelmann, 2004).

All the narratives produced in the interviews shared the above notion of health as a complex issue; however, the subject positions the women took up within the wider medical and health promotion discourses were dynamic and often contradictory and conflicting. While often taking up positive subject positions of healthy eaters and exercisers within discourses of health and healthy lifestyle choices, these conflicted with the subject positions imposed on 'large' people within discourses of weight and illness. These conflicts are articulated by Yvonne and Jenny in the following extracts:

> Yvonne: I go to the gym, I swim, I can do twenty-odd lengths no problem, I get on the rowing machine I'll cycle a mile, so, and my heart recovery rate is good, so *yes*, I'm sort of eighteen-plus stone (.) but in that respect I feel that I'm physically quite healthy /I: mm/ so when I look at sort of textbooks, research articles, the media and say right obesity's the main cause of this /I: mm/ that and the other I think well actually, yes it may be, but it's not the whole picture /I: mm/ because I think it- you know, I'm not trying to fool myself that I'm not going to get cancer or diabetes or whatever down the line (.) but I think actually my general health, if you look at it holistically /I: mm/ *yes* obesity's a factor but I *don't* smoke I *don't* drink and everything else is fallen in line but /I: mm/ but I think it does need to be taken holistically.

> Jenny: Um (..) the obesity epidemic kind of stories (.) I don't know I feel- I guess I feel a bit conflicted 'cause I, I you know I know how comfortable I am /I: mm/ um but I'm not sure that (.) I'm not sure it's necessarily a good thing to be fat you know it's kind of like (.) [sighs] I don't know how um (..)

As in previously quoted accounts, health promotion and medical discourses are drawn on here by Yvonne and Jenny, who construct their own health as good and Jenney construes herself as positively comfortable with her body size. However, both these women produce an image of conflict between this 'healthy' subject position of theirs, and 'textbooks, research articles, the media' (Yvonne) and the 'obesity epidemic kind of stories' (Jenny). Jenny articulates this tension directly, saying she feels 'a bit conflicted' as she is 'not sure it's necessarily a good thing to be fat'. In Yvonne's account, the medical discourse of 'fat equals ill health' is produced as so commonsensical and convincing that not believing it would amount to 'fooling' herself. These accounts draw attention to the increased and extensive medicalisation and pathologisation of our bodies, and the imperialising power of the medical profession, as a result of which people seem to have lost their trust in their own bodies and feelings of well-being (Illich, 1976). The knowledge and power to distinguish between the healthy and pathological have been entirely relinquished to medical professionals – the experts on health and disease. And while fat individuals employ dominant medical discourses to position themselves as 'healthy', the same discourses globally construe fat and as such each fat individual as unhealthy. Despite challenging this medical imperialism on one level, troubling simplistic notions of health and drawing on discourses of holistic well-being, participants at the same time reinforce its power by positioning themselves as conflicted and constituting medical predictions of ill health as truth. These conflicts reflect fat women's struggles within the 'general politics of truth', or Foucault's (1991) regimes of truth in Western societies today, which he explains as follows:

> [T]he types of discourse which it accepts and makes function as true; the mechanisms and instances which enable one to distinguish true and false statements, the means by which each is sanctioned; the techniques and procedures accorded value in the acquisition of truth; the status of those who are charged with saying what counts as true.
>
> (Foucault, 1991, p. 73)

In relation to health and body size, in Western industrialised nations, truths are being constructed through medical/scientific discourses, which are distributed and consumed through a variety of media, from academic literature to the mass media and day-to-day talk. They are 'produced and transmitted [. . .] under the control of a few great political and economic apparatuses' (Foucault, 1991, p. 73), in this case the established medical (and psychological) institutions as well as the diet industry. Standing and arguing outside the prevailing discourses within these established institutions carry the risk of rendering the speaker 'mad' or 'abnormal' (Hook, 2007). As such, dominant discourses also regulate what cannot be said, which is what my participants struggled with in their efforts to position themselves as healthy. Drawing on prevailing medical and health promotion discourses, they simultaneously reproduced the very same discourses that constituted the fat body as always-already pathological. This struggle was further exemplified in another predominant theme in my study and the rejection of the subject position of the 'stupid fat person'.

We are not stupid or ignorant

One of the alleged 'truths' or stereotypes surrounding 'large' people is that they are stupid, ignorant and uneducated (Cordell and Ronai, 1999; Puhl and Brownell, 2003a), particularly in relation to healthy eating and exercise. In contrast to this, the women in my study constituted themselves as knowledgeable about health and healthy lifestyles, and aware of what the medical establishment sees as the risks of 'being large', thus defending themselves against discourses that construct fat individuals as stupid, health-illiterate and not caring about their health.

> Sue: It's not as if we're (.) uneducated people either / I :hmm / I mean this is a big problem that tha that people would stereotype, if you're fat, you're stupid / I: hmm / and we, all the friends I've got who are overweight, my friends and myself all are all people who've got degrees / I: hmm / and got or have had well-paid jobs uhm you know and we fully understand and could, can *read* the literature, and we fully understand what we should eat and what we shouldn't eat.

Similarly to the accounts at the beginning of the chapter, where women managed their spoiled (Goffman, 1963) fat-embodied identity through the construction of health as a multifaceted and broad concept that could not be reduced to 'fat = unhealthy', Sue here rejects the imposed subject position of the uneducated and health-illiterate fat person by positioning herself as an educated person who 'can *read* the literature' and who knows what she should and should not be eating. Sue is drawing on discourses of academia, talking about 'the literature' and 'degrees', thus positioning herself and her friends as educated and well-paid professionals, who understand the issues around health, and generally would not have achieved in life what they had if they were stupid.

Samantha, below, equally rejects the stereotype of the stupid and health-illiterate fat person by displaying nutritional expertise. Talking about the general obsession with dietary fats in society she went on to say:

> Samantha: [A]nd I'm like 'for God's sake', you need raw oil, you need raw fats in your diet to be really healthy / I: hmm / and you know, the (.) oil and fat can actually, you know, *give* health rather than (.) / I: hmm / take health away but that's not what they're focused on, they're focused on, purely on, kind of weight, uhm (.) and, like my mum's just lost a lot of weight recently, done Weight Watchers and she just looks *terrible*, she looks so gaunt and awful cause she's lost it really quickly, as they / I: hmm / encourage you to do, which I think is bad uhm, and I know she'll inevitably put it back on again, and she eats the most tiny portions and she doesn't eat enough (food) and she doesn't eat enough fruit and vegetables.

Drawing on nutritional health promotion discourses, Samantha challenges the often-held notion that all dietary fats are bad and positions herself as better informed than the general public, who have 'a real kind of obsession with fat'. Samantha not only rejects the imposed subject position of the uneducated 'large' person but positions herself as a lay expert in dietary matters, which strengthens her point about quick weight loss and dieting being bad for people (Aphramor, 2005; Ernsberger and Koletsky, 1999). Samantha uses the example of her mother, who has lost weight on a commercial weight loss programme, but who now 'looks terrible' and, she says, is bound to put the weight back on again. She construes the diet as not providing her mother with enough food and nutrients in the form of fruit and vegetables, and diets and quick weight loss are thus constructed as harmful to both one's looks and health. Nutritional health promotion discourses and the importance of a good diet are thus held in place. However, Samantha employs these to position herself as knowledgeable and the quick weight loss mantra that is being used to encourage people to go on diets as harmful and unhealthy. This is also reflected in Sarah's account below, talking about her relationship with her relatives, several of them health professionals, who she construes as putting pressure on her to go on a weight loss diet:

> Sarah: I find myself repeating myself to them, saying you know, yeah, I I do understand this, and I *do* want to but I wonna do it slowly / I: hmm / because I think (inaudible) if you if you do it more slowly you're probably more likely to keep the weight off / I: yeah / so plus, I think the fact that my friends (.) one of my friends who's anorexic . . . I think she uhm (.) I don't wonna get really obsessed.

Sarah in the above extract draws not only on the often-heard notion that slow weight loss is more beneficial to health, but also on psychological discourses of obsession. While she is positioning herself as under attack from her relatives, she also constitutes herself as more informed and more sensible than them in her lifestyle choices and as aware of the potential dangers of dieting in relation to not only physical but also mental health.

Drawing on constructions of academia, nutrition and mental health, Sue, Samantha and Sarah in the above accounts position themselves as intelligent, informed and educated individuals who understand issues of health and lifestyle, thus rejecting the subject position of the stupid 'large' person who is ignorant of and does not care about healthy lifestyles. Being better informed than the general public or their relatives when it comes to nutrition and dieting, they portray themselves as knowing what they are doing. Discourses that connect health and food are being kept in place within the above accounts and deployed for the positioning of fat people as better informed in these matters than the general public and consciously and intentionally practising a healthy lifestyle based on advanced knowledge. The above excerpts also represent a dilemma for fat individuals, however; by rejecting the subject position of the uninformed, stupid fat individual, they simultaneously reproduce the health promotion and medical discourses that produce those health 'truths' which constitute fat and fat people generally as pathological.

The women in my study struggled with the multiple discourses that converge on them and constitute the fat body as abject. Like Charlotte in the following extract, however, most of them positioned themselves as active agents in regard to health and healthy lifestyles. They are making choices for the good of their health, rather than making the wrong choices out of ignorance, which is the picture generally drawn in the media of the stereotypical 'large' person, who needs help from experts (for example, 'documentaries' like *You are What you Eat* (Channel 4), the *Diet Doctors* (ITV), *The Biggest Loser* (ITV)).

> Charlotte: I tend to question quite a lot of things / I: mhm / that I'm told and try and make up my own mind about it / I: hmm / I try and (..) really look at my body (.) and (.) acknowledge and notice what it's capable of, how it, how I'm feeling, what *I need* / I: hmm / so uhm (.) for example I know that for my mental health it's really good for me if I go swimming once / I: hmm / a week so (.) so I do that.

Contrasting previous accounts which draw on more mainstream medical discourses to demonstrate health literacy, thus keeping links between health and lifestyle intact, Charlotte positions herself as critical of the prevailing 'health truths' and her own embodied experience as a potentially more valid source for information on her own health. Within the discourse of well-being and self-care she positions herself in tune with her body, knowing what she needs and doing whatever is good for her health. Charlotte thus constructs the information generally available as not always reliable and herself as the expert on her body, rather than being dependent on generalised health expertise. In doing so, and unlike previously quoted women, Charlotte empowers and enables herself to challenge prevailing discourses on fat, related health risks and recommended health practices – she is the (only) expert on herself and thus knows best what is good for her physical and mental health.

Responsibility for health

The above accounts, and the excerpt from my interview with Charlotte in particular, also draw on neoliberal discourses, with the women in various ways positioning themselves as educated in relation to health (e.g. Sue, Samantha, Sarah) and as proactively and autonomously taking steps to improve their health (e.g. Charlotte). The women position themselves as responsible individuals, taking health seriously and managing their health as best as they can. According to Nikolas Rose (1996), the autonomous and liberated individual, who continuously strives for self-fulfilment and self-realisation, is highly valued in the neoliberal societies that are most Western industrial nations. Individuals are free to choose their path in life and the way they want to live, but with this freedom comes the responsibility or obligation to become the best possible self. 'The practice of freedom appears only as the possibility of the maximum self-fulfilment of the active and autonomous individual' (Rose, 1996, p. 17), which in turn is defined by culturally constructed norms. As such we are 'obliged to be free' (Rose, 1996, p. 17) to choose lifestyles, careers, actions, and so forth that make us acceptable selves within the boundaries set by society. In today's healthist society, being the best possible self is very much linked to staying healthy by making the right choices in terms of lifestyle generally, and diet and exercise in particular. Good dietary and exercise regimes are constructed in medical and health promotion discourses as the basis of a healthy self and as such the health of individuals is being made their own responsibility – all they have to do, allegedly, is to make the right choices in respect to food and physical activity. As quoted earlier, this was clearly set out by Tony Blair (UK Prime Minister at the time in question) in the foreword to the Department of Health (2006) document *Choosing Health*.

Tony Blair's foreword is an appeal to people to make the 'right choices' in order to improve the nation's health 'across society'. He is addressing each and everyone to make (small) changes in their lifestyles, and thus constructs it as each individual's responsibility to look after her or his own health, and equally to make adequate changes necessary for making 'a big difference' nationally. People are free to make 'better' choices 'if they wish to' but at the same time they are being told what choices are the better ones and that they have co-responsibility for improving the nation's health, with the state's responsibility being reduced to the role of educator. The obligation lies with the (good) neoliberal citizen who is 'obliged to be free' (Rose, 1996, p. 17) to make the right choices.

The extracts in this chapter so far were articulated from this neoliberal position of individuals being responsible for their health; the women participants were drawing on health promotion discourses of healthy lifestyles and positioning themselves as healthy and knowledgeable, and as broadly making the 'right' choices. This contrasts with the following extract, where Emily draws on the same discourses, positioning herself, however, as a failed citizen both in respect of responsibility for her own health, as well as, by extension, in regard to each individual's responsibility for the nation's well-being.

I: Hmm (.) what, how do you react to, to the messages on TV, on on the NHS? How do you personally react? How do you feel?

Emily: I agree / I: hmm / (..) [laughs] I don't like (..) I don't like the finger pointing / I: hmm / (..) probably because there is truth in it / I: hm / I overeat and it's gonna cost other people money to look after me because *no doubt* I will become ill because of my overeating (.) it's a fact / I: hm / you can't get away from it. Okay, I could remain fit for the rest of my life but (..) the chances are it won't happen (.) and, despite knowing that / I: hmm / I *still* have to comfort eat / I: hmm / It's a *ridiculous* situation to be in.

Emily constructs it as her responsibility not to become ill and thus not costing 'other people money to look after [her]'. Her overeating can be interpreted as a double violation of the 'regulative ideal of the self' (Rose, 1996, p. 2): not only does she fail to make the right choices to strive towards what is constructed as a well-functioning normative individual, which in our current culture also includes a 'normative body weight and shape' (Malson, 2008, p. 2) that is always a slim body. Emily is also construing herself, and in extension fat individuals generally, as someone who will need looking after in the future as a result of her lifestyle choices. She will therefore also not fulfil her responsibility to be the 'free, autonomous self' (Rose, 1996) that is so highly valued in our society, as she will depend on others to care for her.

However, Emily's construction of herself is not without ambiguity, as while accepting the subject position of the irresponsible overeater, guilty of not shaping her lifestyle in an effective way to realise her potential (Stephenson, 2003) and thereby wasting money, she also construes herself and other fat people at the same time as victims of the urge to comfort eat. Both in the above and the following quote, Emily draws on psychological discourses to position herself as helpless in her efforts to solve this problem, comparing it (below) to addictive behaviours like smoking.

> Emily: I guess the NHS situation (. . .) it is true / I: hmm / We, it's the same, you could say the same about smokers / I: hmm/ you can say the same about people who play football (.) carelessly [laughing] and break their legs / I: mhm / It's (.) we do use up NHS money (.) It's a shame it's not perhaps channelled more into finding out why / I: hmm / (.) and if you sort the head out, the body follows.

Emily draws on discourses of Cartesian dualism, the idea of subjecting the body to the will of the mind: 'if you sort the head out, the body follows'. The body within these discourses is produced as the weaker part of the binary unit that makes up a human being, with the mind being in control. Overeating (as well as smoking and careless exercising) is constituted in the above as a lack of control and as such as a problem caused by the mind, which manifests itself in the body, and which consequently could be solved by 'sorting out' the head. Emily construes this 'mental problem' as something not unique to herself, but as something fat people – 'we' – in general have to deal with and that could be solved if more money was spent on efforts to find out the causes. Thus, while Emily is positioning fat people as responsible for their physical health and the increased expenditures of the NHS on the one hand, she is at the same time rejecting the subject position of the irresponsible 'large' person by constructing the cause of her overeating as a mental problem and thus as something fat people are not entirely in control of and need help with. Within the psy-institutions (psychology, psychotherapy and psychiatry) (Rose, 1996; see also Malson *et al.*, 2006), discourses of Cartesian dualism are held in place and the problem of fat is thus still located in the individual and can be solved by the individual, with the help of some kind of therapy aimed at 'sort[ing] her head out'.

A small number of my participants thus constructed not being in control of one's eating as something that the 'large' person simply could not help, caused by mental health problems, which consequently should reduce the moral judgements made against them. However, uncontrolled eating was also identified as one of the inherently negative connotations which form our 'collective knowingness' about fat people and which are held firmly in predominant discourses about fat. In comparison to the constructions of health and the responsibility each individual bore for it, the responsibility for one's body size was constituted as a lot more ambiguous:

> Norah: Obviously like on uh some of the TV shows like the um, *Celebrity Fit Club* /I: mm/ and *Celebrity Fat Club* and um I just think why do they bother doing it because a lot of the time when you sort of see the shows and think they say they're trying to lose weight if they really wanted to do it /I: mm/ they, they'd just do it, they wouldn't need to go on a TV programme to do it.

> Jenny: I put on um (.) I think it was like three stone in two months, when I was on some medication, and (.) I'd be absolutely lying if I said that that didn't bother me /I: mm/ and if if if I could take some magic pill that would make that go away /I: mm/ 'cause I feel that that was *unfairly* given to me /I: mm/ but then that's kind of makes me think well what what does that say about how I really view fat (.) you know if I think it- if I think it's somehow *wrong* that I had it, that I didn't *deserve* it I didn't *deserve* to be this fat then that's saying on one level that (.) people- some people *do* deserve to be fat and then what does that mean?

In both accounts above, weight loss or weight maintenance is constructed as the responsibility of the individual. The generally prevailing discourse of 'obesity' is held in place by the rearticulation of one of the assumptions the war on obesity is based on, namely that weight loss is achievable for everybody if they 'really wanted to' (Campos, 2004; Cogan and Ernsberger, 1999). In Norah's narrative, she herself and other fat individuals are positioned as simply not wanting to lose weight, thus attributing the responsibility for body size to the individual. Jenny's account on the other hand draws up a much more complex picture. Similar to Emily (above), Jenny offers what Throsby (2007, citing Scott and Lyman, 1968) calls an 'excuse account' by attributing her latest weight gain to medication, thus distancing herself from moral attributions of laziness, gluttony and the like, generally made to 'large' individuals (Cordell and Ronai, 1999; Murray, 2005a). She sees herself as 'not deserving' the fat and with that any negative judgement from others. Jenny construes herself as conflicted over her categorisations of who deserves to be fat, and to be judged for it, and who does not; however, despite her challenging them she keeps discourses of individual culpability for weight and health in place, positioning herself as not being able to avoid them. The notion of not deserving to be fat also implies a construction of fat as something inherently bad, and a state nobody wants to be inflicted with, whether they have brought it on themselves or have been subjected to it through no fault of their own. This generally negative construction of fat is also reflected in Sue's excerpt below:

> Sue: I wouldn't watch those kind of shows / I: hmm / particularly uhm (..) but (..) I mean I, my my my concern is, it *does tend* to be on on the negative side

/ I: hmm / you know and then that's just, that's not really *fair* because there are many reasons why people are obese and it's not always sort of just lack of willpower or or whatever else / I: yeah / you know, and uhm it's the the the education needs to be uhm around the fact that people can be obese for many different *reasons* and there maybe / I: hmm / there be reasons why it's not possible for them to *change* or / I: hmm / you know, whatever so it's it shouldn't be so judgemental.

Sue similarly keeps predominant discourses of 'fat is bad' in place by constructing 'obesity' as something that should be changed, if possible. However, Sue positions 'large' people as often unfairly judged and blamed for their 'obesity' as not everybody is able to do something about it. As with Jenny's account above, some people are construed as 'deserving' fat more than others, but in both narratives, while the discourses on fat are reinforced, the reasons why people are 'large' are being construed as complex and multifaceted.

The ideal of the neoliberal, ever self-improving individual was also challenged as unrealistic in other ways within narratives that positioned the modern individual in a complex web of responsibilities and activities that made it impossible to be perfect in all respects and that saw body size and sometimes healthcare dwarfed in importance.

Life's realities

Doing everything that is beneficial to one's health was often construed as not so easy, and most of the women positioned themselves as restricted in their lifestyle choices by a variety of factors.

I: Mm (..) um how much freedom do you think you have in terms of your lifestyle choice?

Lynn: Um, no freedom at all [laughs].

I: What what do you perceive as restrictions?

Lynn: Time, really, money [laughs] /I: mm/ health [laughs] yeah,

I: Any, sort of um (.) what what do you think would help you to have a bit more sort of have a bit more choice /Ly: um/ what could, could anybody or anything be done?

Lynn: Um have a personal dietician [laughs] someone that would prepare my meals for me [laughs].

Lynn positions herself as trapped and restricted in her lifestyle by a lack of time, money and health. Her lot is construed as something that has to be accepted, however, by herself as well as those who continuously advocate the immense benefit of small lifestyle changes. The idea that somebody could do something to help is constituted as laughable, as it would need extreme measures like a personal dietician to help Lynn. This positions Lynn outside as well as critical of the neoliberal discourses of self-improvement as her living situation simply puts too many restrictions on her choices; she is positioned as not belonging to the, what Jenny terms 'Jamie Oliver', type of people:

> Jenny: A lot of the time all this stuff all the, you know, the press attention it's not about, you know, nice people, middle-class families who've /I: mm/ both got jobs and you know (.) obedient children we're talking about the fat poor, you know, the the *that's* what the obesity time-bomb is, it's mothers who- you know it's single parents who feed their kids McDonald's [laughs] um that's that's the obesity time-bomb it's not the Jamie Oliver /I: mm/ (.) and um that's something that's, you know, kind of kind of goes under the radar again it's not necessarily to do with size it's to do with *class*.

The so-called 'obesity epidemic', and all its related health issues, is constructed in the above excerpt not as an individual but as a class issue, affecting mostly those who cannot afford to live a 'healthy' lifestyle. Attention is thus drawn to income inequalities in society, and a lack of consideration for this economic diversity in health promotion messages. Neoliberal discourses of self-perfection work within an ideal of a classless and economically just society with resources equally available to everyone. While it is often acknowledged that this diversity exists, in as much as different people are seen as having different starting points and foundations (in terms of income and education) to work from, the basic tenet of what it is to be a 'normative' individual with its ideals of self-fulfilment remain similar across the different societal strata, including class divisions (Rose, 1996). Within these discourses of self-improvement, those who cannot live up to the proclaimed standards of self-work are marginalised or, as Jenny calls it, fall 'under the radar'. This is reflected in most mainstream (as opposed to critical) health psychological theories of behaviour change. Despite an acknowledgement of socioeconomic factors in respect to determinants of health (Bennett, 1997), interventions mostly focus on changing the (health) behaviours of the individual, who ultimately bears the responsibility for her/his own health. Such interventions are often based on theories grounded in cognition and social cognition models (Ogden, 2004), for example the Theory of Planned Behaviour (Ajzen, 1985), the Health Belief Model (Rosenstock, 1966), the Health Action Process Approach (Schwarzer, 1992) or Prochaska and DiClemente's (1982) Transtheoretical Model. All these models are based on the assumptions that behaviours in the individual can and must be changed through a manipulation of individual cognitions, motivations and beliefs, in order to achieve the status of best-possible health. As such, the individualising processes Nikolas Rose (1996; Malson *et al.*, 2006) attributes to the psy-institutions, and their role in the constitution of 'regimes of the self' (Rose, 1996, p. 3) can equally be applied to the discipline and institution of health psychology and their efforts to treat individuals to improve their health. What seems to be missing from these neoliberal discourses of health and health psychology is what my participants construed as their lived experience of multiple restrictions in lifestyle choices:

> Eileen: Well I mean obviously everyone's got a right to choose the lifestyle /I: mm/ that they they want to, but I do think that um some people aren't able to choose a lifestyle /I: mm/ [. . .] I think when you're looking at a a lifestyle choice I think if you're on a lower income, I don't think your options are so available to you /I: mm/ um, you know so the lifestyle that you would choose, is not necessarily, it's not all available to you /I: mm/ so I think you know it, some of it is down to education /I: mm/ some of it's down to the fact that you, um fall into maybe a poverty bracket /I: mm/ and then you're not necessarily always, the information's not necessarily so available to you /I: mm/ or you haven't got the ability to, you know, to find out these things.

> Sarah: I think I'm, I'm, I'm a bit (.) lucky at the moment because I'm a student / I: hmm / so uhm there is quite a few activities that we can do uhm and we all get like Wednesday afternoons off anyway / I: hmm / to do what we want [. . .] I think (.) uhm once I leave university I think it might it may probably become a bit more restricted because you have to work so won't have as much free time.

> Sue: It's *not* that somebody is obese because they are lazy / I: hmm / or something you know, and I have a *frantically* busy life (you know), you know *hugely* busy and *that* is probably the reason why I'm not under *control*, you know / I: yeah / because, uhm, you know I (uhm) don't have the *time* / I: hmm / you know.

Restrictions to the freedoms people have in choosing the lifestyle they would like, or are encouraged to live, are portrayed in a number of ways. Eileen and Sarah draw on discourses of inequality in regard to income, education and occupation, which links back to Jenny's comment on class, above. My participants – as well as health promotion agencies (Department of Health, 2004a) – construe it as the right of everybody to choose the lifestyle they want. However, the ability to exercise this right is constructed in the interviews as a matter of knowing about and having access to the relevant resources and choices. In the above accounts, people are positioned on different levels of agency by their level of income, education or current occupation, which are limiting the resources of time and money necessary to exercise their right to choose.

Similarly, Sue is positioning herself as 'frantically busy' and thus not entirely in 'control' of her lifestyle choices, thereby constructing choices as pragmatic but necessary compromises. Life is construed as full of problems and challenges, where big choices have to be made as to what to spend one's time and energies on, and body weight is not necessarily the prime issue in people's lives:

> I: Uhm how do you feel when you, when you see or hear what you, what you perceive as the negative portrayal [of large people]?

> Sue: Well I feel *angry* because I know, (I mean), I know different / I: hmm / you know, I mean some of my some of my good friends are also very large people and, you know, we're all (just) you know we're we're *all* good at our jobs / I: hmm / you know, we *all* have uhm difficult family lives to deal with / I: hmm / and you know, obesity is just *one* problem that we are dealing with which you know, it might not always be the top priority.

> Eileen: Of course so much more is expected of you these days /I: mm/ you're expected to look good, to have a good job /I: yeah/ your kids to be brainy you know /I: mm/ and and the pressures of all those things something gives /I: mm/ and I think sometimes its your weight /I: mm/ I think you know you're trying to be so blimmin' good at everything else /I: mm/ that um sometimes you, personally, and your weight and and and your health comes quite low /I: mm/ on the um, agenda.

The above accounts draw on the discourses of the liberated superwoman who can have it all if she only wants to – from the successful job to a happy family life (Nicolson, 2002). Sue and Eileen are positioning themselves as obliged 'to have it all' and thus, at the same time, challenge the notion that this neoliberal ideal is possible or realistic. Having achieved (legal) equality with men, women now (in theory) can choose any job they like, compete successfully for highly paid positions while also enjoying happy and successful social and family lives. The above accounts reflect what Paula Nicolson refers to when she says that for women '*having it all* has become the same as *doing it all*' (Nicolson, 2002, p. 2). Sue and Eileen similarly construe this ambition not as a choice any more but as an obligation. Rather than being able to choose a career and family life, it is expected of women 'these days', that while leading such busy lives, they also 'look good' and maintain their health. The above accounts construe these neoliberal ideals of the modern superwoman as unrealistic, and position Sue and Eileen as having to prioritise when making choices about where to expend their energies. One's body size and health are construed as not important enough and certainly not the only issue these women have to deal with, and as such size does not take centre stage in their lives.

The constructions of health and well-being, as well as the responsibility for health and body weight, offered by the women in my interviews are much broader than the prevailing discourses of body size, health and illness imply, where health is generally reduced to the absence of medically diagnosable diseases and frequently equated with being thin. While the women use medicalised discourses to position themselves as healthy within them, they reject a reductionist approach taken to health and body size through an active expansion of the perspective on health, by including the notion of well-being, living environment and financial security, and by directly rejecting the 'fat = unhealthy' equation. These positive assertions of well-being are shifting and dynamic, however, and are sometimes articulated against commonly held notions of health.

At the doctors

The multifaceted picture of fat embodiment painted by my participants stands in stark contrast to what the fat body signifies culturally and particularly within medical institutions. While the women in my study often articulated complex and dynamic meanings of health that would accommodate the simultaneous existence of fat and 'health', they construed themselves as mostly being read and treated monolithically by health professionals as a fat person in need of weight loss.

> Louise: I've had medical professionals tell me that you know problems I have had are because of my weight. / I: hmm / ehm when I've had the same problems for a number of years before I was at this weight so there's there isn't a link [between weight and health] but people try and make it easy for medical / I: hmm / professionals not to address people's actual real health problems / I: hmm / and just say well if you go away and lose weight then, you know, you'll be better.

> Charlotte: I think the depth of misinformation (.) and repetitive cliché you get about fat and health are *so* (.) *so* encompassing / I: hmm / are *so* deep that you just can't get a, real information about it / I: hmm / and that really, really, really worries me because I think (.) well, I *know* that I get treated differently as a fat person at the doctors / I: hmm / and going through [. . .] the hospital, the medical process I know that I get treated differently and that is my *lived* experience (.) so that that really really worries me but whether I have higher (.) blood pressure or am more susceptible to cancer or a heart attack / I: hmm / or any of that stuff, I don't really care, I don't think that's true.

Although a couple of women recounted positive experiences with their doctors, these were raised as examples of exceptions and more frequently encounters with the medical system were constructed as annoying and worrying, as in the above two excerpts. What Charlotte calls the 'repetitive cliché . . . about fat and health' can be interpreted as part of the prevailing 'regimes of truth' (Foucault, 1991) relating to body weight, discussed above. Within the discourses of these regimes of truth fat women are positioned as unhealthy *per se* and weight loss is heralded as the cure for any ailment: 'you go away and lose weight then, you know, you'll be better' (Louise). These medical practices are constructed as worrying as the individuals' 'real health problems' are not being considered and consequently fat women do not receive adequate health treatment. The above accounts reflect research findings that 'large' individuals are being stigmatised and discriminated against within the health system (Joanisse and Synnott, 1999; Puhl and Brownell, 2001). By positioning the 'large' person as 'diseased' *per se*, and fat as the cause of all illness, however, fat individuals are simultaneously positioned as not really ill or suffering. They are construed as having brought ill health on themselves, as equally able to 'fix it' again through weight loss, and thus as not needing or deserving treatment. The fat body takes on a master status, blending out any other individual characteristics or health concerns.

The monolithic treatment by health professionals of all 'large' individuals as one and the same is also reflected in society in general through media coverage on the topic of 'obesity' and the portrayal of fat people in news reports. More often than not, such reports are illustrated by pictures of 'large' people's bodies from behind or from their shoulders down, what Charlotte Cooper calls 'headless fatties' (a collection of these can be seen on her website: http://www.charlottecooper.net/docs/fat/headless_fatties.htm).

> As Headless Fatties, the body becomes symbolic: we are there but we have no voice, not even a mouth in a head, no brain, no thoughts or opinions. Instead we are reduced and dehumanised as symbols of cultural fear: the body, the belly, the arse, food. There's a symbolism, too, in the way that the people in these photographs have been beheaded. It's as though we have been punished for existing, our right to speak has been removed by a prurient gaze, our headless images accompany articles that assume a world without people like us would be a better world altogether.
>
> (Cooper, 2007)

These 'headless fatties' are thus not portrayed as individuals; they have no characteristics of their own. The fat person in what Samantha Murray (2005a, p. 154) calls a 'culture of a negative collective "knowingness" about fatness' is always-already constructed as lazy, a glutton, possessing poor personal hygiene (Murray, 2005a) and as unhealthy. In such a culture there is no need to see the person's face or get to know her, it is assumed that all one needs to know about her can be read from her body size. And, as Karen Throsby (2007) points out, there are very few opportunities for 'large' people to narrate their own stories, and this silencing of their voices is both 'reflecting the entrenched nature' (Throsby, 2007, p. 1570) of this 'culture of knowingness' and helping to perpetuate it and the 'regimes of truth' around health and weight.

Health and fat are not simple or monolithic

The constructions of health and responsibility for health in my interviews were multilayered and dynamic. While participants drew on health promotion and biomedical discourses to construct health as a matter of lifestyle choices and positioned themselves as responsible for their health within these, the majority also constructed health as an issue that was much more complex than just a matter of body size. Most of the women positioned themselves as healthy, as well as health-literate individuals within the discourses of healthy lifestyles and holistic well-being, thus constructing health as unrelated to body size. A small number of the women took up the subject position of the unhealthy overeater, reinforcing biomedical discourses that linked body weight with physical health; however they rejected the subject position of the irresponsible fat person, drawing on psychological discourses of mental distress and addictive behaviour. Where fat was associated with health it was construed as a two-way tie-in as much as fat was not just seen as the cause of ill health, but (mental) ill health was equally construed as leading to weight gain, thus attributing less responsibility and consequently less moral judgement to the 'large' individual.

However, the prevailing constructions of 'fat is bad and unhealthy' were also reinforced with the women managing their fat subjectivity within dynamic constructions of responsibility for their body size. While the responsibility for body size was located in the individual, not every person was construed as deserving to be fat to an equal degree. Generally neoliberal discourses of everybody's capability for self-improvement or self-perfection were challenged with constructions of 'real' life as full of challenges and problems, with the choices available being distributed in unequal measures, and individuals having to choose what to focus their energies and time on.

The women in my study rejected imposed subject positions of the lazy, health-illiterate and unhealthy individual, and while health and healthy living were constituted as important and something to be taken seriously, health and life were construed as a lot more complex than just looking after one's weight. The women positioned themselves as active and proactive agents who chose their lifestyles consciously, if not completely freely, and managed life as best as they could. Within what they construed as their lived experiences, body weight was not the prime concern that the media and health promotion messages make it out to be. The multiple and dynamic subject positions taken up and rejected by the women, entrenched not only in discourses of health and weight, but also in those of familial commitment, time pressures and economic circumstances, also draw attention to the inappropriateness of the ill-conceived health promotion strategy of targeting certain sectors in the population delineated by their body mass index only.

The construction and positioning of women as main care-givers (for husbands and children) were among the issues in the current chapter, which draws attention to the various ways in which the politics of body weight and health are clearly gendered. In the following chapter I will further explore the dynamics around body size and gender, drawing on accounts from both women and men.

6   Gendering fat

Ever heard a man ask the question: 'Does my bum look big in this?'? 'Yes', you may say – in jokes about women. Intrigued by the different ways men and women talk about their bodies, and by the potentially artificial (as in interview-related) lack of references to gender in my interviews with women, I am exploring the issues of 'gender', bodies and fat in this chapter.

The gendering of fat is also of particular interest as the war on obesity seemingly targets both women and men in the current atmosphere of neoliberalism and healthism. We are all held responsible for our own health and well-being (see Chapter 5), and health is equated with body size by health professionals, the media and the general public alike. The notions that fat is unhealthy and being slim and weight loss are inherently good have become commonsensical truths to the extent that the conflation of 'being healthy' with 'losing weight' or 'maintaining a low body weight' are omnipresent and go largely unquestioned (Aphramor, 2008b; Malson, 2008). Whilst the neoliberal, healthist discourses on fat converge on fat individuals of any gender, like others (Frost, 2005; Malson, 2008; Monaghan, 2008a) I would argue, however, that gender equality within this 'war on obesity' is still as elusive as in other areas of society. Women's and men's (fat) bodies, femininity and masculinity are construed in qualitatively different ways and inscribed with different meanings.

Women have historically and currently been subject to considerably greater pressures than men to conform to gendered body ideals, and particularly to idealised slimness as a key signifier of 'femininity' (Bordo, 1993; Orbach, 2006b; Smith, 1990). The continuously growing focus on women's appearance is seen by some feminist theories as a backlash against women's liberation and as a means of domination and oppression (Weitz, 2003; Wolf, 1991). As others have observed, appearance pressure on men is indeed also increasing (Bell and McNaughton, 2007; Gill, 2008a), with the ideal masculine body being socially constructed as tall, strong, muscular and lean (Frith and Gleeson, 2004; Gill, 2008a; Monaghan, 2007b). However, the constitution (or performance) of hegemonic masculinity is less dependent on bodily appearance than the socially acceptable performance of femininity (Monaghan, 2007a; Smith, 1990). This gendering of how appearance figures in constructions of sexed/gendered identities can be understood in the discursive context of Cartesian dualism and the culturally entrenched hierarchical binaries of mind/body, man/woman, culture/nature, rational/irrational (Bordo, 1993; Malson, 1998). Within this context, 'women' are discursively produced and regulated, much more than 'men', through the ways in which their bodies and particularly bodily appearance are discursively constituted. Drawing on men's and women's narratives, I will now discuss the multiple and dynamic constructions of femininity and women's bodies and how they differ from constructions of masculinities and men's bodies. I will further explore how the discursive resources available to and deployed by my participants regulate women's and men's practices and what gendered subject positions they make available.

At this point I would like to reiterate a note of caution. As with all qualitative research, and discourse analysis in particular (see Chapter 2), my findings will not lend themselves to, and are not intended for, decontextualised generalisations about how 'large' men and women experience their fat bodies. The focus of this research has been on how 'fat women', and in this chapter 'large' women and 'large' men, are discursively constituted (in both women's and men's talk) and on the gendered constructions of embodied fat, control, dieting and empowerment, rather than on any generalisable statement about, for example, differences between 'large' men and women. Some of my interpretations do not seem to reflect the most recent writings in regard to hegemonic masculinities, and the undisputed fact that men are also targets in the war on obesity, which may or may not be a reflection of the research process in this particular study. The data was collected through open-ended interviews (18 women and three men) and focus groups (six women and two men in two unisex groups), which are always also social interactions in which the interview dynamics, and thus data produced, are affected by the personality and 'gender' of the interviewer and interviewee(s) (Burman, 1994; Burns, 2003; Oakley, 2005). As discussed earlier (Chapter 2), I believe that some of my data may have been influenced, but certainly not devalued, by the fact that I am a normatively sized woman, interviewing 'large' men and women. It is quite possible that a man conducting the interviews and focus groups may have elicited different data; however, whether this data would have been 'better' is up for speculation.

Construction of male and female bodies

According to Bell and McNaughton (2007), men and their struggle with weight and size issues have been somewhat ignored in the literature and research about fat, and the interrogation of the complex interrelationships between gender and fatness has been explored mostly with a focus on women's bodies and/or from a feminist perspective. Bell and McNaughton maintain that, contrary to claims in the more recent literature (citing, for example, Bordo, 1993), it is not a new phenomenon that men have been the targets in a societal disapproval of fatness but that, according to Schwartz (1986) both men and women 'in the USA were caught up in a variety of intersecting and at times contradictory discourses and technologies regarding fat and bodily reduction' in the nineteenth and twentieth centuries (Bell and McNaughton, 2007, p. 113). Notwithstanding these assertions, Bell and McNaughton agree with a great number of writers (Bordo, 1993; Chernin,

1983; Malson, 1998; Tischner and Malson, 2008, 2011) that women are under a lot more societal and individual scrutiny in relation to body weight and size than men are. A slim body is a socially constructed beauty ideal for women (Bordo, 1993; Germov and Williams, 1999) while a 'big albeit lean body', as Lee Monaghan (2007a) put it, is an 'often intentionally developed and valued' signifier of masculinity. This valuing of strength, bigness and muscularity in relation to men's bodies was also articulated by my participants:

> Judy: The breadwinner s-, the traditional tribal breadwinner [. . .] the man is still the, (.) traditionally the breadwinner has to be strong and muscly, go out and kill the animals, so it's gonna take centuries to (.) to completely change that, it's still, it's still there, isn't it, they gotta be fit (.) fitter than women in that sense / hmm /

> Emma: I'd, I was just, the negative images, you know, the negative im-, for a *man* it would be to, to be *weedy* and to be small, wouldn't it, whereas for a woman it's to be big, so it's the reverse image (women's focus group).[5]

Both Judy and Emma construct the 'ideal' masculine body as strong, fit and muscular, certainly not 'small' or 'weedy'. Women on the other hand should be smaller and less physically strong than men, and definitely not big. Words such as 'traditional tribal breadwinner' can be seen as elements of a discourse of the traditional family with its implied 'roles' for men and women (cf. Sayers (1982) for a discussion of the biological determination of gender roles). While Judy with her use of the term 'tribal' construes the traditional family as something that dates back as far as to times when men went out to 'kill the animals', which conjures up pictures of caves and very basic living, theorists like Lupton (1996) associate the notion of the traditional nuclear family with the industrial era, when the places of work and home became separated. Men started to leave the family home to earn a living in the public sphere while the women stayed at home, maintaining a safe place of comfort and nurturing for the man to return to (Bordo, 1993). Within the discourse of traditional family life men are constructed as having to be strong, tough and consequently big enough to compete in the outside world, and on the flip side of the coin, women not only allegedly do not need physical strength and powerful size in the 'romanticized and mystified' (Bordo, 1993, p. 118) domestic arena, but also get their main gratification from nurturing and caring for others, i.e. husbands and children.

Wifely concern or love and maternal love are two of the three types of affection Deborah Lupton (1996) connects with food and women's role in preparing food. The third one is romantic love, which since industrialisation has taken over as the main basis for marital relationships, which were grounded on more pragmatic and economic reasons before. The woman here is seen as the 'emotional centre of the family' (Lupton, 1996, p. 38), while the man is seen as the provider and protector. Traditional heterosexual romantic narratives also construe the ideal feminine woman/heroine as weak, passive, dependent and fragile (Nicolson, 2002; Ussher,

1997; Wetherell, 1986), needing to be rescued by a (strong) man. As such, the discourses of maternal, wifely and romantic love converge on women to produce romantic femininity as signified in the small and thin body (Malson, 1998), which in reverse means the signification of non-femininity for the fat woman's body (Orbach, 2006b; Rice, 2009a). A woman's slim and small body signifies that she does not eat much, that she feeds others before herself, like generations of women have done in a variety of cultures (Orbach, 2006b; Wolf, 1991), and that she will generally not ask for much for herself.

Within heterosexual romantic discourse, femininity is also defined by hetero-sexual attractiveness, which is reflected in the following excerpt. While the dis-cussion draws on constructions of fat and 'curvy' as being naturally feminine, Cathy, Emma and Judy also draw on discourses of heterosexual attraction:

Cathy: I think it [being large] can make you feel *more* feminine, more (.) shapely and *voluptuous* and *sexy*

Emma: Now, see, *those* are *lovely* positive words / yeah / and they *imply* / curvy / *size*, don't they, yes / and touchable / lovely words,

Cathy: You see some men like that don't they?

Judy: Anyway, why is it all about men? (.) Now that's society again, I, I think (women's focus group).

In associating 'large' with feeling 'more feminine', 'shapely', 'voluptuous and sexy', Cathy, as well as several other women in the group, rejects the imposed subject position of the unattractive and unfeminine fat woman. Being fat is construed as curvy and voluptuous, which are exclusively feminised attributes. However, these positive feelings of attractiveness and femininity are still contingent on men liking it. As such, despite the women in the above quote asserting their potential attractiveness, the heterosexual power relations remain the same. They are produced in heterosexual romantic discourses, which construe attractiveness and femininity as dependent on men being attracted to what they see, and the woman being defined as passively hoping to attract a man (Malson, 1998). These dis-cursively produced power relations are maintained in the above excerpts.

However, the women in my study did not construe this societal gendering of body size as unilaterally putting pressure on women only, as the above exchange between Judy and Emma reflects. The need for a strong, big and muscular body is constructed as something imposed on men, something that may cause men similar worries about body size to those of women. The statement 'They gotta be fitter than women', and that they must not be 'small' or 'weedy' acknowledges that men are also subjected to some social pressure to fulfil a certain image. For men thinness, like fatness, has negative connotations (Monaghan, 2007a; Robertson, 2006) and men have come under increasing pressure in regard to body weight over the past 20 years (Bordo, 1993; Frith and Gleeson, 2004); the ideal masculine body shape is now construed as muscular, strong, tall – and lean. This arguably recent increase in pressure on men in respect to body weight was articulated by Don in the focus group:

> Don: I have become (.) a bit shshshy (.) about my (.) shape so that uh, after playing football I don't have a shower [. . .] I don't want the others to see me in the shower, 'cause uh, 'cause because I'm overweight, so (.) uh (.) it affected uh uh my behaviour [. . .]
>
> I: mhm (.) When you say you've *become* more shy, has that that that changed over the years=
>
> =Don: yeah, I think so, maybe I'm feeling more overweight then I was or (.) uh for, for (.) for a reason I'm not particularly aware of / I: mhm / uh, I'm not, so I'm not, I I'm not really sh-, I can't really put my finger on what the reason is, but (.) the last couple of years I've (.) you know I'd be *extremely* reluctant to, to have communal showers (men's focus group).

While constituting himself as reluctant to expose his body to the other men in the football team, Don at the same time constructs this increased weight consciousness as something that has crept up on him, something he 'can't really put [his] finger on what the reason [for it] is'. Worrying about and tending to one's appearance are often socially constructed as feminine (Smith, 1990). Construing his concerns about his weight, and the reasons for his appearance consciousness, as something he is not really sure of, Don can be seen as attending to the potential feminisation his shyness and appearance concerns mobilise.

Bell and McNaugton (2007), as well as Lee Monaghan (2008a), describe how fat men are positioned as non-masculine or feminised. According to the above authors, fat men are thereby positioned doubly negative with a fat body generally being loaded with negative interpretations (as argued in various places throughout this book) but in addition to that, men are being denigrated through the social construction of the feminine body as inferior to men's bodies. Through fat, men are being seen as 'demoted' to women, the 'inferior other'. Apart from constructions of dieting behaviour and health and weight consciousness, the theme of the feminised fat man was not evident in my data. In fact, as I will argue in more detail later on, men seem to have a variety of discursive resources available that allow them to maintain a dominant masculine identity (Coles, 2008), and that are mostly unrelated to their bodily make-up.

Despite the increased social pressure on men to be lean, participants in my study constructed men as still 'better off' in relation to body size issues. While for women, being large in any shape or form is construed as bad, for men it is not as clear cut, and there are some positive significations of a large body:

> =Debbie: I think Marks's [UK shopping chain] do have a men's (.) bigger size [section], it's call-, I can't remember what it's called now, but you know, like High and Mighty (.) it's something along those lines, but, but it's like (.) it's sort of emphasising it's for the taller, broader man / hmm / rather than the fatter man (women's focus group).

I: Uhm (.) what (..) in your views, what does it mean to to be a man, and how does body size come into it, does it come into it at all? (..)

Don: Uh [name], my, my wife (.) she, she's got two views uh (.) she criticises me for being overweight, but (.) [. . .] being large, she's, she sees as an advantage on the street, she feels people were less likely to uh (.) have a go at me, 'cause I'm large, obviously if I was short and overweight (.) that probably wouldn't work / I: hmm / but, being tall and bulky, [. . .] she sees that uh as an advantage uh, that there be (.) you know, less hassle / I: mhm / than, uhm say I, uh, a a man of normal height and weight (men's focus group).

As with High and Mighty, the name of a store for large men, terms like taller, broader and bulky all conjure up positively construed images of the strong, safe and protective man, a man who would not get any hassle on the street. There is a dynamic and ambivalence here around being positioned as the tall, strong masculine man or the fat man who needs to be criticised for his overweight. This ambivalence reflects work by other researchers and theorists (Bell and McNaughton, 2007; Lupton, 1996; Stearns, 1997) who maintain that men are also targeted in the war on obesity, even though they may not talk about it as much. However, in both quoted excerpts, Don does not constitute himself as worried (or even appreciative) of his size. Responding to the question about how body size affected what it meant to be a man, he refers to his wife's opinion rather than giving his own. He thereby construes the issue of body size as something wives and by extension women generally, rather than men, are concerned about. He constitutes himself implicitly as having no view on the topic, which reflects Hannah Frith and Kate Gleeson's (2004) findings that, while body image for men, as for women, is fluid and at times contradictory, it seems that as a man one must not be seen to care about one's appearance.

One of the lads?

In the above quotes, large bodies were associated with masculinity, and these associations were construed as carrying potentially positive connotations for men. Particularly the association of a certain body size with (masculine) strength was constructed as beneficial for men in both work and social situations.

Bill: I negotiate for a living / I: mhm / right so this is why I'm quite comfortable with what we are doing today / I: hmm / I mean I negotiate contracts so (.) under negotiation tactics it can be quite good to be big and and and forceful and aggressive or not / I: hmm / depending on the tactics you need to employ in a situation you're in, uhm but really, uhm appearance is becoming uhm more prevalent [. . .] in some respects professionally it's been an advantage / I: hmm / to being in negotiation and to be uhm you know when you sit comfortably arms crossed and a smile that's fine [. . .] though you have to be very careful cause because uhm particularly with females / I: mhm / they may find that too threatening.

Wynne: You know there (.) there are times when I wish yes I was a bit thinner and there are times I wish I was a bit smaller or a bit shorter 'cos I could then go and buy this pair of trousers or that shirt or. Um, but then I think yeah but if I wasn't 6 ft 5 (.) then [. . .] I couldn't (.) do these jobs that involve me reaching up high, or I couldn't just get out of a situation just by standing up straight and projecting that / I: hmm / I'm bigger than you are look, get away from me kind of aura.

In both excerpts above the sheer presence of a sufficiently large and tall man is constructed as commanding respect and power, and as constituting an advantage in a variety of social situations. Whilst it is acknowledged that this can also be interpreted as threatening, 'particularly with females', overall a large body size for men carries mainly advantages in social interactions and signifies masculinity and power. Being 'large' in height here dwarfed the negative connotations being fat may carry, as Wynne recalls:

Wynne: But I have got friends who are (.) short and fat, so short and round basically and they're, they, they suffer with it.

So it is the tallness or general bigness that signifies masculinity and strength and the fatness thus then seems to become less relevant. Similar constructions were drawn on in the women's focus group, where 'large' bodies and body parts were also construed as masculine, and thus as having a defeminising effect on women.

Debbie: I feel *less* feminine (.) because of my size (..)

Judy: I can't say I have ever felt feminine=

Debbie: =then I also have my father's large hands rather than my mother's small hands, so (.) [. . .] I feel, the bigger I've been, the less feminine I've, I've felt (women's focus group).

Increasing weight in the above excerpt is correlated with an increasing defeminisation, and the same effect is bestowed on the possession of big body parts, like large hands, which are associated, implicitly at least, with men and masculinity.

The thin woman's body signifies the 'ideal' feminine woman; however, at the same time it also signifies the inferiority of women in a patriarchal society. Unlike the powerful large man's body, which may be interpreted as 'forceful and aggressive' (Bill) and thus potentially professionally advantageous, the thin female body represents a person, which one (man) does not have to take seriously, and need not feel threatened by (Bordo, 1993; Malson, 1998; Orbach, 2006b; Wolf, 1991). Smallness, fragility, emotionality and frivolity are all characteristics that constitute and signify the 'feminine' and are simultaneously constructed as inferior to men's rational and unemotional mode of operation (Malson, 1998). As I have argued above, masculinity on the other hand is associated with being strong and big (albeit increasingly also lean) in a physical sense. Since the nineteenth century and the separation of the public and private sphere, masculinity has also been associated with a lack of emotion and the ability to operate rationally in order to succeed in the workplace outside the home (Lupton, 1996). Women on the other hand are construed as emotional, irrational and interested in frivolous things such as fashion and appearance (Frith, 2003; Smith, 1990). This construction of the idealised, i.e. small, female body as being less capable than a man's body was also implicit in the construction of the fat woman's body as capable, in my data. In contrast to the constructions of the fat woman as lacking control and therefore 'being no good' for a job, as discussed below, here her size was construed as working for a woman, gaining her respect in a male-dominated workplace:

> Lucy: I worked for quite a long time, well for *19* years for BT, and 13 of those years I spent as an engineer (.) uhm, I was the second woman in [city] to become (.) an engineer (.) uhm, the girl before me was slim, blonde and (.) the guys used to do everything for her (.) whereas *I* was (.) not as overweight as I am *now* but I was still overweight, and, hence, I (.) more rapidly became accepted because I was seen as being possibly stronger (.) and more able to do the *job* than being a delicate thing / general murmur / I mean one of the guys that was, an out and out, uh, not quite a misogynist but going that way (.) one day at tea break sat down and said, well, yeah, well *you*, Lucy, you're just one of the lads (..) and I actually th- (..) took that as quite a compliment / (inaudible) / in that I've been accepted as being just *me* / yeah / (women's focus group).

Not being slim, or rather being 'large', is again construed as defeminising (Rice, 2009a) in the above excerpt, however, with more positive connotations. Here Lucy and fat women generally are positioned as 'one of the lads', as non-feminine; but Lucy also constructs her 'overweight' as enabling her to gain respect in a male-dominated work environment. By not being 'slim' and 'blonde' she is at the same time disqualified from femininity as well as given qualities that are normally reserved for men – she can hold her own in the male-dominated workplace. Being fat can thus be seen as liberating women from oppressive and restricting 'doctrines of femininity' (Smith, 1990, p. 171). What is socially accepted as feminine is constructed and reconstructed in discourses distributed in the media and day-to-day talk, but is also performed by women through their compliance with these doctrines. While some would point to the choice women have in adopting the various beautifying and feminising practices, it is clearly a lot more complicated than just deciding not to conform, with a woman's worth still to a great extent linked to her (feminine) appearance (Stuart and Donaghue, 2012). This worth is in part secured through the adoption of the practices and appearances prescribed within the doctrines. This performance of femininity, however, also reconstructs and reinforces other signifiers of the feminine, i.e. frail, thin/small, passive and emotional – in the context of the male-dominated workplace this may also translate into less capable or competent (Nicolson, 2002; Orbach, 2006b; Smith, 1990).

When they lose weight, that is, begin to look like a perfect female, they find themselves being treated frivolously by their male colleagues. When women are thin, they *are* treated frivolously: thin-sexy-incompetent worker.

(Orbach, 2006b, p. 22; original emphasis)

Sara Crawley, in her autoethnographic rant (2002), describes her own efforts at breaking out of this interpretative circle. By not complying with the doctrines of femininity, in particular not wearing dresses and make-up and assuming a 'butch' appearance, she tries to avoid the feminine/incompetent complex – not always successfully. I would not want to suggest that my participants, or fat women generally, intentionally became fat in order to improve their chances of success in male-dominated work environments. However, Lucy's account above seems to articulate a sense of positive effects of being fat through not being seen as feminine, and simply being 'accepted as being just *me*', with all the competences that come with her now 'gender-neutral' persona. However, this 'positive' construction of fat women represents a double-edged sword if it means that women have to reject or give up their 'femininity' in order to be accepted and successful in certain fields of work.

In contrast to gaining respect once in a job (as discussed above), and more in line with research on the stigmatisation of 'large' individuals (Cordell and Ronai, 1999; Puhl and Brownell, 2001), securing employment was construed as difficult for 'large' women, in the following quote by Judy:

Judy: if you're going looking for new jobs in new places and you're overweight, you just walk in the room and people get that instant impression 'she hasn't got control over her body, so' you know 'she's no good' / hmm / (..) [sighs] (women's focus group).

In Western industrialised countries, fat bodies are signifiers of a lack of self-control (Germov and Williams, 1999) and, for women in particular, a lean and toned body signifies control and, in extension, success (Gill, 2007). This is articulated in the above focus group excerpt in which finding a job for an 'overweight' woman is construed as very difficult as fat women are immediately judged, purely based on their appearance, as 'no good' due to their 'obvious' lack of self-control. The construction of the female body, and by extension women (of any body size) generally, as a problem and in need of control due to its inherent changeability and uncontrollability, has been theorised by a number of writers (Bordo, 1993; Burr, 1998; Malson, 1998; Wolf, 1991). I find Elizabeth Grosz's (1994) interpretations most apt in relation to fat women's bodies. Similarly to Jane Ussher (2006), Grosz maintains that the 'metaphorics of uncontrollability' (p. 203) which we find in 'literary and cultural representations of women' have their basis in the construction of female bodily processes as irrepressible. Reproductive processes in particular, such as menstrual blood flow and pregnancy, signify uncontrollability and undefined boundaries.

Can it be that in the West, in our time, the female body has been constructed not only as a lack or absence but with more complexity, as a leaking, uncontrollable, seeping liquid; as formless flow; a viscosity, entrapping, secreting; as lacking not so much or simply the phallus but self-containment – not a cracked or porous vessel, like a leaking ship, but a formlessness that engulfs all form, a disorder that threatens all order?

(Grosz, 1994)

Women's uncontrollable, changing and changeable bodies are thus construed as a problem (Rudolfsdottir, 2000), and with fat being equally construed as uncontained, uncontrolled and dangerous (Campos *et al.*, 2006a; Monaghan, 2008a; Orbach, 2006a), the constructions of women's bodies and fat converge on the fat woman's body, as signifying a formlessness, a disorder that threatens Western industrialised, patriarchal order, that must be contained – or literally kept small. The containment of the female body, and as such its apparent threat to cultural/patriarchal order, is in part achieved through the construction of the 'ideal' feminine woman as slim.

Lucy: In a lot of shops you do now also get a petite range / hmm / for small and short people / yeah / I'm torn between the two because I'm not very tall / [laughter] [. . .]

Emma: But isn't petite such a (..) [. . .] connotations / [group comments] / are nicer connotations than *plus* / yeah [laughter] / your petite is one end and plus is the other (women's focus group).

The laughter in the group clearly constitutes Lucy's dilemma as a joke, as although she is 'not very tall' Lucy would not call herself 'petite' in earnest. Petite women are small and thin, or at least not fat, and as a fat woman she is – as Emma puts it – at the other end of the spectrum. Fat, or 'plus-sized' women also find themselves on the opposite end to the nice, positive connotations and images the term 'petite' evokes. 'Plus' conjures up images of 'too much', of something 'extra', of more than the standard – and thereby of excess and of being uncontained. It comes as no surprise to see the 'perfect' woman represented (for example, in adverts) as having 'achieved a state beyond craving' (Bordo, 1993), as not really needing food, and certainly not passionately wanting more ('plus') food than deemed appropriate.

The 'ideal' feminine woman then is frequently construed culturally as small and slim, but also as irrational and frivolous. She is concerned about (trivial) health and appearance matters (which I will expand on below) and, as such, as inferior to men and incapable of achieving in a male-dominated workplace. As such, there are dynamic and at times contradictory constructions of women's fat bodies at play. The slim 'ideal' defeminises 'large' women but positions them thus as capable and competent in a male-dominated work environment. At the same time, however, being 'large' is also construed as uncontrollable and uncontained and thus as 'no good' for any job and in need of control. A large body or body parts were construed as masculine, and as such men were positioned as 'better' off in the 'war on obesity'. However, men were not construed as having an easy life in relation to body weight and size, but rather as being subjected to qualitatively different pressures, for example the need to be strong, or the threat of feminisation through body fat or a concern with their appearance and health.

These multiple and dynamic constructions of 'femininity' and 'masculinity' converge on individuals and their bodies, to produce gendered pressures which regulate women's (and men's) behaviours.

Gendered pressures

Throughout the interviews and focus groups, women were construed as both more size-conscious, as well as more controlling of other people's weight and health. Several of my women participants, for example, constructed their mothers as in some way directly or indirectly responsible for their size, what and how much they were eating, and so forth:

> Debbie: Well I was five and a half pounds [birth weight] / group members: really? – I was 7 13 / because my mum smoked. My mum's going through a stressful time, smoked with me, I came out five and a half pounds, as such a little thing, and she promptly overfed me for the next 2 years / [laughter] alright / which of course then sort of went, I sort of went from being a=

> =Judy?: don't stand a chance (women's focus group).

> Linda: Well, if I'm out with my husband and my son, I'll eat what I want to eat, if I'm out with my mum (.) I eat what my mum wants me to eat / [laughter]

> I: How does that differ?

> Several: a lot [laughter] (women's focus group).

In the first excerpt, Debbie constructs her mother's situation and lifestyle as responsible for her low birth weight, which in turn is construed as the cause for her being overfed as a child and ultimately for her current 'overweight'. She did not 'stand a chance', to use Judy's words. This representation of mothers as responsible for the nutritional health of their children right from the moment they are in their wombs has been discussed by Deborah Lupton (1996) and others (Orbach, 2006b). As soon as women are pregnant, they are expected to 'eat for two' and also look after two people, with a special emphasis of taking extra care with their lifestyle, especially their eating and drinking habits, in order to ensure optimal health of the fetus they carry. A discourse of the traditional family, and its implied gender roles, is being employed here (Lupton, 1996). As I have argued above, this discourse positions men/fathers as the breadwinners of the family, while women/mothers are positioned as caretakers, responsible for the family's diet and health. Buying and preparing food and being in control of the family's eating are construed as 'good mothering' (Beagan *et al.*, 2008). Looking after and caring for others are, however, not just constructed as the maternal role, but are also construed as a sign of femininity. Bordo (1993) summarises the gender difference in relation to food and eating under the heading 'Men eat and women prepare' (p. 117). Being a woman, or rather being feminine, is constructed within the discourse of the family, but in practice extends beyond the family into society as a whole, as seeking gratification in the care for others, wanting only little for oneself (Bordo, 1993; Lupton, 1996).

This construction of women being responsible for everybody else's health, while men do not care about their health unless they are being reminded of it, was also identified in discussions around health in the men's focus group.

> Rich: hmm (.) I think for myself I don't think about it at all, really, uhm (.) I *do* think about, I *do* think about it when it's brought to my attention and, uhm, my wife brings my size to my attention reg- at regular intervals, uhm, but because I'm also diabetic / I: hmm / I, I, it's [laughing] brought to my attention by the diabetic nurse as well / I: hmm / uh, which means that every sort of six months I, I, I'm [laughing] forced to feel guilty about it, and swear that I'll do something about it, and do something about it for about a day and a half (.).

> Don: Uhm, yeah, I mean again, luckily as, as a man it's not an issue that's on my mind much at all, uhm (.) It's, sometimes when I catch a glimpse of myself in profile, I'm, I'm shocked and think that (.) that's pretty bad [. . .] but (.) it's not something that's kind of nagging away at me / I: hmm / (.) uh (.) I, I go for long periods where, you know, it wouldn't even occur to me / I: Hmm / (inaudible) days, so it, it's not something that's (.) pressing on my mind and and worrying me / I: hmm / or anything, and I'm not, most of the time I'm not, I'm not aware of it, they're irrelevant things.

Men are often constructed as not worried about health, as not being in touch with their bodies and health generally and as not engaging in appropriate healthcare (Kimmel, 2004; Messner, 1997). Through their narratives my participants in the men's focus group positioned themselves as men who, in contrast to women, do not worry about health issues as long as they are not reminded by external influences – either by their wives or by, as in the above account, seeing their own profile in the mirror. Even when they are reminded, they construe themselves as not being worried about it, laughing the concerns off, and positioning themselves as 'being forced to feel guilty about it [. . .] for about a day and a half' (Rich). '[A]s a man it's not an issue that's on my mind' (Don). This reflects other writers' argument (Sloan *et al.*, 2010; Will, 2000) that caring about health would reflect a certain vulnerability and thus violate the rules of masculinity.

In Sloan *et al.*'s research, as in my own data, caring for one's health and living a healthy lifestyle were indeed constructed as not very masculine. If health consciousness was admitted to, other discursive repertoires, e.g. of rationality and functionality, were drawn on to maintain a certain status of masculinity. Being concerned about one's body size and health thus is constructed as a feminine trait generally, something that is not on men's mind much. Rich is laughing about his lack of concern, and while Don counts himself lucky for not worrying about his size, he also counts himself lucky to be a man; as a man he positions himself above such frivolous matters like health and body weight issues. These 'women's issues' are construed as laughable or belonging to those 'irrelevant things' men do not think about much.

However, the two excerpts above also serve as examples of how, in my data, women are construed as having responsibility for the health of their husbands or men generally; they are the ones bringing men's body size to their attention in order to spur them into action. Men do not have to care about their size or health, as they have women to care about these things for them. Health behaviour is constructed as clearly gendered in these narratives, and in line with the gender roles that are constructed within traditional family discourses, these are firmly held in place in these excerpts, as well as more contemporary postfeminist cultural discourses of sexualisation (Gill, 2007). Women care for men; they provide food and take responsibility for the overall health and well-being of all family members.

So far in my data, then, mothers and women are constructed as responsible for their children's and husbands' health and weight, while as daughters the women construed themselves also as being pressured by their mothers. Particularly the men in my study also positioned women as being subject to more severe appearance and body size criticisms generally, and from various directions:

> Wynne: I have got friends who are (.) short and fat, so short and round basically and they're, they, they suffer with it a, a whole (lot), and I think it's (.) slightly better being a male than it is for a female (.) on that sort of ratio / I: hmm / uhm, but again I can't speak from experience obviously but er just from observation I think it (.) / I: hmm / they, also the media seems to portray it worse for women / I: mhm / you know, uhm, we as blokes don't necessarily have to (.) have that body image issues that uhm seems to be portrayed (inaudible) throughout the media (interview).

> Bill: I mean I think there is a prevalence to to the being you know very very thin and particular for the females you know the pressure on them is is quite significant particularly for the young you know I mean my daughter uh she comes home with saying oh someone's again promoting being very very thin and and uhm not eating the the stuff that my daughter eats and and there is I think a real peer pressure (interview).

Here the pressure to be a certain size and look a certain way is constructed as higher for women than for men, who 'don't necessarily have to have that body image issue'. Drawing on and thus reproducing body image discourses which constitute being 'very very thin' as the ideal for women, those who do not comply with these slim ideals are depicted as suffering under societal, media and peer pressure. Similarly Don, in the following excerpt, constitutes women as primary targets for cultural appearance pressures, but also brings into view a complex and seemingly contradictory network of power relationships that are active in regard to weight and size scrutiny:

> Don: Well, just reiterating I (..) I thought about it bef-, before I came here that I'm just so lucky (.) to be male in this, in this particular circumstance / I: hmm / I feel very sorry for women that they're under such pressure and uh (.) even my wife (.) uhm [. . .] got involved, we, we were on the bus one day and there was uh, a young woman who was (.) more overweight than my wife, wearing uh incredibly (.) skimpy clothing, and she was nudging me, and winking and so on, uh which was sort of [. . .] here was she, a person who's quite overweight, uh (.) you know, the thing was, you know, criticising another woman uh [. . .] in some ways it was really (inaudible) hypocritical, because I know she doesn't (.) like to be reminded of her size (men's focus group).

Women, here, are not simply constructed as the passive victims of the social pressure to be thin, but also as agentic in maintaining the pressure on women, even if they could be, due to their size, a target for equal pressure and criticism themselves. This links back to Chapter 3, where I used Foucault's concept of the Panopticon to interpret the discourses around being visible and under the gaze of others. There, as here, women construct themselves, and are being constructed, as being in both parts of the Panopticon – in the cell as the watched 'inmate' and at the same time one of the guards in the watch tower. As objects of the male – and female – gaze of normalisation, women will employ technologies of the self (to apply Foucault's term) of self-perfection as well as regulating others.

Discourses of health and beauty have merged in recent years (Arthurs and Grimshaw, 1999) and 'large' women are construed as being in need of improvement in terms of both. Fat is culturally constructed as unattractive and ugly (Malson, 1998), and being thin, albeit 'toned and slightly muscly' (Arthurs and Grimshaw, 1999, p. 2) is considered beautiful or even 'ideal' for women. At the same time, through the near interchangeability of the discourses of health and beauty and the general view that a person's body reflects her interior life (Gill, 2007), beauty 'on the outside' is read as health 'on the inside' (Arthurs and Grimshaw, 1999). Within the neoliberal discourse of self-perfection, everybody is very much held responsible for their own health, and deemed able to change both their health and beauty at will (Rose, 1996; see Chapter 2). To achieve 'perfection' in both is illusory but constantly to be worked on, for all our lives. Dorothy Smith (1990) termed women's work on and communication through their bodies 'femininity as discourse' (p. 159) – I would like to extend this to 'femininity, health and beauty as discourse' in that the doctrines of the three discourses converge on women's bodies, and women are positioned along dimensions of value within them.

In order to position themselves as women, as feminine, within these discourses, women self-discipline their bodies according to cultural standards. However, 'women are not simply duped by patriarchal, capitalist, consumer society' (Frith, 2003, p. 4) but, as already mentioned above, they actively maintain the cultural constructions of femininity and the prevailing power structures through their actions and day-to-day talk. As such, the discursive regulation of these activities should not be read as a simple unidirectional oppression of powerless women by a powerful patriarchal society (not wanting to deny unequal genderised power relations existing here, however). Rather, women are executing some control over their practices and, as well as experiencing anxieties over their bodies, they may also gain some pleasure and self-assurance through these (Lupton, 1996; Stuart and Donaghue, 2012), within the context of a neoliberal society which assigns agency, (professional) success and feminine beauty to young, toned, flawless and slim women (only). Neoliberalism and living in allegedly postfeminist times mean that we now have the 'choice' to engage in these beauty practices, rather than being directly pressured into them. This in turn deproblematises and depoliticises these issues and also means that questioning and challenging them become a lot harder (Gill, 2007; Stuart and Donaghue, 2012); after all, women are doing it all 'for themselves' (Braun, 2009) rather than for men. Thus, in a shift from objectification to subjectification, women get actively engaged in 'doing femininity' through working on their bodies (Smith, 1990), which become body projects of subjectivity, regulated through the discourses of beauty and femininity, but presented as our free choice. The latter is reflected in Debbie's account below, on having to work with what one has got, in her case her father's 'large' hands, which signify masculinity.

> Debbie: =then I also have my father's large hands rather than my mother's small hands, so (.) you gotta work with what you've got (women's focus group).

The imperative to work ('with what you've got') on one's femininity, health and beauty, the valuing of achievements in these domains, but equally the near impossibility of achieving the 'postulated ideals' without special help, were also evident in the following excerpts from the women's focus group discussion. Here, 'large' women celebrities were construed as positive role models for what fat women can achieve. However, if they lost weight they were simultaneously positioned as traitors to those who had looked up to them as through their weight loss they failed in making fat women more visible and acceptable (see Chapter 3; Tischner and Malson, 2008). On the one hand they were positioned as everybody else, and under 'the same pressures to be *normal*', but on the other hand as privileged and thereby not representative of the women in my focus group:

> Debbie: But I also think a lot of the positive, the [fat] women who were positive images on the telly (.) often, I'm not gonna say sell out because that's wrong, because sort, for me losing weight is all about health and not about image / hmm / but they *have* lost weight, so Vanessa Feltz / hmm / and, uhm, Fern Britton.
>
> Emma: But equally, famously they / then put / you know then they put it back on again / yeah / yeah.
>
> Lucy: But aren't they, even though they, we, we're trying to cite them as positive role models, they are still under the same pressures / hmm / to be (.) *normal* / hmm / that we are / hmm / (women's focus group).

'Large' successful celebrities, who are visible in the media, are construed as positive role models for fat women to be happy with their size and as examples for the possibility of being successful and in the public eye, despite being fat. This links back to my arguments in Chapter 3 where I coined the phrase 'fat efficacy' for the potentially positive effect a greater visibility of 'large' women may have on fat acceptance and the experience of 'being large' for fat individuals generally. Despite citing the celebrities as positive role models first of all, Debbie goes on to draw on a medical discourse, constructing fat as unhealthy and thereby positioning herself and other 'large' individuals as unhealthy fat people. This discourse of body size = health is ubiquitous and goes mostly unchallenged; by fat and 'slim' people alike (Campos, 2004; Department of Health, 2008b; Orbach, 2006a). It has taken on the form of a commonsensical truth, which is difficult to reject (Aphramor, 2008b; Malson, 2008). The resulting pressures to be thin are construed as ubiquitous, as not stopping at celebrities, who also have to try and be *'normal'*.

When these celebrities intentionally lose weight, however, it is constructed as a let-down to the cause of fat people, as 'selling out' to society and the pressures there are on them. Their weight loss is construed as sending out the message to other fat individuals and society that being 'large' is bad, and losing weight is healthy and possible to achieve after all. This last message is rejected by the women in the focus group however:

> Judy: But what do they do? Have they got the money to go to a private nutritionist or something?
>
> Debbie: Well, Vanessa did, didn't she, she had her own private fitness instructor and cook (inaudible).
>
> Unidentified: Well, there you go (women's focus group).

In terms of how they cope with the pressures and deal with striving to be normal, that is thin, the celebrities are being construed as different, as not 'one of us', as a privileged group who do not have to deal with the daily grind of losing weight in the same way as everybody else. They have and deploy special resources in the form of personal trainers and nutritionists, which are not accessible to the women in my study. Success or otherwise in the area of weight loss is construed here as dependent on one's financial situation. By referring to the privileged status of fat celebrities, my participants reject the imposed neoliberal subject position of the agentic individual who can easily change her body weight and health at will.

In contrast to the celebrities' privileged way of losing weight, the women in my study construed lifelong overweight as a never-ending battle, a lifelong project of physical improvement:

> Lucy: I went to a dietician when I was 7 / hmm / because I was picked up by the health screening at school as being overweight, and (.) that was the beginning. Dietician when I was 7 and diets (.) ever since (.) (women's focus group).

> Debbie: I was a size 16 going to comprehensive school, and look [. . .] I think, crikey, size 16, I'd *love* to be a size 16 but, looking back I felt enormous going to school / yeah / and I was the biggest girl in the school / hmm (women's focus group).

In the above excerpts, Lucy and Debbie construe their lives as constant, imposed battles with their weight, in relation to both health and appearance, from an early age. As I have argued above, constructs of femininity, health, beauty and fat converge on the fat woman's body, positioning her as inferior and in constant need of improvement, which is reflected in these quotes. In neoliberal Western societies, self-improvement is imperative and considered achievable (Malson, 2008; Rose, 1996); for women generally, and 'large' women in particular, self-improvement is closely associated with controlling one's weight via one's diet.

Diets, food, freedom and trouble[6]

> =Judy: You cannot buy a woman's magazine now, without it offering you a *diet* on the front page, to make you feel as if, if you're a woman you gotta be on a diet, if you're fat you gotta be on a diet / hmm / and you *cannot* get away from it, wherever you move (women's focus group).

Looking at the above quote and (women's) magazines generally, dieting is construed as a woman's and a fat person's duty. In discourses of health, discourses of beauty and discourses of femininity, this imperative for women *not* to eat is multiply and continuously (re)constructed. These discourses are prevalent not only in the media or health promotion literature, however; indeed, we encounter them in common narratives on a daily basis. On a recent trip to Munich, I was reminded of this 'female duty' to watch my calorie intake and to choose diet drinks (and foods) by a (female) member of the cabin crew.

When offered a drink, I asked for a can of Coke, and was promptly presented with a can of *Diet* Coke. I responded to the offer by saying: 'Could I have "proper" Coke, please?' The member of the cabin crew, pointing to the red non-diet Coke can on her trolley, with an incredulous tone in her voice asked: 'This one?' and after my confirmation added: 'It's just that ladies don't ask for Diet Coke, but always mean it'. It seems that Diet Coke is construed as the standard for 'ladies'.

The choices of how much and what we eat, in order to control and influence our health, body size and how other people perceive us, are examples of what Michel Foucault termed technologies of the self:

> [T]echnologies of the self, which permit individuals to effect by their own means, or with the help of others, a certain number of operations on their own bodies and souls, thoughts, conduct, and way of being, so as to transform themselves in order to attain a certain state of happiness, purity, wisdom, perfection, or immortality.

> (Foucault, 1997, p. 225)

What passes as wise or 'perfect', or in terms of my research healthy, beautiful, feminine or sexually attractive, is culturally and socially specific; constructed, maintained and circulated through discourses not only in texts but also images, day-to-day talk and actions. Our technologies of the self, i.e. our health and beauty practices, are regulated in and through these discourses, which are inherently gendered – in contemporary society the culturally produced requirement for continuous self-scrutiny and self-improvement is a lot greater for women than for men (Gill, 2007). As articulated in the excerpt above, there is no escaping the discourses of health and beauty that construct women as 'ideally' always dieting, and dieting/not eating as signifying femininity. This construction of dieting as a feminine practice reflects Vartanian *et al.*'s (2007) findings that what and how we eat is highly gendered and that eating a healthy diet of modest amounts signifies femininity. This social association of femininity/masculinity with eating habits and healthcare practices (Sloan *et al.*, 2010) may have contributed to the reluctance of the men in my study to talk about their own health concerns, and their tendency to construe a focus on appearance and health as feminine. There seems to be a fear of a potential feminisation through health and diet talk, which does not sit well with a hegemonic masculine identity (Robertson, 2006; Watson, 2000). Recent research indicates that, with the increase in pressure on men to fulfil a certain bodily ideal, dieting and looking after one's health as a man seem to be gaining in acceptance, too (Monaghan, 2008b). The extent of self-scrutiny and self-improvement required of men seems generally a lot less, however (Gill, 2007), and in relation to dieting the focus appears to be on health only; men are dieting when weight loss is reconstructed as a positive, healthy behaviour, while for women dieting is associated with health *and* looks, with the latter being the feminised, frivolous purpose of weight loss.

In my research, the increased social pressure on women was constructed in the men's focus group as counterproductive and harmful:

Rich: I think that sort of diet thing is, must be, *must be*, I cannot say *it is*, but I, but I would imagine it must be a great deal worse [for women] / I: hmm / In my view it must be a great deal worse (.)

I: In what way?

Rich: All the social pressure to, to, to not eat / I: mhm / uhm (.) which is basically, I mean, the whole way through, it's an unhealthy thing because what it ends up doing is [. . .] you tend to eat more and more privately / Don: mhm / (.) which means it's actually doing the opposite / Don: mhm / you know the social pressure is actually having the opposite effect to what (.) you would imagine the social pressure would. You'd think the social pressure would, would depress somebody's eating when act-, in fact it's pushing the eating into a private place / I: mhm / where it can actually be (.) uhm (.) more, you know, they could be eating more, and *more* unsuitably, because uhm, because what you eat in private tends to be (.) you know portable (inaudible) tasty foods tend to be much worse for you / Don + I: hmm / (..) (men's focus group).

As in previous accounts, women are depicted as worse off in terms of body size pressures, and here in particular it is 'the diet thing' which women are seen as struggling with to a greater extent. Drawing on everyday understandings of criminal(ised) practices such as drug-taking, Rich construes these pressures as counterproductive, as they only get 'push[ed] . . . into a private place' and thus encourage over-indulgence. 'Counterproductive', presumably in the campaign to reduce the nation's waist line and improve health – importantly, whilst Rich articulates a 'woman-friendly' account in critiquing 'the diet thing', he also reproduces the discourses which constitute good and bad foods and quantities of food, as well as women as 'unsuitably' overindulging in the wrong thing when not under surveillance.

The above reminds us of Susan Bordo's (1993) analysis of advertisements for food products, where she found that if, women were depicted as eating in public, they do so in a constrained way; hidden away, behind 'do not disturb signs', however, we can see them indulging in food. Bordo asserts that 'female eating is virtually always represented as private, secretive, illicit' (p. 129) and she links this also to Victorian times, when the display of unrestrained appetite was deemed unseemly for women. With eating practices thus closely linked to the construction of femininity, Bordo (1993) also associates these cultural rules with disordered eating practices:

> The representation of unrestrained appetite as inappropriate for women, the depiction of female eating as a private, transgressive act, make restriction and denial of hunger central features of the construction of femininity and set up the compensatory binge as a virtual inevitability.
>
> (Bordo, 1993, p. 130)

However, in contrast to the men's focus group, where the act of eating in private was constructed as unsuitable, even illicit and as something detrimental to women, in the women's focus group the same behaviour was constituted as an act of freedom and rebellion.

> Judy: I don't think I was *really* fat until I, after I'd had the children, but the *real* problem started when I left my husband and I was allowed to do what I wanted to do for the first time in my life (..) I can eat when I want, and eat what I want, whenever I want (.)

> Debbie: The same thing happened to me when my mother died. I went from (..) not, only having chocolate on the weekends or whatever and then mum died and I could have chocolate every night of the week if I wanted to, so I did / yeah / and I've grown 10 stone within (.) 3 years / yeah / (women's focus group).

> Linda: I eat, I eat (..) I wouldn't eat a pudding [when eating out with mum] because I would, mum would frown upon that, uhm, I probably wouldn't have starters, I probably just have a main course and it probably would be [collective laughter] salad

Lucy: Trouble *is*, you then go home afterwards =[laughter]= and you make up for it / several: oh yeah / because it's that reaction, it's like 'now I *can* have what *I* want to have' / yeah, it is isn't it / (..) (women's focus group).

After having been controlled by various others in their eating practices, the women construe themselves here as finally grasping some freedom by eating what and how much they choose to. In contrast to the men's accounts, where the pressure was constituted as deriving from society in general, here the control is exerted more directly by close others. With the exception of Judy, the women position themselves as rebelling against maternal (or the spouse's) disapproval. Similar discourses of rebellion are active here as those described by Deborah Lupton (1996) in her work on young adults who enjoy a never-known control over what they could and could eat once they move out from home. Within these discourses the women position themselves as agentic rebels, finally enjoying self-determination over their food consumption. However, this subject position of the indulging and eating rebel is not unambiguous, as this rebellion, this freedom of eating, is still happening in secret, behind the 'do not disturb signs'. Holding the discourses of overeating, which positions the fat woman as overindulging in place, the practice of eating what one wants in private is constituted as 'trouble'. The collective laughter Lucy's comment receives constitutes these eating behaviours as 'naughty', as something they possibly should not do; thus the maternal and patriarchal control is constructed as something they rebel against but, not dissimilar to a mother's control over her children, it is appropriate and/or required to keep them in line, thus also infantilising (fat) women.

Dis/integrated feminine/masculine selves

The issue of 'eating in secret' is close to the theme of in/visibility. As I have argued in Chapter 3, in/visibility plays a vital part in the dynamic construction of fat women's subject positions, which was again articulated during the focus group discussions.

Emma: And I *do*, I *do* find as well when uhm (.) even the really close circle of friends that I got in [city], *really*, really supportive women of similar age and things, I'm, I am always very careful what I eat when I'm with them (.) / hmm / (.) because I don't want to be seen to overeat / several: yeah / by them. (women's focus group).

To be seen to be eating too much, as a fat woman, is construed here as problematic, and how much one is eating is thus subject to self-policing even within a close circle of 'really supportive women'. This awareness of one's visibility, of being seen and what will be 'read' from one's appearance, as well as concerns about certain body parts, is constructed by the women's group as a problem all women, not just fat women, have to cope with:

Emma: Yeah (..) it, what would be interesting would be whether the size, you know, 10s and 11, 12s in this world, how often *they* feel attractive, or whether they think, 'oh my bum looks big in this, or my', you know

Debbie: They *do* actually, I've got a friend /Emma =it's people's perceptions/ she's a size 8 and she, she says 'oh, my bum's really big' / [quiet laughter]/ and I was like 'yeah, right, OK' / [laughter] / and then she, she asked me to go for coffee one day and I went 'couldn't possibly walk down the corridor with you, your bum is *far* too big'=

=[collective laughter]=

=and she felt really upset, and I'm like 'uh, irony?'

[collective laughter]

Debbie: So, yeah, I, I think whatever size you are, you, you hate certain lumps and bumps about yourself (women's focus group).

How often do we encounter the question 'does my bum look big in this?' in day-to-day life and in the media? Frequently used by men (but also women) referring to women's irrational and exaggerated concerns with their appearance, and often in the context of a joke, we are reminded of women's vigilant and constant self-scrutiny over concerns about how others will judge their bodies and individual body parts. Expressions like 'whatever size you are, you, you hate certain lumps and bumps about yourself' reflect the construction of women's bodies as a collection of body parts rather than as an integrated whole, which was apparent in various places in my study. This dislike of, and focus on, often 'imperfect' body parts can be interpreted in the context of the body project, discussed above, where the identification of physical characteristics that need improving is essential. The above account can also be seen as drawing on the discourse of Cartesian dualism in which women are constituted as critical observers of their own bodies such that the scrutinising subject/mind is separated from the body constituted as an object of her critical gaze.

Within Cartesian dualism the body is constructed as a separate, inferior entity to the mind, and as something which needs to be controlled by the mind (Spelman, 1982). And, as argued above, within dualistic patriarchal discourses, women are associated with the (uncontrolled) body, while men are associated with the (rational) mind (Bordo, 1993). As I will outline in the following, my data reflects a complex web of dynamic constructions and subject positions where, on the one hand, women's bodies are constituted as fragmented collections of often faulty body parts (Martin, 1989; Young, 1998/1990) but at the same time women are construed and entirely defined by their bodies. A woman's body, and particularly her body size, is produced as the master signifier of her subjectivities and worth.

This metonymy of the fat woman's body for the woman's entire being was evident within the focus group discussions:

Don: Yeah, I'm I'm sure you're right (.) I can think of one example (.) a work colleague (.) was very upset. She'd been to a night club and (.) and another woman called her a heifer (.) which I think, was to compound a number of insults / I: hmm / but it's clearly ai- uh, aimed at her, her weight, because this person's (.) a b-, a bit overweight (.) and so (..) (inaudible) again no insinuation but I think if a man wanted to insult me, he probably wouldn't say (.) fat bloke or something / I: hmm / uh, probably choose some some other epithet, it wouldn't be, one that would spring to mind / I: mhm / 'cause, because I'm a man (inaudible) my feeling= (men's focus group).

Rich: I think quite often when, when a woman does something wrong, *fat* will get in, will get attached to it / Don: hmm / (.) will get at-, attached to the description / I: mhm / uhm, to to sort of add another bit of edge to the (.) to to to the insult as it were. [. . .] (men's focus group).

Judy: If you're going looking for new jobs in new places and you're overweight, you just walk in the room and people get that instant impression 'she hasn't got control over her body, so' you know 'she's no good' (women's focus group).

While women construct themselves as fragmented, their 'largeness' takes on master status and is read as the whole self. This metonymy of fat for ugly, inferior, out of control, incapable, and so forth is used in insults and negative comments towards and about women. Notwithstanding research reporting otherwise (Lupton, 1996; Monaghan, 2008a), the men in my study construed 'fat as insult' as applying exclusively to women. In the account above, the adjective 'fat' 'adds an edge' to any insult, connoting the general inferiority of the woman in question, precisely because the body stands metonymically for the whole woman and female fat is metonymic of everything negative.

The construction of women's bodies as metonymic of their whole selves was part of a complex and gendered dynamic, apparent in my data, around the signification of the whole body versus parts of the body. Within this dynamic, women and men were positioned in quite different relationships with their bodies. This is evident in the following quote in which men's fatness is construed quite differently to the constructions of women's fatness, discussed above:

Emma: It's probably more acceptable for a man to be heavier than a woman / hmm /

Lucy: That that's partly to do with the way that a man puts on weight in that they tend to put it on here [pointing to stomach area] you know, and their arms and their legs and everything can be relatively *normally* proportioned / I: so it's more the beer belly / with just a big stomach

Judy: yeah and the beer belly is (a cause) of laughter, isn't it / yeah / (women's focus group).

In this excerpt not only is it 'probably more acceptable for a man to be heavier than for a woman' but a 'beer belly' is constructed as just one part of a man's body. It does not much affect the whole, otherwise 'relatively *normally* proportioned' male physique. In the excerpt below men's fatness is again construed as more acceptable and as just *one* aspect of a man.

> Rich: hmm (..) I think the thing I always felt is that I don't *feel* overweight (.) *I* don't, when I look at myself in the mirror I am surprised / I: mhm / at my size (.) because I don't feel like that / I: mhm / probably because (.) nobody *does*, they (know) you are the size *you are*, that's that's *you* / I: mhm / you know, that's, that's how you feel, and you feel completely normal, cause you know nothing, nothing else to judge it on / I: hmm /. [. . .] *if you're*, like I've been all my life (.) chronically overweight (.) *that's*, that's *me* / I: hmm / I don't *feel* overweight / Don: hmm / I feel *me* / I: hmm / I think that's the, the, the (.) the thing, really, uhm it probably is, it's probably (.) *quite* a difference from people who've always been overweight to people who've put on weight / I: mhm / I would guess / I: hmm/
>
> I: You adjust to it
>
> Rich: yes, yeah, I think, cause I've always, I, I mean I'm (.) I'm *more* overweight now than I was in the past / I: hmm / but I have always been overweight / I: hmm / uh, all my life / I: hmm / (.) and uh, so, you know, that's *me*, that's the way I am (..) I'm the same you know (men's focus group).

Whereas, in the excerpt from the women's focus group, male fatness is presented as affecting only part of the male body, in this excerpt men's fatness, and by extension their bodies, are construed as only one part of *them* that does not in itself and by itself define the whole man. This is similar to Wynne's quote above, in which tallness, as a signifier of masculinity and power, dwarfed the negative connotations of fatness, and contrasts strongly with the focus group excerpt where the fat woman at a job interview is judged in her entirety on body size. Rich talks about the reflection of his body in the mirror surprising him, but this is not construed as an ignorance of his body, but rather as an integration, and acceptance of his body size as just one aspect of himself. This integrated whole of a man, fat body and all, is construed as just 'being himself' and being accepted just as he is – by himself and by others. Much like the beer belly which doesn't spill over to produce the rest of the male body as fat, being overweight is just one part of the bigger picture of who Rich is: it doesn't define that picture.

This chimes with Helen Malson's argument (1998) that masculinity is more easily defined 'independently of physical appearance' (p. 106) than femininity. With men being culturally associated with the rational mind, their body does not feature strongly enough to define their whole being solely or their (masculine) identity. Tony Coles' term of 'mosaic masculinities' (2008) lends itself to the interpretation of the way body size is being constructed as only a part of the whole man.

Mosaic masculinities refers to the process by which men negotiate masculinity, drawing upon fragments or pieces of hegemonic masculinity which they have the capacity to perform and piecing them together to reformulate what masculinity means to them in order to come up with their own dominant standard of masculinity.

(Coles, 2008)

As in Rich's account above, the 'fat body' is presented as only one fragment of a man's identity, that is made insignificant in its negative aspects when others, or the men themselves, consider them(selves), their subjectivity and positioning in society and life – other aspects of their lives and/or subjectivities count as much as, or more than, body size and there are alternative discursive repertoires available for men to position themselves as 'proper men' (Sloan *et al.*, 2010). Linked to this is the construction of lifelong overweight as something that one adjusts to, something that just becomes absorbed into a man's being and does not feature separately any more in life's struggles or projects. In contrast to the women's constitution of lifelong fatness as an eternal battle, lifelong fatness, at least in comparison to sudden weight change, is construed by Rich as something that allows him to forget about it, as that is simply how he is.

Rich: I've been all my life (.) chronically overweight (.) *that's*, that's *me* / I: hmm / I don't *feel* overweight / Don: hmm / I feel *me* (men's focus group).

To conclude on gender and fat

Despite an increasing pressure on men to aspire towards an idealised tall, strong, muscular and lean body, 'large' women were construed by both men and women in my study as under more pressure to be slim, and as experiencing greater difficulties due to their body size.

While the 'slim' female body is a signifier of 'ideal' femininity, it also signifies inferiority of women to men, and incapability in socially designated 'masculine' occupations. This construction of femininity as small in effect disqualifies fat women from femininity. However, this 'defeminisation' of 'large' women was construed as positive within the (male-dominated) workplace where being seen as less feminine also meant a recognition of one's capabilities. Their body size allows fat women in these environments to take up 'better', more respected subject positions; however, this dynamic also reflects and reinforces the construction of women as 'other' and inferior to men. Only by reducing their differences to men do they 'rise in status', and what is socially constructed as 'masculine' qualities, and thus men, remains the benchmark (Gatens, 1991; Wetherell, 1986). Certain, very specific, conditions seemed to be a prerequisite for these, what was construed as positive, effects of a 'large' body, while an association of fat with lack of control seems more common.

The issue of control in relation to women's body size was a prominent theme within my research. The discursive constructions and significations of fat and of women's bodies converge on the 'large' woman's body, in as much as her body size is construed as a signifier for a lack of self-control, self-containment and a threat to (patriarchal) order. This threat is contained through a positioning of 'large' women within health, femininity and beauty discourses as in need of improvement through self-perfection, self-scrutiny and a lifelong battle with body weight. Women are not just passive dupes within these complex discursive systems and dynamics of power, however, but position themselves as active agents within these body and femininity projects. They construe themselves as working on and with their bodies. They simultaneously accept and reject the subject positions of the 'troubled' eater on the one hand and rebel on the other hand, in their accounts of eating with other people and in private. There is an ambiguity between taking control over their food intake by eating in private, and at the same time construing this private eating as a problematic course of action.

The final issue I wanted to draw attention to was the complex dynamic around the construction of men's and women's bodies as integrated and fragmented entities respectively, and the contrasting definition of women and men by their bodies. My data reflected what has been theorised elsewhere, that women are defined in their whole being by their body. However, at the same time the women in my study were construing themselves as a mosaic of (faulty) body parts. Men on the other hand construed themselves, and are generally discursively constituted as, whole, integrated selves; here, a socially constructed less than perfect part, for example a beer belly, or one characteristic of their body, for instance being fat, takes back stage, is rendered as less significant. Men seem to have a greater variety of discursive resources available for the construction of their own hegemonic masculinity (Coles, 2008) than women have in relation to femininity. For women the body always takes centre stage and is metonymic for their entire self.

The power relations implicated in the above constructions and accepted/rejected subject positions of fat men and women are still very much signs of masculine hegemony. Fat women are entangled in a discursive health/beauty/femininity triplex which positions them as inferior to slim women as well as (fat and slim) men on a variety of axes. Some of the dynamics around the construction of femininity and masculinity, control, ability, and so forth, are clearly not only applicable to 'large' women and men but to people in Western industrial nations generally. However, although I have also identified a small number of positive constructions of fat bodies, and consequently the availability of more positive subject positions to fat individuals, I would still argue that some of the oppressive and negative effects of the politics around body size and 'gender' are amplified for fat women.

This concludes my empirical analyses of the experience of being 'large'. Not surprisingly, the theme of 'gender' runs through all four themes explored and many of the discourses and power relationships identified are highly gendered. However, the main message I would like to highlight from this analysis is the dynamic, varied and at times contradictory nature of subjectivities and subject positions available, taken up and rejected by fat individuals, which emphasises the heterogeneity within the population of 'large' people, the cultures they live in and the discourses and power relations they are regulated within (Probyn, 2009). This heterogeneity has implications, I believe, not only for health promotion, but also for how we approach researching and advocating for certain population sectors: we cannot afford to treat socially constructed categories as homogeneous groups. The final chapter will draw out these implications further.

7   Conclusions

The experience of being fat

The predominant topics or themes I identified in my exploration of 'fat lives' were 'being in/visible', restrictions in identity construction (and other aspects of life) due to the lack of choice in clothes, health and being always-already constituted as unhealthy, as well as issues of gendered pressures and gender identity. I could have chosen other themes, including matters of space or the topic of relationships and attraction. The chosen subjects were present in the majority of the interviews, but ultimately what I have explored at a deeper level remains my very subjective choice. This inherent subjectivity, as well as my acute awareness of all the power axes that are operational in the embodied lives of the fat person which I have *not* explored or considered, remind me of the following cautionary note by Susan Bordo:

> We also should have learned that while it is imperative to struggle continually against racism and ethnocentrism in all its forms, it is impossible to be 'politically correct'. For the dynamics of inclusion and exclusion . . . are played out on multiple and shifting fronts, and all ideas (no matter how 'liberatory' in some contexts or for some purposes) are condemned to be haunted by a voice from the margins, already speaking . . . awakening us to what has been excluded, effaced, damaged.
>
> (Bordo, 1990, p. 138)

Bordo's statement is somewhat ideologically dis-illusionary, and indeed the lack of discussion around issues such as class, sexuality, religion, physical ability, ethnicity (the list goes on) is concerning me probably more than the satisfaction I feel over drawing attention to the very important issues I have raised in this book. Of course there are valid reasons for the level of analysis undertaken, such as the self-selection of participants who then turned out to be (with one exception) from predominantly white, Caucasian backgrounds. Equally, and as mentioned in previous chapters, the issue of gender was not raised in the interviews with my women participants and similar comments can probably also be made of the other power axes listed above: they did not form predominant themes in my data. Does this sufficiently justify their emission from the discussion of fat embodiment, however? Maybe not, but for myself and the research presented in this book, I answered Bordo's question as to 'just how many axes *can* one include and still preserve analytical focus or argument?' (Bordo, 1990, p. 139), with a 'not that many' and accepted my limitations while acknowledging the 'voices from the margins', hoping to return to them at some point in the future.

As a result of these considerations, however, I would like to distance myself from any potential (mis)reading of my work as an attempt at a generalisation of how fat people see or experience themselves and their bodies. The analysis offered in this book can only ever be an interpretation of the discursive constructions offered by a very particular group of people (i.e. those kind enough to take part in my research), read in consideration and conjunction with a variety of theories on the body and 'obesity'. Subject positions are dynamically constituted and reconstituted in the discourses deployed by participants. Their positioning within them and the subjectivities they produce will always be shifting, varied, diverse and sometimes contradictory. So, despite pointing towards ways for positive changes or reforms, on the basis of my reading and analysis, I would not want to claim that generalisations can be drawn from what is presented here to all fat individuals – this, of course, is the case for any piece of research. I would assert, however, that lessons can indeed be learnt from the narratives of my participants, in particular in relation to health promotion strategies and the construction and use of 'facts' or 'certainties' (Rich and Evans, 2005) within them. The power relations produced within the discourses deployed facilitate inequalities and oppression, to the detriment of many. Notwithstanding the limitations of this research, I believe it reinforces the importance of not treating any research population as one homo-geneous group – whether it be women, men or fat individuals (and from any age, class or religious or ethnic background). In my mind, such a dangerous homo-genisation is currently prevalent in current health promotion campaigns and dominant health discourses generally – I hope I have succeeded in at least challenging this reductionist and harmful take on fat.

In the following I will briefly summarise my analysis, by pulling out some predominant 'themes' that ran through most of the data, namely the construction of the self and the fat body within the narratives of my participants, leading into, and obviously connected to, the construction of femininities and masculinities. I will conclude this section with an exploration of the dis/empowering effects and regulation of practices produced within the discourses drawn on in the interviews. This summary of my analyses will be followed by a discussion of the implications of my work.

Fat feminine and masculine 'selves'

A lot of the subject positions that are regularly imposed on fat individuals were unsurprisingly rejected by the women and men in my research. These stereotypical subject positions include the 'lazy fat individual' who does not move, 'sitting at home flicking round watching the telly uhm (.) with the Chinese on [their] lap' (Ally), the large woman as indifferent to her appearance and the stupid, uneducated fat person who does not know what is or is not considered a healthy lifestyle.

These rejections were quite unanimous, while the constructions of subjectivities and subject positions taken up were a lot more dynamic, multifaceted and in places also contradictory.

Contrary to common constructions – in the general media and by health promotion agencies – of 'large' individuals as not informed or educated enough to know what is 'good for them', most of the women in my study positioned themselves not only as healthy but also as experts on diet, nutrition and exercise. Amongst other discourses they drew on discourses of biomedicine and well-being, constructing 'health' as consisting of biomedical indicators like blood pressure and cholesterol levels and the absence of disease. As I have discussed in Chapter 5, this positioning as lifestyle and health experts can work as a double-edged sword for the fat individual as it is grounded in the very same discourses that constitute fat as disease and the fat individual as pathological. But my participants also deployed discourses of physical and mental well-being and thus broadened the construction of health beyond medical indicators. The choice of a 'healthy' lifestyle was construed as an important factor for this holistic feeling of well-being. And, drawing on discourses of nutrition, psychology and physical activity, the women frequently positioned themselves as 'good citizens' who adhered to all the advice available on healthy lifestyles and in fact as knowing and doing more for their health than the average 'non-obese' person. In some places, losing weight was indeed produced as one aspect of looking after their long-term health, but body weight was constituted by many of the women as not the major problem that it is often constructed as socially; rather body weight figured as just one part of the jigsaw of health. It was constructed as a fragment within a mosaic of health, which sometimes had to be relegated to a lower priority in the bigger scheme of things, and which did not solely determine a person's health or indeed the entire person.

The metonymy of fat for the whole fat person, which is so often constituted in popular discourses like the 'New year, new you' slogans in weight loss promotions, or statements heard on weight loss reality TV shows like 'I'm determined to change the person I am' (ITV, 2012), is thus also challenged. And while these women took up a neoliberal position in rearticulating notions of a lifestyle-induced, personally achievable good state of health, they were also critical of the weight-focused definition of perfect health. This rigid characterisation of health was constructed as unrealistic in today's society. Compromises were seen as unavoidable, and body weight as only one of the factors in a holistic picture of health, which thus should and could not take a superior rank in their decision-making processes around health.

As well as the pathologisation of their fat bodies, some of the women in my study also rejected the construction of their bodies, and by association themselves, as unattractive. Society, on the other hand, was constituted as a problem that made life as a fat person difficult. Most of the women positioned themselves as attractive and/or appearance-concerned women who looked after themselves; the clothes that were available for them to buy on the other hand were constituted as spoiling this positive subject position for them. These inferior, unstylish and at best conformist clothes position 'large' women as scruffy and inferior, and my participants constituted themselves as frustrated and as having an inferior 'self' imposed on them. The women were struggling with the reconciliation of their (naked) sub-jectivities as attractive and lovable people on the one hand, and the prevailing discursive constructions of fat women as unattractive and not worth considering in relation to romantic love on the other. The women in my study constituted themselves as marginalised and excluded from and by society through a nor-malising, judgemental gaze, as well as the built environment which positioned them as not fitting the norm and as inferior.

In general, the subject positions constructed and accepted by my participants were dynamic and multiple and at times contradictory and never monolithic. This was in contrast to their positioning within narratives of discrimination, marginalisation and moral and health judgements. Within these latter discourses the fat female body appeared as metonymic of the whole person, her subjectivity, lifestyle, history, medical status, and so forth. The women construed themselves as judged by others on the basis of their body weight and shape only – their body obtained master status over their whole being. This was quite different for men, for whom body weight was construed as only *one* aspect of themselves, both in the men's and the women's narratives. Considering that generally men are associated with the mind, while women are associated with the body (Bordo, 1993), it should not surprise us that within such discourses of Cartesian dualism, a physical feature will define a woman wholly, while it is just one feature of their whole self for men, or one fragment within what Tony Coles calls 'mosaic masculinities' (Coles, 2008, p. 238). The body can be a major part of a man's subjectivity, or not – depending on what other mosaic fragments are available. Not so for women, as they are always-already defined by their bodies (Bordo, 1993, 1998; Levene and Gleeson, 2003; Weitz, 2003), which may also explain why women's bodies were constituted in the narratives of the women and men as fragmented, with individual body parts receiving special attention. This relates to Iris Young's (1998/1990) analysis of women's bodies being experienced as a burden that has to be dragged around, an object which needs manipulating and correcting in its details. Men's bodies, on the other hand, were construed as a unified whole that formed part of an integrated, embodied self – as Rich said: 'that's *me* [. . .] I don't *feel* overweight [. . .] I feel *me*.

This leads me to the construction of femininities and masculinities in my data. Within contemporary Western cultures, a slim body has more and more become a signifier of femininity and 'being a woman' is inherently linked to the perpetuation of the thin ideal (Germov and Williams, 1999, p. 128); as such being fat defeminises women within discourses of femininity. As discussed above, in contrast to women, the discursive resources available for the construction of a masculine identity are much broader than physical attributes. Femininity on the other hand is signified to a great extent through the body, and the women in my study construed themselves as positioned at the margins of femininity within heterosexual romantic discourses, and narratives on clothes, appearance and beauty, but interestingly also in relation to capability in male-dominated workplaces. Here, being on the margins of femininity seemed to bestow certain male characteristics and thus benefits on fat women and some women constructed the defeminising effect of the fat body thus as empowering. In the men's narratives masculinity was also frequently construed as 'not feminine', that is, as not caring about one's appearance, and as not worrying about one's weight or health, both characteristics associated with women. However, for fat women in male-dominated workplaces, being considered not feminine (as a woman) was also constructed as having additional benefits.

The female body is socially constructed as weaker and generally less able (Weitz, 2003). Being 'large' was construed as attracting more respect and clout in certain situations for both men and women. Similar to Sara Crawley's (2002) account of embodying capability through wearing 'butch' or masculine clothes, being considered less feminine due to being fat was constituted in my research as also being considered stronger and more capable. On the flip side, however, and drawing attention to the imposition rather than choice of femininity/masculinity, fat women were also positioned as not being *allowed* to perform their femininity, for instance through clothes. Going clothes shopping and having an interest in fashion was constructed as something women do and the women in my study felt excluded from this feminine activity by the unavailability of stylish clothes and the segregation of large-size merchandise from the normatively sized one.

Fat politics of power

The power relations implicated in the discourses of body size were equally multiple and dynamic. While men, and some women, felt empowered through their size, generally the women constituted themselves as marginalised in society and as disempowered. While constructing *themselves* as healthy and attractive, for example, women were also caught in and struggled with the dominant discourses of health and beauty that positioned them as pathological and heterosexually unattractive, in need of treatment and a free-for-all target for 'advice', discrimination and insult. Within a neoliberal, healthist and Panopticon culture, the participants in my study constituted themselves as objects of stares, scrutiny and judgement. As such, while rejecting the above-mentioned negative subject positions and forging out positive subjectivities for themselves, most of the women also constituted themselves as evading direct confrontation with the dominant system and its discourses, by avoiding consultations with health professionals, by not watching weight loss TV shows, and by generally hiding their bodies.

However, some of the women also positioned themselves and other women as part of this system of surveillance and regulation, not only in respect to self-scrutiny but also as active agents within this Panopticon system of mutual surveillance. So, while these positionings of fat women reflect Foucault's (1977) notion of the normalising and disciplining gaze and the regulative power relations it produces, these women are not just 'docile bodies' that are merely passively inscribed by the often gendered discourses of fat. They are both subjects and objects within the discourses deployed in the women's narratives, with multiple subject positions being produced, taken up and rejected in dynamic and sometimes contradictory ways. This challenges not only the mainstream psychological perspective of a unified and rational individual mind, which needs to be manipulated by education and intervention in order to produce what is socially constructed as healthy and responsible behaviour. It also raises questions for critical psychology, including feminist research, which in their political endeavours to identify and support disempowered sectors of the population may equally homogenise these groups and thus reinforce societal divisions and regulation (cf. Butler, 1999, on gender).

I agree with Elspeth Probyn (2009) that the issue of fat is way too complex, and subjectivities and bodies too dynamic to be considered just from one perspective. Probyn focuses in her critique on the currently frequent body image approach taken to feminist research on women's bodies and fat bodies in particular (Coleman, 2008). She insists that this 'static' view of the body divorces it from all the other social forces at play in the production of fat-embodied subjectivities, and that economic, social and geopolitical conditions need to be brought into the equation. In relation to fat individuals, if representations of the fat body are the main thing that feminist action and research are indeed concerned about, this strong concentrated focus on the body may also reify and reproduce the metonymy of fat and the fat body.

In this context Probyn (2009) also questions semiotic reversal, that is, a positive constitution of the fat woman through an increase in her visibility in the media, as a valid feminist strategy. I agree that semiotic reversal that focuses purely on images as the only form of representation may be a restrictive and potentially counter-productive strategy. Therefore, I would like to extend 'semiotic reversal' to embodied *practices*, to being seen as a fat woman in clothes, occupations and activities that were commonly 'reserved' for normatively sized individuals. These embodied practices, rather than purely an increase in the 'positive' representation of fat women in the media, were constructed, in my study, as empowering and normalising of the fat woman within society, reducing stigma and discrimination in the long run. Rather than simply trying to reconstruct the 'image' of the fat person and being mainly focused on the empowerment of the individual fat woman – a critique Samantha Murray raises against fat acceptance activism in her excellent book *The Fat Female Body* (2008) – these embodied practices were constituted by my participants as having an effect on society and the positioning of fat individuals within it generally.

It is important, even if only as one facet of a number of possible avenues, to challenge the prevailing discourses on fat, and the representation and positioning of fat individuals within them. Anti-fat discourses are getting stronger and are drawing more and more on neoliberal discourses of responsibility, shame and guilt – not only for the individual but for the nation. This discursive development is noticeable, for example, in the already-mentioned reality TV show *The Biggest Loser*. Over the years, the narrative of responsibility for others has increased, and contestants are increasingly made accountable to the public. For instance, in the most current editions of this programme contestants are weighed, and have to 'confess' their behaviours that allegedly made them fat, in very public places and in front of not only friends and family but the general public. Contestants are portrayed as diseased, unattractive, with a short life expectancy and as incapable of carrying out their duties as husbands, mothers or wives as well as they should. A counter-discourse and counter-representations need to be established to challenge the taken-for-granted truths about fat in official health promotion discourses but also in day-to-day life and popular culture.

The role of the 'right' methodology

My research generally reinforces the poststructuralist notion of the dynamic and fragmented self, and illustrates that we cannot assume homogeneity amongst any population researched – whether this is men and women, 'large' individuals, people with disabilities or any other 'distinct' group. In order to explore the embodied experience of certain groups within society, we need to be open to this heterogeneity and careful not to reduce it to a common denominator. Foucauldian discourse analysis allows this openness by focusing on the discourses available to and deployed by individuals, and the conditions of possibilities produced in them, rather than focusing on individual behaviour (if, as Susan Bordo (1990) emphasises, we take care not to lose sight of the intricacies and complexities involved in any area of life). The multiplicity of discursively constituted and dynamic subjectivities, subject positions and conditions of possibilities identified in my research highlights the value of a poststructuralist discourse analytic approach. Certain discourses, entrenched in and produced by distinctive cultural, social, economic and cultural conditions, make particular subject positions, power relations and practices im/possible. By exploring the discourses at play, under consideration of the cultural conditions they are embedded in and which made them possible, as well as the power relations and practices that are produced within them, we can contribute to the initiation of change. Current body size and weightloss-focused discourses of health and health promotion for example provide 'the cultural conditions that support, rationalise, and to some extent normalise, practices that are described as "bulimic"' (Burns and Gavey, 2008, p. 151) and generally facilitate a 'cycle of disturbed eating' (Orbach, 2006a, p. 68), they foster weight stigmatisation (Cogan and Ernsberger, 1999; Puhl and Brownell, 2003a; Rich and Evans, 2005), and may also prevent individuals of all sizes from receiving the healthcare they need (see above) – the list goes on. While they seem to create harmful conditions for individuals of any size, these discourses and the meaning of body size, weight loss and health produced within them do not seem to produce an improvement in the health of the population (Campos *et al.*, 2006b; Garner and Wooley, 1991). I believe it is time to change our take on, and challenge the dominant discourses about, fat and the alleged 'truths' produced in them. In Michel Foucault's words:

> there is always a little thought occurring even in the most stupid institutions; there is always thought even in silent habits. Criticism consists in uncovering that thought and trying to change it: showing that things are not as obvious as people believe, making it so that what is taken for granted is no longer taken for granted. To do criticism is to make harder those acts which are now too easy.
>
> (Foucault, 2002a, p. 456)

Criticism like this is badly needed in the current fat debate, and poststructuralist discourse analysis is the appropriate methodology to utilise for it.

Implications for research and practice

Through research I wanted to explore what it is like to be living in contemporary society as a 'large' person; that is, how fat women in particular position themselves within society and how the current healthist and neoliberal culture in Western industrial nations and the predominant discourses around body weight, health and appearance play out on their subjectivities and lifestyle practices. Drawing on these investigations, I would like to assert that, regardless of who's right in the debate on the putative health implication of fat (Blair and LaMonte, 2006; Campos, 2004; Campos *et al.*, 2006b; Cogan and Ernsberger, 1999; Ernsberger, 2004; Gard and Wright, 2005; Kim and Popkin, 2006), the current reductionist approach and the global 'war on obesity' are problematic and potentially harmful. I have identified three main implications of my research for the social and political 'management' of the concerns around health and body size.

1. The 'war on obesity' is harming people's well-being in the form of discrimination, alienation, vilification, marginalisation and mistreatment.
2. Potentially inaccurate messages are delivered to a poorly and simplistically defined and identified target group.
3. Individualistic and perfectionist notions of health and beauty should be challenged.

The 'war on obesity' is harming people

The men and women in my study positioned themselves on the margins of society, as excluded from social activities, as denied the right to self-expression and to have their voices heard. Despite rejecting many of the negative subject positions imposed on them, they constructed their lives as affected through discrimination and a culture of surveillance and moral judgement, which were constituted as affecting their and other fat people's mental health and well-being. In relation to lifestyle, it is difficult to see how being, or positioning oneself as, excluded from society will encourage individuals to join in with physical exercise or other activities that are considered beneficial for people's health. The weight-focused discourses at play currently seem to be restricting rather than facilitating health-producing conditions of possibilities for individuals of any body size.

Potentially inaccurate messages are delivered to a poorly and simplistically defined and identified target group

The equation 'fat is unhealthy' is nowadays taken as almost commonsensical truth, with 'large' individuals seen as unhealthy by association (Burns and Gavey, 2008; Cogan and Ernsberger, 1999). A simplistic energy balance approach is taken, from which follows the assumption that fat people eat too much and exercise too little, and in conjunction with the above are therefore both unhealthy and responsible for their allegedly poor state of health. While the evidence for the assertion of the above link between fat and health seems to enjoy 'immunity from scrutiny' (Aphramor, 2010; Bacon and Aphramor, 2011) in the academic literature, my participants rejected the subject position of the unhealthy and health-illiterate fat person and positioned themselves as well educated or indeed experts in relation to healthy lifestyles, as active and as taking health seriously. They drew on biomedical and nutritional discourses to construct their lives and themselves as healthy. As such the messages of the health promotion agencies, urging 'large' people to change their lifestyles to healthier ones, are not necessarily or exclusively relevant for this group of people. In their document on social marketing (Department of Health, 2008c), the UK Department of Health recognises that they had to put people at the 'heart of policy' and that there was a need to get to know their 'target audience'. Underlying this plea, however, seems to be the assumption that this target audience can be and has been correctly identified, i.e. that fat people need to be targeted in relation to the alleged 'obesity epidemic'. This target audience is assumed to be a homogeneous group whose collective characteristics in relation to health and lifestyle can be known by just looking at them (or weighing them) (Murray, 2005a).

If based on the biological processes in the human body, an 'unhealthy' diet and sedentary lifestyle should have the same detrimental effects on the health of individuals of all sizes. Thus, rather than focusing on a group who are identified as the 'correct' target by crude measures of body shape and body mass index, a Health At Every Size (HAES) (Aphramor, 2008b; Burgard, 2006; Miller and Jacob, 2001) approach could be taken. This links back to my point above and the dangers inherent in the division of people into discrete and homogeneous groups, as within the HAES approach not only the fat kids and adults are getting help and advice for a healthier lifestyle, but anybody can be included. This would mean that 'large' people will not automatically get constructed as health villains but 'slim' people, who may need and welcome support, would also not remain ignored in this respect. Additionally, certain potentially harmful weight loss practices and medication could not be sanctioned, as they potentially can now, within the 'slim and weight loss are always good' discourses. Burns and Gavey (2008) make a similar point in asserting that the discourses that construct any weight gain as potentially dangerous, and weight loss as always healthy, produce a rationale that allows for problematic dietary practices like the purging of food to be constructed as healthy. People cannot be categorised and targeted in terms of healthy lifestyles by their body size, but the discourses used in an attempt to do so have the potential to produce practices and meanings that can be harmful to people of any size.

The HAES model does not mean that everybody should be targeted with health interventions. We are already living in a healthist culture where people are held responsible for a great number of conditions and health has become a duty rather than a free choice (Cheek, 2008). This individualisation of health also reduces the responsibility of the state (Illich, 1976) to foster and support a society where well-being can be achieved, and links into what could be termed an 'offsetting culture'.

The term 'health-offsetting' could be applied to the collective belief that, no matter how damaging our present culture and societal systems are for people's mental and physical health, the individual who suffers under the consequences can be 'fixed' with psychotherapeutic, health behaviour or medical interventions. The HAES approach would potentially help alleviate the vilification, mistreatment and stigmatisation of 'large' individuals, while also improving people's health, but it is still very much located within the current discourses of individual responsibility and the biomedical model of health. As I have argued in Chapter 6, my participants not only positioned themselves as healthy, but, in contrast to the narrow and reductionist biomedical model of health, they also drew on discourses of physical and mental, that is holistic, well-being. The women contributing to my research constructed well-being as multifaceted and complex and not contingent on the fulfilment of each and every one of the neoliberal imperatives of health. As such, more inclusive and less perfectionist notions of health may facilitate and allow for greater well-being for the majority of people, rather than positioning everybody who does not fit into narrowly drawn delimitations of health as pathological.

Individualistic and perfectionist notions of health should be challenged

Lifestyle choices generally, and 'healthy' diet and physical activity in particular, were constructed as important factors in relation to health by the participants in my study. However, the women and men also construed the picture that is drawn by health promotion agencies and the government of the ideal lifestyle as unrealistic and impossible to achieve in real life. As such this neoliberal perfectionist ideal of health was also sometimes rendered as irrelevant and not to be taken seriously. This last message is partly reflected by the Department of Health, which acknowledges that the information about health is sometimes 'out of step with the way people actually live their lives' (Department of Health, 2008c, p. 3). However, this admission only refers to the uncoordinated and inconsistent nature of the health information provided, not to the fact that healthy lifestyles, as defined by the Department of Health, are just one of the balls people have to keep up in the air. This also reflects Elspeth Probyn's (2008, 2009) point that bodies and embodied experiences like being fat, and I would include health and well-being here, are located in cultural, societal and economic contexts, and cannot be considered in a unilateral or static way (see above). When the women in my research talked about well-being, it was about life generally, including housing, work, financial security, family commitments, leisure time, self-expression, and so forth. They were drawing on the discourses of the twenty-first-century superwoman – now that women have achieved legal equality with men in terms of education and career prospects, expectations are high for women to achieve in all areas of life: career, family, household, friends, appearance, and so on (Nicolson, 2002). However, the women in my research also constituted this 'superwoman' as a myth (Nicolson, 2002), as something that was impossible to accomplish. For the achievement of overall well-being, which they constructed as the overall aim rather than a restrictive definition of medical 'health', choices had to be made; body weight was constituted as frequently having to take a lesser (or even just the same) priority as multiple other factors. Within this context, my participants constituted the status of perfect health (as defined by lifestyle) promoted by health promotion agencies as impossible to achieve.

This reflects Julianne Cheek's (2008) argument: she maintains that the more we know about health, the more we are dissatisfied with our health, and aware that there is something else to worry about; as such the perfect state of health is unattainable. She calls therefore on all health researchers to question unchallenged assumptions about health and healthcare practice. I would like to join her and call for a major reconsideration of our policies and strategies in relation to public health generally, and the issue of body weight in particular. We need to move away from an approach which is focused on the individual and body weight, and towards an inclusive model concerned with the well-being of the nation – whatever their size.

Final words

Throughout this book, but predominantly in the first two chapters, I have frequently drawn on my own experiences, weight history and positioning in the fat debate. I guess I was broadly heeding Susan Bordo's (1990) warning that we 'need to guard against the "view from nowhere"' (p. 140) in our efforts to consider and acknowledge as many complexities and power axes as possible. As researchers we do not analyse, read or think in a vacuum, but will always look at any phenomenon from certain – i.e. our own – standpoints, and it is important to make these as transparent as possible. I was certainly very aware of the fact that I was not 'coming from nowhere', but the directions I was coming from shifted and were as dynamic as the experience of being fat I explored.

I was also very aware of the fact that I am a woman interviewing men and women and that this gendered interaction will have produced different accounts from what may have been talked about had a man run the groups. I felt very strongly during the interviews and the focus group in particular that the men oriented their talk towards me, a woman. This was especially noticeable in relation to the issue of greater pressures to be thin being levied on women. I had wanted to include men in my research partly in reaction to criticisms (Bell and McNaughton, 2007) that men do not get considered much in research on body shape and size. I also believed that I would be able to say more about 'gender' if I included men, as their embodied experiences of fat are as gendered as women's experiences. I wanted to give fat men a voice and was also interested in whether I would detect any differences (without looking for generalisable gender differences) in the constructions of fat and 'health' and the constitution of 'large' women and 'large' men in the articulations offered by women and men. Throughout my research, however, the continued gender imbalance related to pressures around the issues of fat, appearance and health drew my attention – both in the women's and men's narratives. This may have been influenced by the fact that, like some other qualitative researchers (Butera, 2006), I found it difficult to recruit men. Men, no doubt, are targets in the 'war on obesity', which warrants further exploration (Monaghan, 2007a, 2008a, b); for the above two reasons, however, I decided in the end to concentrate on women's experiences for this book.

Taking all these factors into account, the explorations of fat lives presented in this book are inevitably subjective interpretations of the narratives of a small group of participants, who oriented towards me, a normatively sized white middle-aged woman. However, Foucauldian discourse analysis concerns itself with the global discourses that are available to individuals or groups in society, how certain objects and subjectivities are constructed, and how people are positioned within them – the focus is on 'discourses that operate independently of the intentions of the speakers' (Parker, 1994a, p. 92) as any speaker can only deploy the discourses that are available to her within a certain culture. Thus, a different researcher would no doubt have obtained different data in regard to the content and topics covered, but this data would nevertheless be no more or less valid for an analysis of the identified discourses.

My work to date has expanded the research on being 'large' in relation to the discursive regulatory processes at play in contemporary Western societies, the gendered power relationships constituted within them and how these impact on the embodied experience of fat women (and men). This research adds to others that point towards ways of reforming health promotion strategies, towards the adoption of a less harmful, discriminatory and oppressive framework on fat. I believe that I have also further illustrated that poststructuralist discourse analysis is a useful and important method for the exploration of embodied experiences, and have highlighted the dangers of homogenisation of populations studied. My own future work will expand on these issues, and I hope that I have stimulated and encouraged some readers to think again when they hear the all too familiar chants about being healthy by losing weight. To stop, think and potentially also to investigate and challenge the current 'war on obesity' because 'as soon as people begin to have trouble thinking things the way they have been thought, trans-formation becomes at the same time very urgent, very difficult, and entirely possible' (Foucault, 2002a, p. 457). And transformation, in my mind, is what is needed in the way we think about, talk about and handle the issue of 'obesity'. There may or may not be health risks associated with certain body weights (at both ends of the scale), but fat women's lives deserve more than the currently prevailing heavily gendered and reductionist approaches, and often very one-sided debates, which have not improved matters for anybody so far, whatever perspective one may take; but they may be responsible for a great deal of oppression, dis-crimination and pain.

Appendix 1
Theory in the exploration of fat lives

In the following I will outline the epistemological, theoretical and methodological foundations of the critical psychological approach I have taken in exploring fat embodiment; as will be evident, this approach does not lend itself to truth-finding or generalisations.

I am employing a feminist poststructuralist perspective informed by Michel Foucault's as well as feminist theories. As there are multiple variances of post-structuralism as well as feminism, however, it does not suffice simply to name the perspective taken; the theoretical positioning of my research (and myself) thus warrants further explanation and exploration, which follow below. Before I go on, however, I should mention one aspect of feminist thinking that is close to my heart and which has influenced the general approach I have taken to writing this book. It is the notion that feminist writing, as well as research itself, is part of the feminist political struggle, and should thus be accessible to all women, both inside and outside academia, in terms of writing style and terminology employed (Gill, 1998). As such I have tried to keep the language used throughout this book as straightforward as possible, but admit that I may not always have succeeded in doing so.

As mentioned previously, the 'scientific' foundations on which the 'war on obesity' is built are highly contested. Researchers and writers from a number of disciplines, including health professionals, lawyers, sociologists and psychologists (Campos, 2011; Orbach, 2006a; Rich *et al.*, 2011b; Throsby, 2009) challenge the medical 'facts' that are disseminated, as well as the general reductionist and individualistic approach taken in health promotion and practice. The mainstream psychological approach taken to the bulk of the research in regard to being fat, in my view, has added to the potentially harmful focus on body weight as a problem which has to be solved by/through the individual. Psychology does not give us any insight into the subjective experience of 'being large' or the complex interactions between society/culture and individuals, including fat individuals' constitution and reconstitution through talk (as well as practices) around body size, health, well-being and lifestyles. In fact, mainstream psychology – or rather the proliferation of psy(chological) knowledge and methods since the middle of the nineteenth century – was fundamental in the emergence of the unitary and stable individual that we take for granted in Western societies today (Hook, 2007; Rose, 1996).

In its endeavour to be taken seriously and be recognised as a science, mainstream psychology took on scientific methods and belief systems and a focus on categorisation and diagnosis (Fox *et al.*, 2009; Gough and McFadden, 2001; Henriques *et al.*, 1984b). These methodologies aid the distancing of individuals from their surroundings and cultural contexts, and reduce them and any complex 'psychological' and sociological issues to 'predictable' and measurable stimulus–response mechanisms (Gough and McFadden, 2001), or matters of individual information processing. Through the emphasis on generalisation in most mainstream psychology, and a focus on discovering common truths, minority groups and their issues can get diluted out (or appear as 'outliers' in statistical tests), which perpetuates inequalities and oppression. As a subdiscipline of psychology, mainstream health psychology takes a primarily functional biopsychosocial model, mainly concerned with input/output processes (Stam, 2004). In practical terms this translates into the development (and evaluation) of behaviour change interventions to improve each individual's self-regulation towards a 'healthier' lifestyle, and thus the health of the population (British Psychological Society, 2009; Stam, 2000); the responsibility for an individual's (and the nation's) health, and associated costs, is thus firmly laid at each individual's feet. This is not surprising if one considers that health psychology in part developed out of an economic crisis in the late 1970s/early 1980s which called for action to reduce public spending in relation to health and social care (Murray, 2004). This action took the form of government policies and initiatives that celebrated individuals' empowerment and responsibility for their own health. Consequently, theories and interventions of behaviour change, which encouraged people to take up lifestyles that maintained health and prevented illness, were very welcome indeed (Hepworth, 2006; Murray, 2004). Mainstream (health) psychology thus cannot, and will not, challenge the generalised and reductionist 'scientific' findings most health promotion and media projects on 'obesity' are based on. It thereby not only plays a part in the over-simplification of the issues of fat and health, but also promotes a neoliberalist and healthist culture in Western societies, which contributes to the marginalisation, oppression and vilification of fat individuals.

A critical psychological approach respects and addresses the multilayered and dynamic societal and individual complexities inherent in the experience of being fat, thus diverting the focus away from individual responsibility (and related blame cultures) and towards a promotion of diversity and social equality. Critical psychologists challenge current mainstream psychology's emphasis on cognitivism (Willig, 2008) and the individual–society dualism underlying much psychology (Henriques *et al.*, 1984a). Most critical psychology is located within a broadly social constructionist framework, which in short assumes reality, knowledge and consequently the perception of objects and subjects to be constructed socially and as forever shifting and dynamic (Gough and McFadden, 2001; Hollway, 1989; van Langenhove and Harré, 1999). There are multiple forms of critical psychology, but they share a focus on 'the way psychological theory and practice operate to reduce social phenomena to the level of the individual and to normalize certain kinds of behaviour and experience' (Parker, 1999, p. 62), as well as sharing a concern with explicating how experience and subjectivity are discursively produced and regulated. Both critical social and critical health psychology see the individual as socially and politically located (Gough and McFadden, 2001; Murray, 2004), and encourage researchers to adopt a broader perspective than the reductionist and individualistic approach taken by mainstream psychology (Marks, 2008).

Like other critical psychologists, I would argue that individuals, as well as health and illness, are socially and politically located, and thus subject to multiple and shifting power dynamics in society. Of course, the need to consider the social context of an individual's behaviour and mental state has been recognised by many psychologists for a long time. However, frequently the social is included in psychological theories in a unidirectional capacity only, that is, the cultural or societal context is merely considered *one* of the factors impacting on the individual: the individual–society dualism is thus still maintained (Henriques *et al.*, 1984a; Hollway, 1989).

This dualism is challenged by critical psychology (Henriques *et al.*, 1984a), which maintains that the subject is constituted through and positioned in relation to multiple and shifting discourses and practices, which are contingent on social and historical contexts. Thus, the critical psychological 'self' is multiple and dynamic rather than unitary and stable. Critical psychology set out to theorise the individual or subject newly and to challenge social practices and institutions (Gough and McFadden, 2001, p. 2). Psychology as a discipline is seen as playing a major role in the constitution and maintenance of these practices and institutions (Fox *et al.*, 2009; Parker, 1999). Thus, critical psychology raises these issues within psychology as well as society, seeking to challenge 'taken-for-granted' truths and knowledges with the aim not only of understanding but also of changing society (Gough and McFadden, 2001). In this challenge of commonsensical truths, critical psychologists frequently draw on social constructionist and poststructuralist epistemologies generally, and Michel Foucault's theories in particular.

Poststructuralism – knowledge production

The status of knowledge, and the conditions it is being produced in, is at the heart of poststructuralist theory, based on the notion that there is no pre-given, observable reality or truth (Gergen, 2009; Lupton, 1996):

> The object does not await in limbo the order that will free it and enable it to become embodied in a visible and prolix objectivity; it does not pre-exist itself, held back by some obstacle at the first edges of light. It exists under the positive conditions of a complex group of relations. [. . .] These relations are established between institutions, economic and social processes, behavioural patterns, systems of norms, techniques, types of classification, modes of charac-terization; and these relations are not present in the object; [. . .] they do not define its internal constitution, but what enables it to appear.
>
> (Foucault, 1972, p. 49)

For Foucault then, and within poststructuralist theory, there are no pre-existing objects, and there is no reality existing before 'relations . . . between institutions, economic and social processes, behavioural patterns, systems of norms, techniques, types of classification [and] modes of characterization' (Foucault, 1972). As such it is the interrelations between these institutions and people, and their social and institutional practices, that objects and by extension realities are produced in.

These relations in turn are constituted in discourses, which are historically and culturally specific and always provisional and in a state of change. Whilst noting the ambiguity of the meaning of the term 'discourse', for the purpose of his analyses Foucault defines it as a group of statements, of ideas, values and descriptions that 'belong to a single system of formation' (Foucault, 1972, p. 120), i.e. to specific institutions, social and economic practices, systems of norms and the like. As such we can talk of economic discourses, patriarchal discourses, biomedical discourses, psychological discourses, and so forth. These discourses construct and maintain truths and knowledges within these domains, but they are forever dynamic, in flux, never stable or discrete and delineable. This does not mean, as Derek Hook (2007) reminds us, that we are left with a state of ubiquitous relativity, where 'anything goes', or constantly faced with changing truths or knowledges. The circumstances required for certain discourses to emerge and certain knowledges to be accepted as truths, what Foucault calls the conditions of possibility, are materialist and sociohistorically contingent conditions, and as such fairly rigid within any given place and historical time.

Foucault draws on Greek poets to underline this historical contingency of 'truth', which then was what 'inspired respect and terror, that to which one submitted because it ruled, that which was pronounced by men who spoke as of right and according to the required ritual' (cited by Hook, 2007, p. 104). A contemporary example is the already-mentioned (Chapter 1) immunity to scrutiny, enjoyed by any 'facts' about the threat to health and longevity that obesity allegedly presents. Knowledges and truths, then, are whatever is accepted and functions as true within any particular society (Grosz, 1994). The cultural and historical specificity of a society produces the 'conditions of possibility' for certain discourses to emerge, which in return produce the truths or regimes of truth accepted in a society (Foucault, 1972). Discourses, however, are both constituted by, as well as constitutive of, conditions of possibilities, and hence knowledges are constantly discursively produced and reproduced, and as such never fixed.

Equally, or consequently, human experiences and perceptions are (discursively constructed) readings of historical, cultural and linguistic conditions, rather than straightforward reflections of observations (Willig, 2008). Any observations, which form the building blocks of empiricist scientific approaches, can only be described with, and are thus constructed through, language. Within poststructuralist theories, the dynamic nature of language, or discourse, is at the centre of the production of meaning (Lupton, 1996), and knowledges and truths are historically and culturally located and produced in and by societies through discourse. As such, whilst most of us would probably welcome a level of certainty provided by empirical research findings, there cannot be *one* objective and empirically verifiable truth; or, in Ann

Oakley's words (2009, p. 118), much of the academic writing that we are seeking certainties from 'was (is) [just] a concealed form of fiction'. There are always a variety of ways in which social reality can be and is constructed in a culture, and as such there will always be several knowledges available, produced in multiple as well as fragmented discourses. And whilst the above examples of economic or psychological discourses may imply a discrete discourse for each of these domains, according to Foucault there can exist various, and contradictory, discourses within each such 'fields of force relations' (Foucault, 1978, p. 101), and discourses themselves are not unitary systems but of a fragmented nature.

The *oeuvre* serves Foucault (1972) as an example for the interconnectedness and fragmentary nature of discourses. While the *oeuvre* of, for example, a writer, her complete output, could be seen as a discrete and closed 'piece' of work on the topic explored within it, for Foucault it only represents one fragment within an interconnected and dynamic system of texts produced. This particular *oeuvre* could not exist, or rather would not mean anything in a vacuum, without reference to other works and other writers' *oeuvres*. There is a network of works that feed into and off each other, and depend on each other for the construction of meanings, which is only possible in interaction. Extended to society, we can never find a discrete and detached piece of discourse. Any discourse is contingent on the cultural and historical context in which it exists and is constituted and reconstituted through practical and discursive social interaction.

As such, for every (empirical) fact or truth we encounter, we should ask ourselves where, when and by whom this knowledge was produced. The discourses produced by the Conservative government during times of austerity following the banking crisis and subsequent recession in the early twenty-first century lend themselves as prime examples for this theory. In defending harsh cutbacks and austerity measures, the terminology changed: It was not government or social services any more who were paying for services provided centrally, but the 'tax payer' – as in each one of us was paying individually for everybody else who was using public services. We all thus also had the responsibility to use as little of these services as possible – the discourses drawn on in times of 'austerity' thus also produced discourses of individual responsibility for the nation's financial health and blame.

Poststructuralism – knowledge/power

Back to Foucauldian poststructuralist theory, however, and the link that Foucault saw between knowledge and power. This power–knowledge relationship is closely linked with the 'emergence' of the individual or the subject, which can be traced back to the beginning of the nineteenth century, and, for Foucault, is associated with the penal, or disciplinary system. In *Discipline and Punish* (1977), Foucault outlines how technologies of power have evolved from a pre-modern sovereign power to a new disciplinarity, based on knowledge (and psychological knowledge in particular) as a modality of power, surveillance, and the self-regulation of subjects. Under the influence of humanism, the focus of the penal system shifted from deterrence (in the form of very public and violent physical punishment) to correction and prevention. The latter was pursued through the simultaneous subjectification and objectification of the individual, drawing on what Derek Hook[7] (2007, p. 12) calls 'proto-psychological' knowledge. Subjectification here involves the collection and recording of detailed (psychological) knowledge of individuals (or offenders), their state of mind, their attitudes, how they live, and so forth. The subject thus becomes very visible, and at the same time treatable or correctable, towards a desired norm which will ensure the efficient and economical running of a society (or an institution).

Objectification is also grounded in knowledge; categories of desirable and undesirable types of individuals (offenders, homosexuals, mentally ill) are created and defined, to aid the prediction of subjects' behaviour and the identification and treatment of the deviant subject. The more knowledge is produced in this way, the more it needs experts both to supply the knowledge and to treat the deviant subject, which in turn creates unequal power relationships between those who know (the experts) and those who don't. This mechanism of power is succinctly described by Hook in the following excerpt:

> Knowledge, as a modality of power, thus grew in two different directions at the same time, producing profiles of troublesome persons and related behaviours, while simultaneously refining the techniques of measurement, comparison and surveillance able to render such problematic individuals in ever more detail. This led to a circular relation: objectifying knowledge came to persuasively sanction prescriptions of expert intervention, which, in turn, intensified the procedures of individualization able to capture the problematic facets of deviant subjects.
>
> (Hook, 2007, p. 15)

This combination of subjectification and objectification, supplemented by the technology of extensive examination, measurements and data recording, thus brought about a shift in disciplinarity from a focus on the offence to a focus on offenders in their 'entire way of being' (Hook, 2007, p. 17), produced within a psychologico-moral discourse.

Another important factor in this new form of power – disciplinarity – was the role played by the in/visibility of its mechanisms and technologies, on the one hand, and the individual on the other hand. The subject became more and more transparent or visible, in what Foucault considers a 'compulsory visibility' (1977, p. 187): through 'the examination', i.e. multiple measurements, record-taking. the individual becomes subject to a permanent gaze, known in every detail and thus 'fixed' and objectified. This at the same time produces norms and measures of distinction; it produces unitary individuals and at the same time objectifies them – creates objects that can be categorised, judged and treated (or punished if deviant from the norm). The 'war on obesity' in contemporary society lends itself as a prime example here, with its insistence in the measurement and recording of every person's weight, height and body mass index. Recent campaigns to measure, record and correct every child's body size details illustrate this worrying trend further.

The mechanisms of disciplinarity itself stay largely hidden, as they are not concentrated in one body, one institution or sovereign. This continuous visibility to invisible 'agents' of power is exemplified in Foucault's concept of panopticism. Foucault (1977) uses Bentham's conception of the Panopticon as a model for how being continuously visible – or the ever-present potential of being watched, i.e. under surveillance – creates power inequalities and acts as a 'discipline-mechanism' (p. 209) of normalisation. Bentham's Panopticon was the plan for a prison constructed in a way that allowed prison guards in a watch tower to watch inmates in their cells constantly (but without being seen themselves). This creates a visibility and power asymmetry, with the power lying with the invisible but monitoring prison guards. Expanding this idea to society more generally, Foucault talks about a normalising and regulating gaze, as when there is a constant possibility that people are being watched and judged, individuals start watching or disciplining themselves. They are making sure they do not step out of line (i.e. that they fit the culturally constructed normative rules of appearance, behaviour, and so forth) as someone may see them, judge them or even punish them.

Permanent visibility goes together with the above-mentioned increasing individualisation within a disciplinary system. Visibility – or this normalising omnipresent gaze – is thus a prerequisite for discipline and the development of a society where each person scrutinises him- or herself according to societal regulations and norms. It also means that:

> [p]ower is everywhere; not because it embraces everything, but because it comes from everywhere. . . . power is not an institution, and not a structure; neither is it a certain strength we are endowed with; it is the name that one attributes to a complex strategical situation in a particular society.
>
> (Foucault, 1978, p. 93)

As I have argued above, however, these 'strategical situations in a particular society' (Foucault, 1978, p. 93) are constituted in discourse and discourse produces knowledge. For Foucault, then, power and knowledge are inextricably linked, which is signified in his use of the term 'power-knowledge' (1977). Knowledge produces power but power also produces knowledge, in terms of what (knowledge-producing) discourses are allowed, in other words, what is possible to be said and by whom (Foucault, 1978). This power–knowledge interaction in Western industrial nations particularly applies to the human sciences and the medical system (Hollway, 1989), where the status of 'the expert' empowers researchers and health professionals while disempowering patients or, in the example of the 'war on obesity', the fat individual or lay activist in the fat acceptance movement.

As such, I believe that Foucault's theories, with their focus on a complex analysis of governmentality, disciplinarity, control and power relationships, lend themselves particularly well to an exploration of fat embodiment, in the context of the current 'war on obesity'. It seems important to acknowledge, however, that my discussions of poststructuralist theories and approaches represents yet another construction of these, and the knowledges produced within them. I am offering my interpretation of poststructuralism and poststructuralist feminism in the context of the exploration of fat lives, and grounded in my own social, political and historical experiences and beliefs, which I cannot avoid (Bordo, 1990).

Poststructuralist feminism

Some quarters of feminism have embraced poststructuralism for decades now. Di Stefano goes as far as to claim that 'contemporary Western feminism is firmly, if ambivalently, located in the modernist ethos' and continues to say that 'Western feminism was finally able to deconstruct the presumably fixed and universal association between femininity and the biology of reproduction' (Di Stefano, 1990, p. 64). This claim was never wholeheartedly accepted by all feminist writers at its point of publication, and our relationship with poststructuralist theories is currently still a matter of debate. At the heart of the argument lie different conceptions of gender differences, and of the structure and cause of gendered power inequalities, which result in the oppression of women.

Historically, there are a number of different strands within feminism, with different takes on gender and gender differences. For the purpose of this book, I will briefly summarise the standpoints taken by liberal, radical and poststructuralist feminism as these in my view represent the different perspectives in relation to gender differences most clearly (see Weedon, 1999, for a comprehensive discussion of feminist theories).

Liberal feminism is rooted in liberal humanism and thus has freedom, choice, self-determination and equality at the centre of its fight for women's rights. Based on the notion of 'sameness', women and men are considered equal in all respects relevant to the above cornerstones of liberalism. As liberalism in general, this approach has Cartesian dualism, with its separation of the superior mind from the inferior body at its heart and assumes a rational human being; it neglects the importance of the body in (gender) politics, as well as the role of emotions (Weedon, 1999). This neglect is one critique raised against liberal feminism, as well as its lack of consideration for social contexts and circumstances, and their inherent structural power relations. With its insistence on 'sameness' between women and men, and ignoring certain biological and societal factors (e.g. that women are the child bearers and predominant family caretakers), liberal feminism can therefore be seen as contributing to the creation of the 'superwoman'. The modern 'super-woman' is entitled and thus expected to fulfil her potential in all areas of modern life (in the spheres of domestic life, paid work and public life) and thus also faced with a multiplication of life burdens (Nicolson, 2002; Weedon, 1999). This neoliberal take on women's equality, that they indeed can choose what they want in terms of their careers, family lives or body projects, is reflected in a number of studies which indicate a fading of feminism; particularly young women seem to see feminism as a nowadays unnecessary thing of the past, and women as free to choose their actions in life (Rudolfsdottir and Jolliffe, 2008; Stuart and Donaghue, 2012).

Apart from their argument of 'sameness' of the sexes, the neglect of the body in liberal feminist theories is one of the most crucial critiques levied against them.

Radical feminism carried these criticisms forward by asserting that women, and in particular women's bodies, are different from men and men's bodies, and by making the female body and female sexuality the centre of women's domination. Radical feminism generally identifies patriarchy and thus men as the clear oppressors of women, whose true essence is obscured and oppressed and thus does not find expression, with cultural feminism going as far as asserting that women are naturally superior to men (Weedon, 1999). This commitment to a difference between the sexes and the focus on patriarchy and men as the oppressors gives radical feminism (in all its guises) a clear structure and target to fight and overcome.

This clear structure of how women's oppression works, and a distinct powerful agent or agents who can be challenged, is, according to critics, missing in postmodern/poststructuralist feminist perspectives, allegedly making them less useful for women's struggle against oppression and for equality. Poststructuralist feminism sees power as dispersed and dynamic, ubiquitous and not centred within one person, gender or societal group. Of course this does not mean that power is spread equally among everybody (Bordo, 1999) and the multiple and dynamic positioning of people and groups within power systems results in power inequalities and oppression. The dispersed nature of power, however, makes it difficult to identify, and thus challenge, the active agent(s) in oppression. In the same vein, poststructuralist feminism does not offer any generalisations on the concept of 'woman', her experiences, or subjectivity; in short, there is no true experience or essence of woman which can be drawn on for the feminist cause. As Helen Malson contends (1998, p. 25), 'Women's subjectivity might then be best theorised in terms of "plural collectivities" of often contradictory subject positions constituted in and by various socio-historically specific discourses'. According to poststructuralism's critics, this means among other things that the grounds for feminist (but equally racial, class, religious[8]) politics are equally destabilised or removed (Gill, 1995). If only abstract and dynamic genders and individuals can be theorised, it is impossible to ground oppression in gender relations and thus to fight the inequalities inherent in them, as they cannot be concretised, or generalised to women as a homogeneous and oppressed group.

The notion of power being ubiquitous and not fixed within one or another gender also seems to play into the hands of those who claim that we are in a postfeminist era where feminism is not necessary any more. Feminism is seen by many as a spent force, as something that was necessary in the past but has in effect achieved equal opportunities for women (in term of education and careers). Allegedly, it is thus now each individual woman's (free) choice and responsibility to take up these opportunities. Free choice is something we, in Western neoliberal societies, value highly, and together with empowerment, choice is sold to women by government policies as well as popular culture as synonymous with equality (Malson *et al.*, 2011; McRobbie, 2009; Rudolfsdottir and Jolliffe, 2008). In other words, if we cannot generalise a relatively homogeneous women's experience, if each individual (dependent on class, race and socioeconomic status) is experiencing life in a number of various and inherently individualised ways, the poststructuralist notion of a dispersed power could be interpreted as just another individualistic (neoliberal?)

version of power. And with no generalisations across women possible, can we still speak of women's oppression?

Equally, if every account, every version of events produced in discourse is as valid as the other, how can we claim that our, feminist, version of oppression is real and serious enough to take action against? This is a dilemma often faced by my students when they struggle with the concept of social constructionism generally. They ask, for example, if child sexual abuse is socially constructed, based on our construction of innocent and asexual childhood, does that mean it's not intrinsically bad – only socially constructed as bad? Shall we thus not persecute the offender (Gill, 1995, drawing on Stevi Jackson, 1992)? It is thus not only my students' view that taking a poststructuralist perspective may leave us with no clear definition of 'good' and 'bad', no direction, and in terms of research, with no goal other than pure enquiry and scepticism. Put differently, if you cannot get a clear picture of how a system (or society) works, if you do not know the structure of this system, how can you know how to change it? In Nancy Hartsock's words:

> Those of us who are not part of the ruling race, class, or gender, not a part of the minority which controls our world, need to know how it works. . . . What systematic changes would be required to create a more just system?
>
> (Hartsock, 1990, p. 159)

Poststructuralism can offer us no such clear picture, and thus no simple solution, in the feminist fight against the rather real and lived oppression of women. However, what if there is no such clear structure and vision to be had? I would argue that the above concerns and critiques are based in positivistic epistemologies, in a belief that there are truths and facts which can and need to be countered in a straight-forward and often binary way. Drawing on works by Jane Flax and Judith Butler, Gill (1995) asserts that 'what we as feminists want is not truth but *justice*', which may not be attainable by establishing another 'truth'. From a poststructuralist feminist standpoint, it is crucial, however to question, challenge and deconstruct the truth claims and values which are often at the basis of oppression and discrimination, and thus enable transformation. Only if we engage in this type of criticism, making it harder for people to believe taken-for-granted truths or thoughts, can we make change possible. Or, in Michel Foucault's words, 'as soon as people begin to have trouble thinking things the way they have been thought, trans-formation becomes at the same time very urgent, very difficult, and entirely possible' (Foucault, 2002a, p. 457).

This point is particularly important for the subject matter explored in this book: the embodied experience of being fat. We cannot offer an opposing 'truth' to the discursively produced, but taken-for-granted 'fact' that being fat is always bad for us. Just as there is no proof for this statement, we cannot offer a counter-argument, like, for example, that fat is good for us, against this ill-evidenced (see Chapter 1) but nevertheless strong and dominant piece of health 'knowledge'. However, we can try and deconstruct it, dismantle and contest the basis of its truth claim. For the sake of justice and equality, we need to throw as much doubt at it as possible, to make it difficult for people automatically to think and utter the taken-for-granted statements that equate (ill) health with body size and a great number of negative characteristics and behaviours with the fat individual.

I appreciate the concerns of poststructuralism's critics and acknowledge the inherent difficulties of fighting a non-discrete and non-unitary oppressive power, but would like to advocate a critical and reflective use of poststructuralist feminism rather than its abandonment. One of the important benefits of a poststructuralist methodology, in my view, is a smaller risk of falling prey to 'centrisms'; something feminism generally has been critiqued for in as much as it (historically) was supported by, and focused predominantly on, white, middle-class women of Western nations. Of course a total avoidance of centrisms, even by the 'right' choice of methodology, is impossible; we cannot avoid focusing, explicitly or implicitly, on the culture and other groupings of society we belong to, as we cannot stand outside these. We will make more or less intentional choices of attention and consideration, based on our own background, history, experience and political orientation. And this 'orientation' (struggling for a better word than bias) will need to be acknowledged and attended to, made transparent and reflected on. However, the relativism and pluralism inherent in poststructuralist approaches make it possible to consider multiple, dispersed and dynamic powers that work on equally heterogeneous and dynamically assembled societal groups – producing oppressors and those being oppressed, the powerful and powerless, within the same groups and individuals. Thus, the risk of 'gloss[ing] over other dimensions of social identity and location, dimensions which, when considered, cast doubt on the proposed gender (or racial, or class . . .) generalizations' (Bordo, 1990, p. 137) is reduced.

So, while the lack of a direction and unified force to fight against can be frustrating, circular and infuriating, to abandon poststructuralist theory despite all indications for its applicability seems to be misguided. While a united fight against a clearly defined target seems appealing and to promise results, I suspect it would not deliver. 'Battling on one front' is not sufficient in a complex web of power relations, where power cannot be constituted as purely a negative force of oppression – for Foucault, power is also productive. In contemporary Western societies, the domination of women is the result of discipline and governance, effected through processes of self-discipline and self-regulation, rather than unilateral direct oppression (Saukko and Reed, 2010). This (self) governance is to a great extent played out on women's bodies, which is no doubt one reason why being fat is very much a gendered issue.

Appendix 2
Transcription conventions

[laughing/laughter] spoken whilst laughing

[ ] passages (e.g. names) anonymised by researcher or additional explanations that are not part of the original interview

[. . .] deleted passages

(.) pauses – more dots denote longer pauses

( ) inaudible or unclear passages, so the accuracy of the transcription is not guaranteed

do italics denote words/phrases that were emphasised/stressed by the interviewee

/ / interjections

= beginning and end of overlapping speech or if there was no break between the two speakers' utterances

Notes

1   The adjectives 'fat' and 'large' are used throughout this book instead of 'obese' or 'overweight' or any other descriptor, as the majority of the participants in my research seemed to deem these terms acceptable. I am aware that there may be many people who will dislike the terms 'fat' or 'large', and that the positive opinions about these terms in my group of participants were in parts created by using 'large' in my recruitment material. I may have only recruited individuals who were not offended by the word 'large'. Within the field of fat studies, the term 'fat' is commonly used, but, lacking a term that does not bear any negative connotations in society, I continue to use 'large' as well as 'fat', but express a certain unease by putting 'large' in quotation marks.

2   Parts of the data and analysis presented in this chapter have been reported on before in an article published in *Feminism and Psychology* (Tischner & Malson, 2008).

3   All excerpts quoted in Chapters 3–5 are taken from interviews with women only. Interview participants chose their own pseudonyms.

4   See also Tischner and Malson (2012).

5   The excerpts used in this chapter are from the women's and men's focus groups and the individual interviews with men.

6   See also Tischner and Malson (2011).

7   For a comprehensive and accessible discussion of the links between psychology and power in Foucault's theories, I would like to direct the reader to Derek Hook's excellent book *Foucault, Psychology and the Analytics of Power* (2007), which I am drawing heavily on in my – necessarily very simplified – exploration of poststructuralism, knowledge and power.

8   By talking about women's and feminist struggles against oppression I do not want to belittle or devalue other, similar power struggles in (global) society, but merely choose not to add an inclusive qualifier for pragmatic and readability reasons.

References

Abbott, P. and Sapsford, F. (2001). Young women and their wardrobes. In A. Guy, E. Green and M. Banim (Eds.), *Through the Wardrobe* (pp. 21–37). Oxford: Berg.

Adam, A. (2001). Big girls' blouses: learning to live with polyester. In A. Guy, E. Green and M. Banim (Eds.), *Through the Wardrobe* (pp. 39–51). Oxford: Berg.

Ajzen, I. (1985). From intention to actions: a theory of planned behaviour. In J. Kuhl and J. Beckman (Eds.), *Action-control: From cognition to behavior* (pp. 11–39). Heidelberg: Springer.

Alcoff, L. (2006). *Visible Identities : Race, gender, and the self.* New York: Oxford University Press.

Annis, N. M., Cash, T. F. and Hrabosky, J. I. (2004). Body image and psychosocial differences among stable average weight, currently overweight, and formerly overweight women: the role of stigmatizing experiences. *Body Image,* 1(2), 155–167.

Aphramor, L. (2005). Is a weight-centred health framework salutogenic? Some thoughts on unhinging certain dietary ideologies. *Social Theory and Health,* 3(4), 315–340.

Aphramor, L. (2008a). Ten things that scare me about 'Obesity'. Talk at Fat Studies UK Event, 2 May 2008, University of York.

Aphramor, L. (2008b). Weight and health: changing attitudes and behaviours. *Health Psychology Update,* 17(1), 42–45.

Aphramor, L. (2010). Validity of claims made in weight management research: a narrative review of dietetic articles. *Nutritional Journal,* 9(30) (retrieved from BioMed Central database).

Arthurs, J. and Grimshaw, J. (1999). Introduction. In J. Arthurs and J. Grimshaw (Eds.), *Women's Bodies: Discipline and transgression* (pp. 1–16). London: Cassell.

Austin, S. B. (1999). Fat, loathing and public health: the complicity of science in a culture of disordered eating. *Culture, Medicine and Psychiatry,* 23(2), 245–268.

Bacon, L. and Aphramor, L. (2011). Weight science: evaluating the evidence for a paradigm shift. *Nutritional Journal,* 10(9) (retrieved from BioMed Central database).

Bandura, A. (1994). Self-efficacy. In V. S. Ramachaudran (Ed.), *Encyclopedia of Human Behavior* (pp. 71–81). New York: Academic Press.

Bartky, S. L. (1988). Foucault, femininity, and the modernization of patriarchal power. In I. Diamond and L. Quinby (Eds.), *Feminism and Foucault – Reflections on resistance* (pp. 61–86). Boston: Northeastern University Press.

Bartky, S. L. (1990). *Femininity and Domination: Studies in the phenomenology of oppression.* London: Routledge.

Bayer, B. M. and Malone, K. R. (1998). Feminism, psychology and matters of the body. In H. J. Stam (Ed.), *The Body and Psychology* (pp. 94–119). London: SAGE.

BBC. (2009). *Radio 4 news,* 6th April 2009, 7 am.

BBC News. (2011). *UK women are 'fattest in Europe'.* Retrieved 24 February 2012, from http://www.bbc.co.uk/news/health-15901351.

Beagan, B., Chapman, G. E., D'Sylva, A. and Bassett, B. R. (2008). 'It's just easier for me to do it': Rationalizing the family division of foodwork. *Sociology,* 42(4), 653–671.

Beckers, S., Mertens, I., Peeters, A., Van Gaal, L. and Van Hul, W. (2006). Screening for melanocortin-4 receptor mutations in a cohort of Belgian morbidly obese adults and children. *International Journal of Obesity,* 30(2), 221–225.

Befort, C. A., Thomas, J. L., Daley, C. M., Rhode, P. C. and Ahluwalia, J. S. (2008). Perceptions and beliefs about body size, weight, and weight loss among obese African American women: A qualitative inquiry. *Health Education and Behavior,* 35(3), 410–426.

Bell, K. and McNaughton, D. (2007). Feminism and the invisible fat man. *Body and Society,* 13(1), 107–131.

Bennett, P. (1997). *Psychology and Health Promotion.* Buckingham: Open University Press.

Berger, J. (1972). *Ways of Seeing.* London: BBC/Penguin Books.

Bianchini, F., Kaaks, R. and Vainio, H. (2002). Weight control and physical activity in cancer prevention. *Obesity Reviews,* 3(1), 5–8.

Blaine, B. (2008). Does depression cause obesity? A meta-analysis of longitudinal studies of depression and weight control. *Journal of Health Psychology,* 13(8), 1190–1197.

Blaine, B. E., Rodman, J. and Newman, J. M. (2007). Weight loss treatment and psychological well-being: a review and meta-analysis. *Journal of Health Psychology,* 12(1), 66–82.

Blair, S. N. and LaMonte, M. J. (2006). Commentary: Current perspectives on obesity and health: black and white, or shades of grey? *International Journal of Epidemiology,* 35(1), 69–72.

Bogle, V. and Sykes, C. (2011). Psychological interventions in the treatment of childhood obesity: what we know and need to find out. *Journal of Health Psychology,* 16(7), 997–1014.

Bordo, S. (1990). Feminism, postmodernism, and gender-scepticism. In L. J. Nicholson (Ed.), *Feminism/Postmodernism* (pp. 133–156). New York: Routledge.

Bordo, S. (1993). *Unbearable Weight, Feminism, Western Culture, and the Body.* Berkeley, CA: University of California Press.

Bordo, S. (1998). Bringing body to theory. In D. Welton (Ed.), *Body and Flesh – A philosophical reader* (pp. 84–97). Oxford: Blackwell Publishers.

Bordo, S. (1999). Feminism, Foucault and the politics of the body. In J. Price and M. Shildrick (Eds.), *Feminist Theory and the Body: A reader* (pp. 246–257). Edinburgh: Edinburgh University Press.

Bordo, S. (2009). Not just 'a white girl's thing': the changing face of food and body image problems. In H. Malson and M. Burns (Eds.), *Critical Feminist Approaches to Eating Dis/Orders* (pp. 46–60). London: Routledge.

BPS Obesity Working Group. (2011). *Obesity in the UK: A psychological perspective.* Leicester: British Psychological Society.

Brady, E. (2011). *Cancer 'caused by obesity and bad diet'.* Retrieved 7 December 2011 from http://uk.news.yahoo.com/cancer-caused-obesity-bad-diet-235904488.html.

Braun, V. (2000). Conceptualizing the body. *Feminism and Psychology,* 10(4), 511–518.

Braun, V. (2009). 'The women are doing it for themselves'. *Australian Feminist Studies,* 24(60), 233–249.

Brighenti, A. (2007). Visibility: a category for the social sciences. *Current Sociology,* 55(3), 323–342.

British Psychological Society. (2009). Retrieved 18 July 2012 from http://www.bps. org.uk/careers-education-training/how-become-psychologist/types-psychologists/ becoming-health-psychologis-0.

Brown, I. (2006). Nurses' attitudes towards adult patients who are obese: literature review. *Journal of Advanced Nursing,* 53(2), 221–232.

Brown, S. D., Reavey, P., Cromby, J., Harper, D. and Johnson, K. (2009). On psychology and embodiment: some methodological experiments. *Sociological Review,* 56, 199–215.

Burgard, D. (2006). *Body positive.* Retrieved 15 November 2006, from www.bodypositive. com/HAES.htm.

Burgin, V. (1982). *Thinking Photography.* London: Methuen.

Burman, E. (1994). Interviewing. In P. Banister, E. Burman, I. Parker, M. Taylor and C. Tindall (Eds.), *Qualitative Methods in Psychology: A research guide* (pp. 49–71). Buckingham: Open University Press.

Burns, M. (2003). I. Interviewing: Embodied communication. *Feminism and Psychology,* 13(2), 229–236.

Burns, M. and Gavey, N. (2004). 'Healthy weight' at what cost? 'Bulimia' and a discourse of weight control. *Journal of Health Psychology,* 9(4), 549–565.

Burns, M. and Gavey, N. (2008). Dis/orders of weight control: bulimic and/or 'healthy weight' practices. In S. Riley, M. Burns, H. Frith, S. Wiggins and P. Markula (Eds.), *Critical Bodies – Representations, identities and practices of weight and body management* (pp. 139–154). Basingstoke: Palgrave Macmillan.

Burr, V. (1998). *Gender and Social Psychology.* London: Routledge.

Butera, K. J. (2006). Manhunt: the challenge of enticing men to participate in a study on friendship. *Qualitative Inquiry,* 12(6), 1262–1282.

Butler, J. (1999). *Gender Trouble: Feminism and the subversion of identity* (10th edn). New York: Routledge.

Cachelin, F. M., Striegel-Moore, R. H. and Brownell, K. D. (1998). Beliefs about weight gain and attitudes toward relapse in a sample of women and men with obesity. *Obesity Research,* 6(3), 231–237.

Campos, P. (2004). *The Obesity Myth.* Camberwell, Australia: Viking.

Campos, P. (2011). Does fat kill? A critique of the epidemiological evidence. In E. Rich, L. F. Monaghan and L. Aphramor (Eds.), *Debating Obesity: Critical perspectives* (pp. 36–59). Basingstoke: Palgrave.

Campos, P., Saguy, A., Ernsberger, P., Oliver, E. and Gaesser, G. (2006a). The epidemiology of overweight and obesity: Public health crisis or moral panic? *International Journal of Epidemiology,* 35(1), 55–60.

Campos, P., Saguy, A., Ernsberger, P., Oliver, E. and Gaesser, G. (2006b). Response: Lifestyle not weight should be the primary target. *International Journal of Epidemiology,* 35(1), 81–82.

Carryer, J. (2001). Embodied largeness: a significant women's health issue. *Nursing Inquiry,* 8(2), 90–97.

Chandler, D. (1998). *Notes on "the gaze".* Retrieved 16 October 2008, from www.aber. ac.uk/media/Documents/gaze/gaze12.html. Chapman, C. (1987). Putting the issue on the boards. In M. Lawrence (Ed.), *Fed Up and Hungry: Women, oppression and food* (pp. 136–144). London: Women's Press.

Chapman, G. E. (1999). From "dieting" to "healthy eating". In J. Sobal and D. Maurer (Eds.), *Interpreting Weight* (pp. 73–87). New York: Aldine de Gruyter.

Cheek, J. (2008). Healthism: a new conservatism? *Qualitative Health Research,* 18(7), 974–982.

Chernin, K. (1983). *Womansize: The tyranny of slenderness.* London: Women's Press.

Clarke, V. and Turner, K. V. (2007). Clothes maketh the queer? Dress, appearance and the construction of lesbian, gay and bisexual identities. *Feminism and Psychology,* 17(2), 267–276.

Cogan, J. C. and Ernsberger, P. (1999). Dieting, weight, and health: Reconceptualizing research and policy. *Journal of Social Issues,* 55(2), 187–205.

Coleman, R. (2008). The becoming of bodies. *Feminist Media Studies,* 8(2), 163.

Coles, T. (2008). Finding space in the field of masculinity: lived experiences of men's masculinities. *Journal of Sociology,* 44(3), 233–248.

Colquitt, J. L., Picot, J., Loveman, E. and Clegg, A. J. (2009). Surgery for obesity. *Cochrane Database of Systematic Reviews, 2011*(2), article no.: CD003641.

Cooper, C. (1998). *Fat and Proud: The politics of size.* London: Women's Press.

Cooper, C. (2007). *Headless fatties.* Retrieved on 7 May 2012 from: http://www.charlotte cooper.net/docs/fat/headless_fatties.htm.

Cordell, G. and Ronai, C. R. (1999). Identity management among overweight women. In J. Sobal, and D. Maurer (Eds.), *Interpreting Weight* (pp. 29–47). New York: Aldine de Gruyter.

Craik, J. (1994). *The Face of Fashion.* London: Routledge.

Cramer, P. and Steinwert, T. (1998). Thin is good, fat is bad: how early does it begin? *Journal of Applied Developmental Psychology,* 19(3), 429–451.

Crandall, C. S. and Martinez, R. (1996). Culture, ideology, and antifat attitudes. *Personality and Social Psychology Bulletin,* 22(11), 1165–1176.

Crandall, C. S., D'Anello, S., Sakalli, N., Lazarus, E., Wieczorkowska, G. and Feather, N. T. (2001). An attribution-value model of prejudice: anti-fat attitudes in six nations. *Personality and Social Psychology Bulletin,* 27(1), 30–37.

Crawley, S. L. (2002). "They still don't understand why I hate wearing dresses!" an autoethnographic rant on dresses, boats, and butchness. *Cultural Studies, Critical Methodologies,* 2(1), 69–92.

Csordas, T. J. (1994). Introduction: The body as representation and being-in-the-world. In T. J. Csordas (Ed.), *Embodiment and Experience* (pp. 1–24). Cambridge: Cambridge University Press.

Davies, D. (1998). Health and the discourse of weight control. In A. R. Petersen and C. Waddell (Eds.), *Health Matters: A sociology of illness, prevention and care* (pp. 141–155). Buckingham: Open University Press.

Davies, B., Browne, J., Gannon, S., Hopkins, L., McCann, H. and Wihlborg, M. (2006). Constituting the feminist subject in poststructuralist discourse. *Feminism and Psychology,* 16(1), 87–103.

Del Busso, L. (2007). III. Embodying feminist politics in the research interview: material bodies and reflexivity. *Feminism and Psychology,* 17(3), 309–315.

Department of Health. (2004a). *Public Health White Paper: Choosing health; making healthy choices easier.* Retrieved 16 May 2007, from www.dh.gov.uk/publications.

Department of Health. (2004b). *Secondhand Smoke: Review of evidence since 1998, update of evidence on health effects of secondhand smoke.* Retrieved 16 May 2007, from www.dh.gov.uk/publications.

Department of Health. (2006). *Choosing Health: Obesity bulletin.* Retrieved 16 July 2012 from http://www.dh.gov.uk/assetRoot/04/13/44/73/04134473.pdf.

Department of Health. (2008a). *£30m Healthy Towns Kick Start Change4life*. Retrieved 16 July 2012 from http://www.noo.org.uk/news.php?nid=346.

Department of Health. (2008b). *Healthy Weight, Healthy Lives – A cross government strategy for England*. Retrieved 6 July 2012 from http://www.dh.gov.uk/en/Publichealth/Health improvement/Obesity/DH_082383.

Department of Health. (2008c). *Social Marketing*. Retrieved 1 December 2008 from http://www.dh.gov.uk/en/Publichealth/Choosinghealth/DH_066342.

Department of Health. (2010). *Healthy Lives, Healthy People: Our strategy for public health in England*. Norwich: The Stationery Office.

Di Stefano, C. (1990). Dilemmas of difference: feminism, modernity, and postmodernism. In L. J. Nicholson (Ed.), *Feminism/Postmodernism* (pp. 63–82). New York: Routledge.

Douglas, M. (1966). *Purity and Danger: An analysis of concepts of pollution and taboo* (2nd edn). London: Routledge and Kegan Paul.

Durgadas, G. (1998). Fatness and the feminized man. In D. Atkins (Ed.), *Looking Queer: Body image and identity in lesbian, bisexual, gay and transgender communities* (pp. 367–371). New York: Haworth.

Edwards, P. and Roberts, I. (2008). Transport policy is food policy. *The Lancet, 371*(9625), 1661.

Edwards, P. and Roberts, I. (2009). Population adiposity and climate change. *International Journal of Epidemiology, 38*, 1137–1140.

Egger, G. and Swinburn, B. (1997). An "ecological" approach to the obesity pandemic. *British Medical Journal, 315*(7106), 477–480.

Elliott, R. M. and Johnson, I. T. (2007). Nutrigenomic approaches for obesity research. *Obesity Reviews, 8*, 77–81.

Engel, S. G., Crosby, R. D., Kolotkin, R. L., Hartley, G. G., Williams, G. R., Wonderlich, S. A. *et al.* (2003). Impact of weight loss and regain on quality of life: mirror image or differential effect? *Obesity Research, 11*(10), 1207–1213.

Entwistle, J. (2000). Fashion and the fleshy body: dress as embodied practice. *Fashion Theory, 4*(3), 323–347.

Entwistle, J. (2001). The dressed body. In J. Entwistle and E. Wilson (Eds.), *Body Dressing* (pp. 33–58). Oxford: Berg.

Ernsberger, P. (2004). Foreword. In P. Campos (Ed.), *The Obesity Myth* (pp. ix–xiv). Camberwell, Australia: Viking.

Ernsberger, P. and Koletsky, R. J. (1999). Biomedical rationale for a wellness approach to obesity: an alternative to a focus on weight loss. *Journal of Social Issues, 55*(2), 221–259.

Fairclough, N. (2001). *Language and Power* (2nd edn). Harlow: Longman.

Farooqi, I. S. and O'Rahilly, S. (2007). Genetic factors in human obesity. *Obesity Reviews, 8*, 37–40.

Field, A. E., Barnoya, J. and Colditz, G. A. (2002). Epidemiology and health and economic consequences of obesity. In T. A. Wadden and A. J. Stunkard (Eds.), *Handbook of Obesity Treatment* (pp. 3–18). New York: Guilford.

Flegal, K. M., Graubard, B. I., Williamson, D. F. and Gail, M. H. (2005). Excess deaths associated with underweight, overweight, and obesity. *JAMA: The Journal of the American Medical Association, 293*(15), 1861–1867.

Flodgren, G., Deane, K., Dickinson, H. O., Kirk, S., Alberti, H., Beyer, F. R. *et al.* (2010). Interventions to change the behaviour of health professionals and the organisation of care to promote weight reduction in overweight and obese adults. *Cochrane Database of Systematic Reviews*, CD000984, accessed 18 July 2012.

Foster, G. D., Wadden, T. A., Makris, A. P., Davidson, D., Sanderson, R. S., Allison, D. B. *et al.* (2003). Primary care physicians' attitudes about obesity and its treatment. *Obesity Research,* 11(10), 1168–1177.

Foucault, M. (1972). *Archaeology of Knowledge.* London: Routledge.

Foucault, M. (1977). *Discipline and Punish* (A. Sheridan trans.). London: Penguin.

Foucault, M. (1978). *The Will to Knowledge, The history of sexuality,* vol. 1. London: Penguin Books.

Foucault, M. (1988). Technologies of the self. In L. H. Martin, H. Gutman and P. H. Hutton (Eds.), *Technologies of the Self* (pp. 16–49). London: Tavistock.

Foucault, M. (1991). Truth and power. In P. Rabinow (Ed.), *The Foucault Reader* (pp. 51–75). London: Penguin Books.

Foucault, M. (1997). In Rabinow P. (Ed.), *Ethics: Subjectivity and truth.* New York: New Press, Penguin Books.

Foucault, M. (2002a). So is it important to think? In J. D. Faubion (Ed.), *Power – Essential works of Foucault 1954–1984* (pp. 454–458). London: Penguin.

Foucault, M. (2002b). The subject and power. In J. D. Faubion (Ed.), *Power – Essential works of Foucault 1954–1984* (pp. 326–348). London: Penguin.

Fox, D., Prilleltensky, I. and Austin, S. (2009). Critical psychology for social justice: concerns and dilemmas. In D. Fox, I. Prilleltensky and S. Austin (Eds.), *Critical Psychology* (2nd edn, pp. 3–19). Los Angeles: SAGE.

Friedman, K. E., Reichmann, S. K., Costanzo, P. R., Zelli, A., Ashmore, J. A. and Musante, G. J. (2005). Weight stigmatization and ideological beliefs: relation to psychological functioning in obese adults. *Obesity Research,* 13(5), 907–916.

Frith, H. (2003). Introducing the body: (in)visibility and the negotiation of embodied identities. *Psychology of Women Section Review,* 5(2), 3–6.

Frith, H. and Gleeson, K. (2004). Clothing and embodiment: men managing body image and appearance. *Psychology of Men and Masculinity,* 5(1), 40–48.

Frost, L. (2005). Theorizing the young woman in the body. *Body and Society,* 11(1), 63–85.

Gard, M. and Wright J (2005). *The Obesity Epidemic: Science, morality and ideology.* London: Routledge.

Garner, D. M. and Wooley, S. C. (1991). Confronting the failure of behavioral and dietary treatments for obesity. *Clinical Psychology Review,* 11(6), 729–780.

Gatens, M. (1991). *Feminism and Philosophy: Perspectives on difference and equality.* Cambridge: Polity.

Gergen, K. J. (2009). *An Invitation to Social Construction* (2nd edn). London: SAGE.

Germov, J. and Williams, L. (1999). Dieting women. In J. Sobal and D. Maurer (Eds.), *Weighty Issues* (p. 117). New York: Walter de Gruyter.

Giddens, A. (1991). *Modernity and Self-identity: Self and society in the late modern age.* Cambridge: Polity Press.

Gill, R. (1995). Relativism, reflexivity and politics: interrogating discourse analysis from a feminist perspective. In S. Wilkinson and C. Kitzinger (Eds.), *Feminism and Discourse: Psychological perspectives* (pp. 165–186). London: Sage.

Gill, R. (1998). Dialogues and differences: writing, reflexivity and the crisis of representation. In K. Henwood, C. Griffin and A. Phoenix (Eds.), *Standpoints and Differences: Essays in the practice of feminist psychology* (pp. 18–44). London: SAGE.

Gill, R. (2007). Postfeminist media culture. *European Journal of Cultural Studies,* 10(2), 147–166.

Gill, R. (2008a). Body talk: negotiating body image and masculinity. In S. Riley, M. Burns, H. Frith, S. Wiggins and P. Markula (Eds.), *Critical Bodies – Representations, identities and practices of weight and body management* (pp. 101–116). Basingstoke: Palgrave Macmillan.

Gill, R. (2008b). Empowerment/sexism: figuring female sexual agency in contemporary advertising. *Feminism and Psychology,* 18(1), 35–60.

Gillies, V., Harden, A., Johnson, K., Reavey, P., Strange, V. and Willig, C. (2004). Women's collective constructions of embodied practices through memory work: Cartesian dualism in memories of sweating and pain. *British Journal of Social Psychology,* 43(1), 99–112.

Glenny, M. A. and O'Meara, S. (1997). *Systematic Review of Interventions in the Treatment and Prevention of Obesity.* Retrieved 18 July 2012 from http://www.york.ac.uk/inst/crd/CRD_Reports/crdreport10.pdf.

Goffman, E. (1963). *Stigma: Notes on the management of spoiled identity.* New Jersey: Prentice-Hall.

Gortmaker, S. L., Swinburn, B. A., Levy, D., Carter, R., Mabry, P. L., Finegood, D. T. *et al.* (2011). Changing the future of obesity: science, policy, and action. *The Lancet,* 378 (9793), 838–847.

Gough, B. and McFadden, M. (2001). *Critical Social Psychology: An introduction.* Basingstoke: Palgrave.

Griffin, C. (2007a). Being dead and being there: research interviews, sharing hand cream and the preference for analysing 'naturally occurring data'. *Discourse Studies,* 9(2), 246–269.

Griffin, C. (2007b). Different visions: a rejoinder to Henwood, Potter and Hepburn. *Discourse Studies,* 9(2), 283–287.

Grogan, S. (1999). *Body Image: Understanding body dissatisfaction in men, women and children.* London: Routledge.

Grosz, E. A. (1994). *Volatile Bodies: Toward a corporeal feminism.* Bloomington, IN: Indiana University Press.

Guy, A. and Banim, M. (2000). Personal collections: women's clothing use and identity. *Journal of Gender Studies,* 9(3), 313.

Hall, K. D., Sacks, G., Chandramohan, D., Chow, C. C., Wang, Y. C., Gortmaker, S. L. *et al.* (2011). Quantification of the effect of energy imbalance on bodyweight. *The Lancet,* 378(9793), 826–837.

Halliwell, E., Malson, H. and Tischner, I. (2011). Are contemporary media images which seem to display women as sexually empowered actually harmful to women? *Psychology of Women Quarterly,* 35(1), 38–45.

Hallschmid, M., Benedict, C., Schultes, B., Born, J. and Kern, W. (2008). Obese men respond to cognitive but not to catabolic brain insulin signaling. *International Journal of Obesity,* 32(2), 275–282.

Harre, R. and Secord, P. (1972). *The Explanation of Social Behaviour.* Oxford: Blackwell.

Hartsock, N. (1990). Foucault on power: a theory for women? In L. J. Nicholson (Ed.), *Feminism/Postmodernism* (pp. 157–175). New York: Routledge.

Harvie, M., Hooper, L. and Howell, A. H. (2003). Central obesity and breast cancer risk: a systematic review. *Obesity Reviews,* 4(3), 157–173.

Haug, F. (Ed.) (1987). *Female Sexualisation.* London: Verso.

Henderson, N. J. and Huon, G. F. (2002). Negative affect and binge eating in overweight women. *British Journal of Health Psychology,* 7(1), 77–87.

Henriques, J., Hollway, W., Urwin, C., Venn, C. and Walkerdine, V. (1984a). Introduction to section 1: From the individual to the social – a bridge too far. In J. Henriques,

W. Hollway, C. Urwin, C. Venn and V. Walkerdine (Eds.), *Changing the Subject* (pp. 11–25). London: Routledge.

Henriques, J., Hollway, W., Urwin, C., Venn, C. and Walkerdine, V. (1984b). Introduction: The point of departure. In J. Henriques, W. Hollway, C. Urwin, C. Venn and V. Walkerdine (Eds.), *Changing the Subject* (pp. 1–9). London: Routledge.

Heo, M., Pietrobelli, A., Fontaine, K. R., Sirey, J. A. and Faith, M. S. (2006). Depressive mood and obesity in US adults: comparison and moderation by sex, age, and race. *International Journal of Obesity,* 30(3), 513–519.

Hepburn, A. and Wiggins, S. (2005). Developments in discursive psychology. *Discourse and Society,* 16(5), 595–601.

Hepworth, J. (2006). The emergence of critical health psychology: can it contribute to promoting public health? *Journal of Health Psychology,* 11(3), 331–341.

Herndon, A. M. (2005). Collateral damage from friendly fire? Race, nation, class and the 'war against obesity'. *Social Semiotics,* 15(2), 127.

Hilbert, A., Dierk, J., Conradt, M., Schlumberger, P., Hinney, A., Hebebrand, J. *et al.* (2009). Causal attributions of obese men and women in genetic testing: implications of genetic/biological attributions. *Psychology and Health,* 24(7), 749.

Hivert, M., Langlois, M. and Carpentier, A. C. (2007). The entero-insular axis and adipose tissue-related factors in the prediction of weight gain in humans. *International Journal of Obesity,* 31(5), 731–742.

Hollander, A. (1980). *Seeing Through Clothes.* New York: Avon Books.

Holliday, R. (1999). The comfort of identity. *Sexualities,* 2(4), 475–491.

Hollway, W. (1989). *Subjectivity and Method in Psychology.* Thousand Oaks, CA: Sage.

Holt, C. L., Clark, E. M. and Kreuter, M. W. (2001). Weight locus of control and weight-related attitudes and behaviors in an overweight population. *Addictive Behaviors,* 26(3), 329–340.

Hook, D. (2007). *Foucault, Psychology and the Analytics of Power.* Basingstoke: Palgrave Macmillan.

Illich, I. (1976). *Limits to Medicine.* London: Marion Boyars.

ITV. (2012). *The Biggest Loser.* Tuesday 3 January, 9 pm.

Jackson, S. (1992). The amazing deconstructing woman. *Trouble and Strife* 25, 25–31.

Joanisse, L. and Synnott, A. (1999). Fighting back. In J. Sobal, and D. Maurer (Eds.), *Interpreting Weight* (pp. 49–70). New York: Aldine de Gruyter.

Joseph, N. and Alex, N. (1972). The uniform: a sociological perspective. *The American Journal of Sociology,* 77(4), 719–730.

Jutel, A. (2005). Weighing health: the moral burden of obesity. *Social Semiotics,* 15(2), 113.

Kiefer, I., Leitner, B., Bauer, R. and Rieder, A. (2000). Body weight: the male and female perception. *Sozial- und Präventivmedizin,* 45(6), 274–278.

Kim, S. and Popkin, B. M. (2006). Commentary: Understanding the epidemiology of overweight and obesity – a real global public health concern. *International Journal of Epidemiology,* 35(1), 60–67.

Kimmel, M. S. (2004). *The Gendered Society* (2nd edn). New York: Oxford University Press.

Kokkonen, R. (2009). The fat child: a sign of bad motherhood? An analysis of explanations for children's fatness on a Finnish website. *Journal of Community and Applied Social Psychology,* 19(5), 336–347.

Kugelmann, R. (2004). Health and illness: a hermeneutical phenomenological approach. In M. Murray (Ed.), *Critical Health Psychology* (pp. 44–57). Basingstoke: Palgrave Macmillan.

Latner, J. D. and Stunkard, A. J. (2003). Getting worse: the stigmatization of obese children. *Obesity Research,* 11(3), 452–456.

Latner, J. D., Wilson, G. T., Jackson, M. L. and Stunkard, A. J. (2009). Greater history of weight-related stigmatizing experience is associated with greater weight loss in obesity treatment. *Journal of Health Psychology,* 14(2), 190–199.

Lawrence, V. J. and Kopelman, P. G. (2004). Medical consequences of obesity. *Clinics in Dermatology,* 22(4), 296–302.

LeBesco, K. (2004). *Revolting Bodies? The struggle to redefine fat identity.* Amherst, MA: University of Massachusetts Press.

LeBesco, K. (2009). Weight management, good health and the will to normality. In H. Malson, and M. Burns (Eds.), *Critical Feminist Approaches to Eating Dis/Orders* (pp. 146–156). London: Routledge.

LeBesco, K. and Braziel, J. E. (2001). Editors' introduction. In J. E. Braziel, and K. LeBesco (Eds.), *Bodies out of Bounds: Fatness and transgression* (p. 360). Berkeley, CA: University of California Press.

Levene, R. and Gleeson, K. (2003). Standing apart – sizing up social identity. *Psychology of Women Section Review,* 5(2), 17–21.

Lupton, D. (1996). *Food, the Body and the Self.* London: SAGE.

Lyons, P. and Miller, W. C. (1999). Effective health promotion and clinical care for large people. *Medicine and Science in Sports and Exercise,* 31(8), 1141–1146.

Malson, H. (1998). *The Thin Woman: Feminism, post-structuralism and the social psychology of anorexia nervosa.* New York: Routledge.

Malson, H. (2008). Deconstructing un/healthy body-weight and weight management. In S. Riley, M. Burns, H. Frith, S. Wiggins and P. Markula (Eds.), *Critical Bodies – Representations, identities and practices of weight and body management* (pp. 27–42). Basingstoke: Palgrave Macmillan.

Malson, H. and Swann, C. (1999). Prepared for consumption: (dis)orders of eating and embodiment. *Journal of Community and Applied Social Psychology,* 9(6), 397–405.

Malson, H., Schmidt, U. and Humfress, H. (2006). Between paternalism and neo-liberal regulation: producing motivated clients of psychotherapy. *Critical Psychology,* 18, 107–135.

Malson, H., Halliwell, E., Tischner, I. and Rudolfsdottir, A. G. (2011). Post-feminist advertising laid bare: young women's talk about the sexually agentic woman of 'midriff' advertising. *Feminism and Psychology,* 21(1), 74–99.

Marks, D. F. (2008). The quest for meaningful theory in health psychology. *Journal of Health Psychology,* 13(8), 977–981.

Martin, E. (1989). *The Woman in the Body.* Milton Keynes: Open University Press.

Matz, P. E., Foster, G. D., Faith, M. S. and Wadden, T. A. (2002). Correlates of body image dissatisfaction among overweight women seeking weight loss. *Journal of Consulting and Clinical Psychology,* 70(4), 1040–1044.

McCracken, G. (1990) *Culture and Consumption: New approaches to the symbolic character of consumer goods and activities.* Bloomington, IN: Indianapolis University Press.

McDowell, C. (1984). *McDowell's Directory of Twentieth Century Fashion.* London: Frederick Muller.

McDowell, C. (1992). *Dressed to Kill.* London: Hutchinson.

McFarlane, T., Polivy, J. and McCabe, R. E. (1999). Help, not harm: psychological foundation for a non-dieting approach toward health. *Journal of Social Issues,* 55(2), 261–276.

McPherson, K., Marsh, T. and Brown, M. (2007). *Foresight – Tackling obesities: Future choices – modelling future trends in obesity and the impact on health* (2nd edn). Department of Innovation Universities and Skills. Retrieved 18 July 2012 from http://www.bis.gov.uk/assets/foresight/docs/obesity/17.pdf.

McRobbie, A. (2009). *The Aftermath of Feminism: Gender, culture and social change.* Los Angeles, CA: SAGE.

Medina, J. X. (2011). Body politicking and the phenomenon of 'passing'. *Feminism and Psychology,* 21(1), 138–143.

Melchionda, N., Besteghi, L., Di Domizio, S., Pasqui, F., Nuccitelli, C., Migliorini, S. *et al.* (2003). Cognitive behavioural therapy for obesity: one-year follow-up in a clinical setting. *Eating and Weight Disorders: EWD,* 8(3), 188–193.

Merleau-Ponty, M. (1962). *Phenomenology of Perception.* London: Routledge & Kegan Paul.

Messner, M. A. (1997). *Politics of Masculinities: Men in movements.* Thousand Oaks, CA: Sage.

Miles, A., Rapoport, L., Wardle, J., Afuape, T. and Duman, M. (2001). Using the mass-media to target obesity: an analysis of the characteristics and reported behaviour change of participants in the BBC's 'fighting fat, fighting fit' campaign. *Health Education Research,* 16(3), 357–372.

Miller, W. C. (1999). Fitness and fatness in relation to health: implications for a paradigm shift. *Journal of Social Issues,* 55(2), 207–219.

Miller, W. C. (2005). The weight-loss-at-any-cost environment: how to thrive with a health-centered focus. *Journal of Nutrition Education and Behavior,* 37(Suppl. 2), S89–S93.

Miller, W. C. and Jacob, A. V. (2001). The health at any size paradigm for obesity treatment: the scientific evidence. *Obesity Reviews,* 2(1), 37–45.

Monaghan, L. F. (2007a). Body mass index, masculinities and moral worth: men's critical understandings of appropriate weight-for-height. *Sociology of Health and Illness,* 29(4), 584–609.

Monaghan, L. F. (2007b). *Men, Dieting and the War on Obesity: Understandings from a sociological study.* Coventry: Coventry University.

Monaghan, L. F. (2008a). *Men and the War on Obesity.* London: Routledge.

Monaghan, L. F. (2008b). Men, physical activity, and the obesity discourse: critical understandings from a qualitative study. *Sociology of Sport Journal,* 25(1), 97–129.

Moreno-Aliaga, M., Santos, J. L., Marti, A. and Martínez, J. A. (2005). Does weight loss prognosis depend on genetic make-up? *Obesity Reviews,* 6(2), 155–168.

Morris, M. J., Chen, H., Watts, R., Shulkes, A. and Cameron-Smith, D. (2008). Brain neuropeptide Y and CCK and peripheral adipokine receptors: temporal response in obesity induced by palatable diet. *International Journal of Obesity,* 32(2), 249–258.

Mulvey, L. (1999). Visual pleasure and narrative cinema. In J. Evans and S. Hall (Eds.), *Visual Culture: The reader* (pp. 381–389). London: Sage.

Murray, M. (2004). Introduction: criticizing health psychology. In M. Murray (Ed.), *Critical Health Psychology* (pp. 1–11). Basingstoke: Palgrave Macmillan.

Murray, S. (2005a). (Un/be)coming out? Rethinking fat politics. *Social Semiotics,* 15(2), 154.

Murray, S. (2005b). Introduction to 'thinking fat' special issue of social semiotics. *Social Semiotics,* 15(2), 111–112.

Murray, S. (2008). *The Fat Female Body.* Basingstoke: Palgrave Macmillan.

NAAFA. (2011). *National Association for the Advancement of Fat Acceptance – mission.* Retrieved October, 2011, from http://www.naafaonline.com/dev2/about/index.html.

National Health Service. (2011). *Change4Life*. Retrieved 7 January 2012 from http://www.nhs.uk/Change4Life/Pages/change-for-life.aspx.

Nicolson, P. (2002). *Having it All? Choices for today's superwoman*. Chichester: John Wiley.

Nicolson, P. (2004). I. Biological politics: challenging man-made science. *Feminism and Psychology,* 14(3), 411–414.

Oakley, A. (2005). Interviewing women: a contradiction in terms? In A. Oakley (Ed.), *The Ann Oakley Reader: Gender, women, and social science* (pp. 217–231). Bristol: Policy.

Oakley, A. (2009). II. Fallacies of fact and fiction. *Feminism and Psychology,* 19(1), 118–122.

Ogden, J. (2004). *Health Psychology: A textbook* (3rd edn). Maidenhead: Open University Press.

Ogden, J. (2006). The experience of being obese and the many consequences of stigma. Keynote speech at Appearance Matters 2, Bath, UK.

Ogden, J., Clementi, C. and Aylwin, S. (2006). The impact of obesity surgery and the paradox of control: a qualitative study. *Psychology and Health,* 21(2), 273–293.

Oliver, M. (1990). *The Individual and Social Model of Disability*. Joint Workshop of the Living Options Group and the Research Unit of the Royal College of Physicians. Retrieved 18 July 2012 from http://www.leeds.ac.uk/disability-studies/archiveuk/Oliver/in%20soc%20dis.pdf.

Orbach, S. (2006a). Commentary: There is a public health crisis – it's not fat on the body but fat in the mind and the fat of profits. *International Journal of Epidemiology,* 35(1), 67–69.

Orbach, S. (Ed.), (2006b). *Fat is a Feminist Issue: The anti-diet guide; fat is a feminist issue II : Conquering compulsive eating*. London: Arrow.

Orbach, S. (2008). *Bodies*. London: Profile.

Papadopoulos, D. (2008). In the ruins of representation: identity, individuality, subjectification. *British Journal of Social Psychology,* 47(1), 139–165.

Paquette, M. C. and Raine, K. (2004). Sociocultural context of women's body image. *Social Science and Medicine,* 59(5), 1047–1058.

Parker, I. (1992). *Discourse Dynamics. Critical analysis for social and individual psychology*. London: Routledge.

Parker, I. (1994a). Discourse analysis. In P. Banister, E. Burman, I. Parker, M. Taylor and C. Tindall (Eds.), *Qualitative Methods in Psychology: A research guide* (p. 92). Buckingham: Open University Press.

Parker, I. (1994b). Reflexive research and the grounding of analysis: social psychology and the psy-complex. *Journal of Community and Applied Social Psychology,* 4(4), 239–252.

Parker, I. (1997). Discursive psychology. In D. Fox and I. Prilleltensky (Eds.), *Critical Psychology: An introduction* (pp. 284–298). London: SAGE.

Parker, I. (1999). Against relativism in psychology, on balance. *History of the Human Sciences,* 12(4), 61–78.

Parker, I. (2011). Discursive social psychology now. *British Journal of Social Psychology,* doi: 10.1111/j.2044-8309.2011.02046.x

Peel, E., Parry, O., Douglas, M. and Lawton, J. (2006). "It's no skin off my nose": Why people take part in qualitative research. *Qualitative Health Research,* 16(10), 1335–1349.

Pepper, A. C. and Ruiz, S. Y. (2007). Acculturation's influence on antifat attitudes, body image and eating behaviors. *Eating Disorders,* 15(5), 427.

Polhemus, T. (1988). *Bodystyles*. Luton: Lennard.

Porter, J. A., Raebel, M. A., Conner, D. A., Lanty, F. A., Vogel, E. A., Gay, E. C. *et al.* (2004). The long-term outcomes of sibutramine effectiveness on weight (LOSE weight) study: evaluating the role of drug therapy within a weight management program in a group-model health maintenance organization. *American Journal of Managed Care,* 10(6), 369–376.

Poston, W. S., Reeves, R. S., Haddock, C. K., Stormer, S., Balasubramanyam, A., Satterwhite, O. *et al.* (2003). Weight loss in obese Mexican Americans treated for 1 year with orlistat and lifestyle modification. *International Journal of Obesity and Related Metabolic Disorders,* 27(12), 1486–1493.

Potter, J. and Hepburn, A. (2005). Qualitative interviews in psychology: problems and possibilities. *Qualitative Research in Psychology,* 2, 281–307.

Potter, J. and Hepburn, A. (2007). Life is out there: a comment on Griffin. *Discourse Studies,* 9(2), 276–282.

Probyn, E. (2008). IV. Silences behind the mantra: critiquing feminist fat. *Feminism and Psychology,* 18(3), 401–404.

Probyn, E. (2009). Fat, feelings, bodies: a critical approach to obesity. In H. Malson and M. Burns (Eds.), *Critical Feminist Approaches to Eating Dis/orders* (pp. 113–123). London: Psychology Press.

Prochaska, J. O. and DiClemente, C. C. (1982). Transtheoretical therapy: toward a more integrative model of change. *Psychotherapy: Theory, Research and Practice,* 19, 276–288.

Puhl, R. M. and Brownell, K. D. (2001). Bias, discrimination, and obesity. *Obesity Research,* 9(12), 788–805.

Puhl, R. M. and Brownell, K. D. (2003a). Psychosocial origins of obesity stigma: toward changing a powerful and pervasive bias. *Obesity Reviews,* 4(4), 213–227.

Puhl, R. M. and Brownell, K. D. (2003b). Ways of coping with obesity stigma: Rerview and conceptual analysis. *Eating Behaviors,* 4, 53–78.

Raisborough, J. (2006). Getting onboard: women, access and serious leisure. *The Sociological Review,* 54(2), 242–262.

Ramazanoglu, C. and Holland J. (2002). *Feminist Methodology: Challenges and choices.* London: Sage.

Rana, J. S., Nieuwdorp, M., Jukema, J. W. and Kastelein, J. J. P. (2007). Cardiovascular metabolic syndrome – an interplay of obesity, inflammation, diabetes and coronary heart disease. *Diabetes, Obesity and Metabolism,* 9(3), 218–232.

Rand, C. S. W. and MacGregor, A. M. C. (1991). Successful weight loss following obesity surgery and the perceived liability of morbid obesity. *International Journal of Obesity,* 15, 577–579.

Reed, L. S. (2010). Gender, pathology, spectacle. In L. S. Reed and P. Saukko (Eds.), *Governing the Female Body: Gender, health, and networks of power* (pp. 59–82). Albany, NY: SUNY Press.

Rennie, K. L. and Jebb, S. A. (2005). Prevalence of obesity in Great Britain. *Obesity Reviews,* 6(1), 11–12.

Rice, C. (2009a). How big girls become fat girls: the cultural production of problem eating and physical inactivity. In H. Malson, and M. Burns (Eds.), *Critical Feminist Approaches to Eating Dis/Orders* (pp. 97–109). London: Routledge.

Rice, C. (2009b). Imagining the other? Ethical challenges of researching and writing women's embodied lives. *Feminism and Psychology,* 19(2), 245–266.

Rich, E. (2005). Young women, feminist identities and neo-liberalism. *Women's Studies International Forum,* 28, 495–508.

Rich, E. and Evans, J. (2005). 'Fat ethics' – the obesity discourse and body politics. *Social Theory and Health,* 3(4), 341–358.

Rich, E., Monaghan, L. F. and Aphramor, L. (2011a). Introduction: Contesting obesity discourse and presenting an alternative. In E. Rich, L. F. Monaghan and L. Aphramor (Eds.), *Debating Obesity: Critical perspectives* (pp. 1–35). Basingstoke: Palgrave.

Rich, E., Monaghan, L. F. and Aphramor, L. (Eds.). (2011b). *Debating Obesity: Critical perspectives.* Basingstoke: Palgrave Macmillan.

Riebe, D., Blissmer, B., Greene, G., Caldwell, M., Ruggiero, L., Stillwell, K. M. *et al.* (2005). Long-term maintenance of exercise and healthy eating behaviors in overweight adults. *Preventive Medicine: An International Journal Devoted to Practice and Theory,* 40(6), 769–778.

Robertson, S. (2006). 'I've been like a coiled spring this last week': Embodied masculinity and health. *Sociology of Health and Illness,* 28(4), 433–456.

Rogge, M. M., Greenwald, M. and Golden, A. (2004). Obesity, stigma, and civilized oppression. *Advances in Nursing Science,* 27(4), 301.

Rose, N. (1996). *Inventing Our Selves: Psychology, power, and personhood.* Cambridge: Cambridge University Press.

Rosenstock, I. M. (1966). Why people use health services. *Millbank Memorial Fund Quarterly,* 44, 94–124.

Rudolfsdottir, A. G. (2000). 'I am not a patient, and I am not a child': The institutionalization and experience of pregnancy. *Feminism and Psychology,* 10(3), 337–350.

Rudolfsdottir, A. G. and Jolliffe, R. (2008). 'I don't think people really talk about it that much': Young women discuss feminism. *Feminism and Psychology,* 18(2), 268–274.

Russell-Mayhew, S. (2006). Stop the war on weight: obesity and eating disorder prevention working together toward health. *Eating Disorders,* 14(3), 253–263.

Ryan-Flood, R. and Gill, R. (2010). Introduction. In R. Ryan-Flood, and R. Gill (Eds.), *Secrecy and Silence in the Research Process: Feminist reflections* (pp. 1–11). London: Routledge.

Saguy, A. and Riley, K. W. (2005). Weighing both sides: morality, mortality, and framing contests over obesity. *Journal of Health Politics, Policy and Law,* 30(5), 869–921.

Sampson, E. (1998). Establishing embodiment in psychology. In H. J. Stam (Ed.), *The Body and Psychology* (pp. 30–53). London: SAGE.

Sassatelli, R. (2011). Interview with Laura Mulvey. *Theory, Culture and Society,* 28(5), 123–143.

Saukko, P. (2000). Between voice and discourse: quilting interviews on anorexia. *Qualitative Inquiry,* 6(3), 299–317.

Saukko, P. and Reed, L. S. (2010). Introduction: Governing the female power. In L. S. Reed and P. Saukko (Eds.), *Governing the Female Body: Gender, health, and networks of power* (pp. 1–16). Albany, NY: SUNY Press.

Schwartz, H. (1986). *Never Satisfied: A cultural history of diets, fantasies and fat.* New York: Free Press, Collier Macmillan.

Schwartz, M. B. and Brownell, K. D. (2004). Obesity and body image. *Body Image,* 1(1), 43–56.

Schwartz, M. B., Chambliss, H. O., Brownell, K. D., Blair, S. N. and Billington, C. (2003). Weight bias among health professionals specializing in obesity. *Obesity Research,* 11(9), 1033–1039.

Schwarzer, R. (1992). Self efficacy in the adoption and maintenance of health behaviors: theoretical approaches and a new model. In R. Schwarzer (Ed.), *Self Efficacy: Thought control of action* (pp. 217–243). Washington, DC: Hemisphere.

Seacat, J. D. and Mickelson, K. D. (2009). Stereotype threat and the exercise/ dietary health intentions of overweight women. *Journal of Health Psychology,* 14(4), 556–567.

Scott, M. and Lyman, S. (1968). Accounts. *American Sociological Review,* 33, 46–62.

Sekine, M., Yamagami, T., Handa, K., Saito, T., Nanri, S., Kawaminami, K. *et al.* (2002). A dose–response relationship between short sleeping hours and childhood obesity: results of the Toyama birth cohort study. *Child: Care, Health and Development,* 28(2), 163–170.

Shapses, S. and Cifuentes, M. (2003). Weight reduction and bone health. In S. New and J. P. Bonjour (Eds.), *Nutritional Aspects of Bone Health* (pp. 589–608). London: Royal Society of Chemistry.

Shaw, K., O'Rourke, P., Del Mar, C. and Kenardy, J. (2005). Psychological interventions for overweight or obesity. *Cochrane Database of Systematic Reviews,*CD003818.pub2.

Shaw, A. K., Gennat, C. H., O'Rourke, P. and Del Mar, C. (2006). Exercise for overweight or obesity. *Cochrane Database of Systematic Reviews,* (4), CD003817.

Siegel, J. M., Yancey, A. K. and McCarthy, W. J. (2000). Overweight and depressive symptoms among African-American women. *Preventive Medicine,* 31(3), 232–240.

Sloan, C., Gough, B. and Conner, M. (2010). Healthy masculinities? How ostensibly healthy men talk about lifestyle, health and gender. *Psychology and Health,* 25(7), 783–803.

Smith, D. E. (1990). *Texts, Facts, and Femininity: Exploring the relations of ruling.* London: Routledge.

Smith, J. A. (1998). Towards a relational self: social engagement during pregnancy and psychological preparation for motherhood. *British Journal of Social Psychology,* 38, 409–426.

Sobal, J. and Maurer, D. (Eds.). (1999). *Weighty Issues – Fatness and thinness as social problems.* New York: Walter de Gruyter.

Soper, K. (2001). Dress needs: reflections on the clothed body, selfhood and consumption. In J. Entwistle and E. Wilson (Eds.), *Body Dressing* (pp. 13–32). Oxford: Berg.

South Gloucestershire Council. (2006). *Active for Life.*

Spelman, E. (1982). Woman as body: ancient and contemporary views. *Feminist Studies,* 8(1), 109–131.

Stam, H. J. (1998). The body's psychology and psychology's body. In H. J. Stam (Ed.), *The Body and Psychology* (pp. 1–12). London: SAGE.

Stam, H. J. (2000). Theorizing health and illness: functionalism, subjectivity and reflexivity. *Journal of Health Psychology,* 5(3), 273–283.

Stam, H. J. (2004). A sound mind in a sound body: a critical historical analysis of health psychology. In M. Murray (Ed.), *Critical Health Psychology* (pp. 83–100). Basingstoke: Palgrave Macmillan.

Stearns, P. N. (1997). *Fat History: Bodies and beauty in the modern west.* New York: New York University Press.

Stephenson, N. (2003). Interrupting neo-liberal subjectivities. *Continuum: Journal of Media and Cultural Studies,* 17(2), 135.

Stuart, A. and Donaghue, N. (2012). Choosing to conform: the discursive complexities of choice in relation to feminine beauty practices. *Feminism and Psychology,* 22(1), 98–121.

Stunkard, A. J., Faith, M. S. and Allison, K. C. (2003). Depression and obesity. *Biological Psychiatry,* 54(3), 330–337.

Stutzmann, F., Cauchi, S., Durand, E., Calvacanti-Proença, C., Pigeyre, M., Hartikainen, A. *et al.* (2009). Common genetic variation near MC4R is associated with eating behaviour patterns in European populations. *International Journal of Obesity,* 33(3), 373–378.

Swinburn, B. A., Sacks, G., Hall, K. D., McPherson, K., Finegood, D. T., Moodie, M. L. *et al.* (2011). The global obesity pandemic: shaped by global drivers and local environments. *The Lancet,* 378(9793), 804–814.

Taylor, J. (2009). Being fat is bad for you – and the environment. *Metro,* 19 April.

Teachman, B. A. and Brownell, K. D. (2001). Implicit anti-fat bias among health professionals: Is anyone immune? *International Journal of Obesity and Related Metabolic Disorders: Journal of the International Association for the Study of Obesity,* 25(10), 1525–1531.

The Editor. (2011). Urgently needed: a framework convention for obesity control. *The Lancet,* 378(9793), 741.

Thomas, D., Elliott, E. J. and Baur, L. (2007). Low glycaemic index or low glycaemic load diets for overweight and obesity. *Cochrane Database of Systematic Reviews,* CD005105.

Throsby, K. (2007). "How could you let yourself get like that?" Stories of the origins of obesity in accounts of weight loss surgery. *Social Science and Medicine,* 65, 1561–1571.

Throsby, K. (2008). Happy re-birthday: weight loss surgery and the 'new me'. *Body and Society,* 14(1), 117–133.

Throsby, K. (2009). 'There's something in my brain that doesn't work properly': weight loss surgery and the medicalisation of obesity. In H. Malson and M. Burns (Eds.), *Critical Feminist Approaches to Eating Dis/orders* (pp. 321–340). London: Psychology Press.

Tischner, I. and Malson, H. (2008). Exploring the politics of women's in/visible 'large' bodies. *Feminism and Psychology,* 18(2), 260–267.

Tischner, I. and Malson, H. (2011). 'You can't be supersized?' A discursive exploration of femininities, body size and control within the obesity terrain. In E. Rich, L. F. Monaghan and L. Aphramor (Eds.), *Debating Obesity: Critical perspectives* (pp. 90–114). Basingstoke: Palgrave.

Tischner, I. and Malson, H. (2012). Deconstructing health and the un/healthy 'fat' woman. *Journal of Community and Applied Social Psychology,* 22(1): 50–62.

Tseëlon, E. (1995). *The Masque of Femininity: The presentation of woman in everyday life.* London: SAGE.

Tyner, K. and Ogle, J. P. (2007). Feminist perspectives on dress and the body: an analysis of ms. magazine, 1972 to 2002. *Clothing and Textiles Research Journal,* 25(1), 74–105.

Ussher, J. M. (1991). *Women's Madness: Misogyny or mental illness?* London: Harvester Wheatsheaf.

Ussher, J. M. (1997). *Fantasies of Femininity: Reframing the boundaries of sex.* London: Penguin.

Ussher, J. M. (2006). *Managing the Monstrous Feminine: Regulating the reproductive body.* Hove: Routledge.

Ussher, J. M. (2008). Challenging the positioning of premenstrual change as PMS: the impact of a psychological intervention on women's self-policing. *Qualitative Research in Psychology,* 5(1), 33–44.

Ussher, J. M. (2011). *The Madness of Women: Myth and experience.* London: Routledge.

van Langenhove, L. and Harré, R. (1999). Introducing positioning theory. In R. Harré and L. van Langenhove (Eds.), *Positioning Theory* (pp. 14–31). Oxford: Blackwell.

Vartanian, L. R. and Shaprow, J. G. (2008). Effects of weight stigma on exercise motivation and behavior: a preliminary investigation among college-aged females. *Journal of Health Psychology,* 13(1), 131–138.

Vartanian, L. R., Herman, C. P. and Polivy, J. (2007). Consumption stereotypes and impression management: how you are what you eat. *Appetite,* 48(3), 265–277.

Wang, Y. C., McPherson, K., Marsh, T., Gortmaker, S. L. and Brown, M. (2011). Health and economic burden of the projected obesity trends in the USA and the UK. *The Lancet,* 378(9793), 815–825.

Wangsness, M. (2000). Pharmacological treatment of obesity. past, present, and future. *Minnesota Medicine,* 83(11), 21–26.

Watson, J. (2000). *Male Bodies: Health, culture and identity.* Buckingham: Open University Press.

Wecker, K. (1989). *Die schoenen Leute. Stilles Glück, Trautes Heim.* Munich: Globale Musikverlage Muenchen.

Weedon, C. (1997). *Feminist Practice and Poststructuralist Theory* (2nd edn). Oxford: Blackwell.

Weedon, C. (1999). *Feminism, Theory, and the Politics of Difference.* Oxford: Blackwell.

Weitz, R. (2003). A history of women's bodies. In R. Weitz (Ed.), *The Politics of Women's Bodies: Sexuality, appearance, and behavior* (2nd edn, pp. 3–11). New York, NY: Oxford University Press.

Well, T. and Cruess, D. (2006). Effects of partial sleep deprivation on food consumption and food choice. *Psychology and Health,* 21(1), 79–86.

Welton, D. (1998). Introduction: Situating the body. In D. Welton (Ed.), *Body and Flesh – A philosophical reader* (pp. 1–8). Oxford: Blackwell Publishers.

Wetherell, M. (1986). Linguistic repertoires and literary criticism: new directions for a social psychology of gender. In S. Wilkinson (Ed.), *Feminist Social Psychology: Developing theory and practice.* Milton Keynes: Open University Press.

Widdicombe, S. (1993). Autobiography and change: rhetoric and authenticity of 'gothic' style. In E. Burman and I. Parker (Eds.), *Discourse Analytic Research: Repertoires and readings of texts in practice* (pp. 94–113). London: Routledge.

Wiggins, S. and Potter, J. (2008). Discursive psychology. In C. Willig and W. Stainton Rogers (Eds.), *The SAGE Handbook of Qualitative Research in Psychology* (pp. 73–90). Los Angeles, CA: SAGE.

Wilkinson, S. (2004). Feminist contributions to critical health psychology. In M. Murray (Ed.), *Critical Health Psychology* (pp. 83–100). Basingstoke: Palgrave Macmillan.

Wilkinson, S., Joffe, H. and Yardley, L. (2004). Qualitative data collection: interviews and focus groups. In D. F. Marks and L. Yardley (Eds.), *Research Methods for Clinical and Health Psychology* (pp. 39–55). London: SAGE.

Will, H. C. (2000). Constructions of masculinity and their influence on men's well-being: a theory of gender and health. *Social Science and Medicine,* 50(10), 1385–1401.

Willig, C. (2004). Discourse analysis and health psychology. In M. Murray (Ed.), *Critical Health Psychology* (p. 155). Basingstoke: Palgrave Macmillan.

Willig, C. (2008). *Introducing Qualitative Research in Psychology: Adventures in theory and method* (2nd edn). Maidenhead: Open University Press.

Wilson, P. W., D'Agostino, R. B., Sullivan, L., Parise, H. and Kannel, W. B. (2002). Overweight and obesity as determinants of cardiovascular risk: the Framingham experience. *Archives of Internal Medicine,* 162(16), 1867–1872.

Wolf, N. (1991). *The Beauty Myth.* London: Vintage.

Wooley, C. S. and Garner, D. M. (1994). Controversies in management: dietary treatments for obesity are ineffective. *British Medical Journal,* 309, 655.

World Health Organization. (2012). *Obesity and overweight.* Retrieved 15 July 2012 from www.who.int/topics/obesity/en/.

Yang, Y. K. and Harmon, C. M. (2003). Recent developments in our understanding of melanocortin system in the regulation of food intake. *Obesity Reviews,* 4(4), 239.

Yanovski, S. Z. (2000). Overweight, obesity, and health risk: national task force on the prevention and treatment of obesity. *Archives of Internal Medicine,* 160(7), 898–904.

Young, I. M. (1998/1990). Situated bodies – throwing like a girl. In D. Welton (Ed.), *Body and Flesh – A philosophical reader* (pp. 259–273). Oxford: Blackwell Publishers.

Zhao, H. L., Sim, J.., Shim, S. H., Ha, Y. W., Kang, S. S. and Kim, Y. S. (2005). Antiobese and hypolipidemic effects of platycodin saponins in diet-induced obese rats: evidences for lipase inhibition and calorie intake restriction. *International Journal of Obesity,* 29(8), 983–990.

Zitzelsberger, H. (2005). (In)visibility: accounts of embodiment of women with physical disabilities and differences. *Disability and Society,* 20(4), 389.

Index

acceptance, fat 15–16
activism 15–16
Adam, A. 63
Alcoff, L. 16
Alex, N. 64
anti-fat prejudice 18–19
Aphramor, L. 13, 14, 15, 74–5
appearance 47; gendered pressures 94,
    106–7; and power relations 58; *see also*
    beauty, clothes
attractiveness 97, 122–3; *see also* beauty
austerity discourses 136

backlash against feminism 8, 22, 60–1
Bacon, L. 13, 14, 15
baggy t-shirts and leggings 64, 66, 73
Bartky, S. 47, 50, 60
BBC news website 3
beautification 8, 53, 60–1
beauty 1–3, 23, 72, 110–11;
    food/health/beauty triplex 21; gendered
    pressures 107–8; need to challenge
    individualistic and perfectionist notions
    of 127, 129–30; wanting to be seen
    52–4; *see also* appearance,
    attractiveness
'beauty myth' 22
beer bellies 115–16
behaviour change 17–18
'being-in-the-world' embodiment 30
Bell, K. 25, 95–6
Bentham, J. 45, 138
Biggest Loser, The 6, 125–6
biomedical view 10–13, 26, 27, 74, 79–80,
    122, 132
Blair, T. 75–6, 84
bodiliness 37–43
body: construction of male and female
    bodies 95–9; and mind 23, 29–30, 85,
114, 123, 139; and psychology
    29–32; significance of 28–32; 'static'
    view of 125
body dissatisfaction 18–19, 25
body image 18–19, 23, 24
body mass index (BMI) 10–11, 13
body Panopticon 50–1
body parts, concern about 113–14
Bordo, S. 23, 31, 105, 112, 120–1, 130
branding 67
British Psychological Society (BPS) 17
Brown, S.D. 29, 30, 32
built environment 49–50
Burns, M. 128

Campos, P. 11, 13, 13–14, 24
cancer 4
Cartesian dualism 23, 29–30, 85, 114, 123,
    139
causes of obesity 5, 11, 17, 74
celebrities 108–9
centrisms 142
Changed4Life programme 4–5
Cheek, J. 6, 130
choice 6, 19, 20, 59, 140; lack of choice in
    clothes 61–2, 71; restricted and lifestyle
    87–90
Choosing Health 75–6, 84
Clarke, V. 68
clothes 9, 57–73, 122–3, 124; being seen
    and hiding 72; branding vs conformity
    67; containment and regulation 62–4;
    femininity and feminism 69–71;
    identity construction through 67–9;
    self-expression through 58–9, 62, 67–9,
    73; signifying function of 57, 58, 64;
    unavailability of desirable clothes
    61–4; unavailability of work uniforms
    66; uniform of fat women 64–6, 73

cognitive behavioural therapy 17
Coles, T. 26, 116–17
collective knowingness 7, 20, 75, 92
comfort eating 85
complexity 11–12
compulsory visibility 137
conditions of possibility 135
conformity 67
constructionism 133, 141
containment 62–4
control 117–18; controllability of body
    weight 19
Cooper, C. 16, 92
Crawley, S. 102, 124
critical health psychology 79, 134
critical psychology 133–4
culture 30, 58; cultural specificity of
    discourses 37

defeminisation of large women 100,
    101, 117
Department of Health 4–5, 13, 128,
    129
depression 18
Di Stefano, C. 139
dietary fats 81–2
dieting 21; gender and 110–13; *see also*
    weight loss
difference 140
disability 49–50
disciplinarity 32, 37, 136–9
discipline 45
discourse analysis 33–43, 126–7, 131;
    Foucauldian 33, 34–43, 131
discourses 34, 135–6, 138
discrimination 18–19, 123, 127
discursive fields 34–5, 36
discursive psychology (DP) 33–4
dispersed power 140–1
docile bodies 45
domination 50, 59–61

eating 48, 49; comfort eating 85; gender
    and 112–13, 118; overeating 74, 85;
    representations in the media 23; *see*
    also food
education 81, 89
efficacy, fat 54–5, 56, 109
Elisabeth, Empress 2
embodied practices 125
empowerment 54–5, 56
energy balance approach 11, 74
Entwistle, J. 57
epistemological reflexivity 37–8

exclusion 72–3
excuse account 86–7

family 96, 104–5
fashion 57, 58, 69–70; *see also* clothes
fat acceptance 15–16
fat activism 15–16
fat efficacy 54–5, 56, 109
Fat Underground (FU) 16
feminine selves: dis/integrated 113–17;
    fat 121–4
femininity 59, 123–4; and body shape
    and size 96–7, 100–4; clothes 69–71;
    norms of 47; performance of 3, 69,
    101–2
feminisation: of consumerism 57–8; of
    male fat 25, 98
feminism 7–8, 21–4, 26, 27–8, 132;
    backlash against 8, 22, 60–1; and
    clothes 69–71; feminist theory and the
    body 31–2; liberal 139; poststructuralist
    139–42; radical 16, 139, 140
food 23; food/health/beauty triplex 21;
    gender and 110–13; *see also* eating
Foucauldian discourse analysis (FDA) 33,
    34–43, 131
Foucault, M. 8, 27, 28, 32, 34–5, 44, 45,
    55, 56, 65, 67, 72, 80, 110, 124, 126,
    134–5, 136, 137, 138, 141
fragmentation 113–17, 118
freedom 110–13
fun 63–4

Gavey, N. 128
gaze: judgemental 51, 61–2, 72, 123,
    124; male 46, 53; normalising and
    regulating 45, 51, 60, 107, 137–8
gender 1–2, 3, 7–8, 9, 44, 94–119, 130;
    construction of male and female bodies
    95–9; diets, food and freedom 110–13;
    dis/integrated selves 113–17; gendered
    pressures 22–3, 104–10; work
    environment 99–104, 117; *see also*
    femininity, masculinity
generalisation 121
Gill, R. 24, 25, 28, 141
global action 12–13
global discursive fields 36
government: austerity discourses 136; role
    and health 75–6
Grosz, E 102–3

Hartsock, N. 141
headless fatties 92

health 3–7, 9, 23, 74–93, 107–8, 110–11, 122; biomedical view 11–13, 74, 79–80; constructions of 76–80; food/health/beauty triplex 21; gender and 105–6; individual responsibility for 3, 15, 19, 46, 74, 75–6, 83–6, 88, 133; lifestyle choices 87–90; need to challenge individualistic and perfectionist notions of 127, 129–30; stupidity or ignorance 81–3; visibility and 45–6
Health At Every Size (HAES) 13–15, 26, 75, 128–9
health-offsetting 128–9
health professionals 18, 80, 91–2
health promotion 4–5, 19, 21, 75, 121; discourses 79–80; potentially inaccurate messages 127, 127–9
health psychology 133
Healthy Community Challenge Fund 4
Healthy Lives, Healthy People 13
Healthy Town initiatives 4
Healthy Weight, Healthy Lives programme 4
hiding/being hidden 51–2, 72
hijab 58
historical specificity of discourses 37
Holliday, R. 68
homogenisation 121
Hook, D. 137

'ideal' feminine woman 103
identity *see* self
ignorance 81–3
income inequalities 88–9
individual–society dualism 133–4
individual responsibility: austerity discourses 136; for body size 74, 86–7; for health 3, 15, 19, 46, 74, 75–6, 83–6, 88, 133
individualism 4–7; need to challenge individualistic notions of health and beauty 127, 129–30
inequality 88–9
Inside Health 5–6
insider/outsider problematic 39
insults 115
integration 113–17, 118
interviews, research 38–42
invisibility *see* visibility/invisibility

job searching 102
Joseph, N. 64
judgemental gaze 51, 61–2, 72, 123, 124
justice 28, 141–2

knowledge: construction of 36; and power 35, 136–9; production 134–6

Lancet, The 2, 3; obesity series 12, 13
language 34, 38, 39
leggings and baggy t-shirts 64, 66, 73
liberal feminism 139
lifelong overweight 116–17
lifestyle 5, 20, 127; health and 6–7, 15, 74–6, 77–9, 122; restricted choices 87–90
literature review 9, 10–26; biomedical view 10–13, 26; fat acceptance and activism 15–16; feminist contributions 21–4, 26; HAES 13–15, 26; masculinities and fat 24–6; neoliberal constructions of fat 20–1; psychology 16–19, 26
Lupton, D. 21, 96, 113

magazines 1–2, 58
male gaze 46, 53
Malson, H. 75, 116, 140
marginalisation 52, 123, 127; clothes and 57, 60, 63–4, 72–3
masculine selves: dis/integrated 113–17; fat 121–4
masculinity 24–6, 123–4; and body shape and size 96, 97–100, 104; mosaic masculinities 26, 116–17, 123
materiality of the body 31–2
maternal love 96–7
McCracken, G. 59
McNaughton, D. 25, 95–6
measurement 137
media 23, 24, 92
medical discourses 10–13, 26, 27, 74, 79–80, 122, 132
medical professionals 18, 80, 91–2
Medina, J. 58
memory 29
mental health 14, 18
Merleau-Ponty, M. 30
methodology 33–43, 126–7
metonymy of fat for the whole person 75, 114–15, 122–3
military school ranks 65
Miller, W.C. 14–15
mind, and body 23, 29–30, 85, 114, 123 139
moral judgement 65–6, 127; *see also* judgemental gaze
morbidity 15

mortality 13
mosaic masculinities 26, 116–17, 123
mothers/mothering 96–7, 104–5
Mulvey, L. 46
Murray, S. 16, 20, 75, 92, 125
muscularity 96
Muslim women 58

nakedness 61
National Association to Aid Fat Americans (NAAFA) 15–16
National Health Service 19
neoliberalism 5–6, 107–8, 125–6, 133; constructions of fat 20–1; and health 75, 83–4, 88–90, 93; *see also* individual responsibility
news reports 3–4, 92
normalising and regulating gaze 45, 51, 60, 107, 137–8
norms of femininity 47
nutrition 81–2

'obesity epidemic' 3, 12, 13, 48–9, 88
objectification 29–30, 50, 60, 137
objects, construction of 36
occupation 89
offsetting culture 128–9
Orbach, S. 21–2, 23, 102
outsider/insider problematic 39
overeating 74, 85

panopticism 48, 55, 138
Panopticon 45, 48, 72, 107, 138
Parker, I. 36
patient information 14
patriarchy 140
penal system 136–7
perfectionism 107; need to challenge 127, 129–30
performance of femininity 3, 69, 101–2
'personal is political' 40–1
personal reflexivity 37–9
phantom limb 30
phenomenology 30–1
physical activity 78
physical environment 49–50
pluralism 142
Porter, M. 5
poststructural discourse analysis 33–43, 126–7, 131
poststructuralism 26, 28, 30–1, 32, 132, 134–9; knowledge/power 136–9; knowledge production 134–6
poststructuralist feminism 139–42

potentially inaccurate messages 127, 127–9
power 28, 31, 32, 118, 142; appearance, clothes and 59–61; dispersed 140–1; dynamics and interviews 40–2; fat politics of 124–6; knowledge and 35, 136–9; visibility and 45, 46–7
practices, regulation of 37
prefabricated codes 59
pressures, gendered 22–3, 104–10
prevention of obesity 12
prison (Panopticon) 45, 107, 138
Probyn, E. 24, 125, 129
psychology 16–19, 26, 27, 132–3; body and 29–32; critical 79, 133–4; discursive 33–4

radical feminism 16, 139, 140
ranks, military school 65
reality, construction of 36
rebellion 112–13
record-taking 137
reflexivity 37–9, 42
regimes of truth 8, 35, 80, 91, 135
regulation 32; normalising and regulating gaze 45, 51, 60, 107, 137–8; of practices 37; unfashionable clothes and 62–4
relativism 142
research interviews 38–42
research perspective 9, 27–43; discursive psychology 33–4; Foucauldian discourse analysis 33, 34–43, 131; methodology and method 33–43; significance of the body 28–32
responsibility: individual *see* individual responsibility; women's for other people's health 104–6
restricted lifestyle choices 87–90
romantic discourses 53–4
romantic love 96–7
Rose, N. 20, 83

sameness 139
self 20; dis/integrated selves 113–17; fat selves 121–4; feminine selves 113–17, 121–4; identity construction through clothes 67–9; masculine selves 113–17, 121–4; technologies of the self 67, 75, 110–11
self-control 20, 24–5, 102–3
self-efficacy 54, 55
self-expression, clothes and 58–9, 62, 67–9, 73

self-improvement 107–10
self-knowledge 83
self-management 59
self-surveillance 47
semiotic reversal 125
sexualisation 60–1
shopping 48, 49; with friends 63
signifying function of clothes 57, 58, 64
smokers 5
social constructionism 133, 141
social status 38–9, 58, 59
society–individual dualism 133–4
Soper, K. 62
'static' view of the body 125
Stearns, P.N. 2
stigmatisation 5, 7, 18–19, 46
strength 96
stupidity 81–3
subcultures 68–9
subject positions 36
subjectification 35, 137
subjects, construction of 36
superwoman 90, 129, 139
surgery, weight loss 11, 20–1
surveillance 45, 48–52, 55–6, 72, 124, 127
systems approach 12

technologies of the self 67, 75, 110–11
Throsby, K. 20, 92
transformation 28, 131, 141
'trouble' 113
truth 135–6; challenging truth claims 28,
    141–2; regimes of 8, 35, 80, 91, 135
Turner, K. 68

unavailability of fashionable clothes 61–4
uncontrollability 102–3

'undeserved' fat 86–7
uniforms 65–6; unavailability of work
    uniforms 66; uniform for fat women
    64–6, 73

visibility/invisibility 5, 9, 44–56, 113;
    clothes and 72; continuous visibility
    137–8; deconstructing 44–7; fat
    efficacy 54–5, 56; surveillance 45,
    48–52, 55–6; wanting to be seen
    52–4

Wann, M. 16
'war on obesity' 2, 3–5, 12–13, 24–5, 27,
    86, 132, 137; assumptions underlying
    13–14; harming people 127
Wecker, K. 57
weight loss 4, 6–7, 14, 15, 74–5, 81–2; by
    celebrities 109; global objective 10–13;
    messages in magazines 1–2; risks of 7,
    14; surgery 11, 20–1; *see also* dieting
weight loss interventions 11; psychological
    17
weight loss simulation model 12
weight stigma 5, 7, 18–19, 46
well-being 78, 129–30
wellness-centred approach 75
'what if' approach to health 6
Widdicombe, S. 68
wifely love 96–7
Willig, C. 36
Wolf, N. 22
women's magazines 1, 58
work environment 99–104, 117
work uniforms 66

Young, I.M. 123